D1759188

1 9 0069524   4

FIFTY YEARS IN POLITICS AND THE LAW

FIFTY YEARS IN POLITICS AND THE LAW

LORD MORRIS OF ABERAVON

UNIVERSITY OF WALES PRESS
CARDIFF
2011

To Margaret, for her encouragement and support
on the long journey we have shared together.

This book is written for my grandchildren:
Harry, Charlie, Millie, Henry, Llewelyn, Arthur, Atticus,
Joe-Joe and Balthazar, so that they will not forget
from whence they came.

y Graig y naddwyd hwynt ohoni

ACKNOWLEDGEMENTS

I am grateful for all the help I have received in providing material and checking facts.

My friends Lord Prys-Davies, Lord Rowlands, Dr Brinley Jones and Lord Elystan-Morgan have made important observations which I have taken into account. I have also benefited from factual assistance by Sir Richard Lloyd-Jones, KCB, formerly of the Welsh Office, and a number of other senior civil servants I have worked with, but the book is, of course, my sole responsibility. The staff of the House of Lords Library, the Cabinet Office and the Attorney General's Department have also provided considerable documentation, as well as the Public Records Office at Kew.

Lord Donoughue's Diaries were an invaluable quarry for ministerial discussions in the 1970s, as were Dick Crossman's diaries for an earlier period.

My secretary, Maggie Stevenson, has been indefatigable in typing over 500,000 words and shown great patience in construing my offerings. I owe a great deal to my editor, Penny Thomas, for her valuable improvements to the text.

© The Rt Hon the Lord Morris, KG, QC, 2011

All rights reserved. No part of this book may be reproduced in any
material form (including photocopying or storing it in any medium
by electronic means and whether or not transiently or incidentally
to some other use of this publication) without the written permission
of the copyright owner. Applications for the copyright owner's written
permission to reproduce any part of this publication should be addressed
to the University of Wales Press, 10 Columbus Walk, Brigantine Place,
Cardiff CF10 4UP.

www.uwp.co.uk

British Library CIP Data
A catalogue record for this book is available from the British Library

ISBN   978-0-7083-2418-9
e-ISBN   978-0-7083-2421-9

The right of the Rt Hon the Lord Morris, KG, QC, to be identified as author
of this work has been asserted by him in accordance with sections 77 and
79 of the Copyright, Designs and Patents Act 1988.

Designed by Chris Bell

Printed in Wales by Gomer Press, Llandysul

CONTENTS

LIST OF ILLUSTRATIONS

between chapters 9 and 10 (pp. 66–7)
Tom and John Morris with cousins on the eve of war, August 1939
In Germany as a young officer, 1955
As Deputy General Secretary and legal adviser with the Farmers' Union
   of Wales, 1955
With Harold Wilson, 1963
Speaking at Kenfig Hill, 1964
The All-Party Welsh MPs, 1964
Election address leaflet, 1966
At induction to the Gorsedd of Bards, Newtown Eisteddfod, 1965
As Defence Minister on Cairngorms, 1969
As Defence Minister, with Indira Gandhi, Mumbai, 1969
Launch of HMS Courageous, Barrow-in-Furness, 1970

between chapters 22 and 23 (pp. 194–5)
Taking constituents around the House of Commons, c.1970
Taking Silk, 1973
Cabinet of the Wilson government, c.1974
Declaration of election result, Aberavon, 1974
All five Secretaries of State for Wales together, 1974–5
Prince Charles visiting St John's Pit, Bridgend, 1976
With James Callaghan, Cynheidre Colliery, 1976
With James Callaghan at the Welsh Office, Easter 1976
At Port Talbot Steel Works with Sir Brian Moffatt, MD, c.1990
With grandson Harry on the way to be sworn in as Attorney General, 1997
With HM The Queen and Lord Elis-Thomas at the Welsh Assembly, 1999
Garter Ceremony, 2003

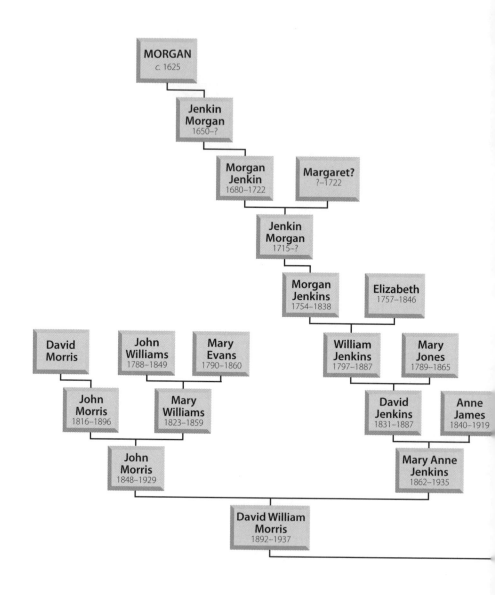

FAMILY TREE OF JOHN MORRIS

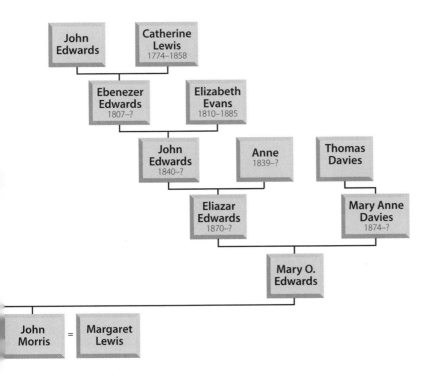

one
IN THE BEGINNING

MY FATHER DIED on Christmas Eve 1937, leaving my mother with three children under seven.

He had been a farmer and 'a noted breeder and judge of Welsh stock', according to the *Western Mail* of the day. He had won some of Wales's premier awards – no mean achievement for a small producer. He died having apparently been struck by a fatal germ when judging Highland and Welsh cattle at the Smithfield Fat Stock Show in London. Antibiotics were things of the future. He was forty-four. His death was to have a profound influence on the young lives of my brothers and myself.

Sadly I have little memory of him – I do recall a large happy gathering of London family and friends for a Christmas wedding a year earlier at our lowland farm Penywern, Talybont, Cardiganshire, overlooking the Dyfi Estuary. I also remember him taking me to my maternal grandparents on a Sunday evening, at their farm, Dolcniw Capel Bangor, where I was born, so I could be ready for school. This was always a bit of a wrench, I had a birthday party there when I was six and my father and mother came over to take home afterwards, just weeks before he died. He was a good horseman and a first class shot – our home was full of stuffed animals, as was the custom of the period. I have inherited his interest in shooting, with less success. On the farm he was in charge of the horses with his workmen; I remember him binding the corn, handling two horses while sitting high on the corn-binder, as seen from a small boy's perspective. I also remember sitting with him in the deacon's seat in his chapel on a Sunday morning, the best place to keep me quiet with pencil and paper.

It was riding his horse or motorcycling to one of his hill farms some ten miles away that he met my mother, Olwen. Apparently on one occasion he suffered unbearable toothache while driving his sheep to a hill farm and called on Dr Williams at nearby Tre'rddol. The doctor said, 'hold this candle, my boy', and promptly did an extraction. My mother was a London-trained district nurse and midwife in Glandyfi, Cardiganshire, which was conveniently on the way to the farms.

My mother was a brave and resourceful woman. She successfully let our farms as the agricultural depression was coming to an end and moved to one of my grandfather's farmhouses, Bwlch, twenty miles away. During the war she was occasionally the unofficial and unpaid district nurse in her new area in Capel Seion and anybody who called was given help.

Within a few years she married a neighbouring farmer, Evan Lewis, and together they brought us up. We could not have had a better stepfather and my gratitude to him is immense. They made sacrifices to see me through two universities, and I am grateful to my mother and also my grandmother for having nurtured whatever genes of public service I inherited.

My mother had six boys and one daughter, with all of her sons becoming farmers except me; I suppose I am the black sheep of the family. We all marvel now at how she organised the feeding and clothing of us all, as well as steering us onto our careers. I have no idea how she had the energy to achieve it all.

One of the regrets of my life is that the demands of a constituency, ministerial life and my profession have denied me the opportunity to try my hand at farming, though I came very near to acquiring a farm once. Common sense prevailed, but to follow man's first craft, *crefft gyntaf dynolryw*, would have given me immense pleasure.

But it was my maternal grandfather, Eliazar Edwards, who had the biggest influence on me. When I went to school at five and a half, I and my brother Tom lived with our grandparents during the week, at their home some fifteen miles away. It was thought that my father's farm was too remote from the local school. This continued until I was sixteen; I only returned home full-time when my mother went into hospital for nearly a year after the birth of my sister, so that I could help to care for the family.

My grandfather sold milk in Aberystwyth, some four or five miles away, and the greatest pleasure I had was to go with him on his rounds. A neighbour would bring his milk for us to sell as well. He would ford the river Rheidol on a pony and trap, provided it was not in flood.

My grandfather's family were originally lead miners. Baroness Symons is a blood relative; she very properly referred to me once in the House as her kinsman. When the lead was no longer mined and his mother, another midwife, died, my grandfather went with his father over the hills to the Rhondda to dig coal at the age of thirteen. Two of his brothers qualified as mining engineers in the Rhondda, presumably at whatever facilities pre-dated the School of Mines, the origin of the University of Glamorgan, of which I am now Chancellor. My great uncles eventually emigrated to the South African gold fields and their descendants were kind to us during the war, sending very welcome food parcels.

My grandfather left the pits to work in insurance and married my grandmother, who was the daughter of a Rhondda farmer and builder. Many years later I was to inherit one of the small houses he built in Gunnor Place in the Rhondda – named after Llangunnor in Carmarthenshire. He originally came from Llangain in that county.

My grandfather returned to the pits in the 1914–18 war and became chairman of the Miners' Lodge at the Wattstown Colliery in the Rhondda. He was one of the Liberal foot-soldiers of the Lib-Lab pact in South Wales and I once saw a telegram sent to him from Mabon, the miners' leader and local MP, asking him to chair a meeting that weekend. I suspect the relationship between the two sides of the pact could be quite strained and meetings called, possibly deliberately, for Sunday clashed with the chapel Sunday school where he taught.

In the meantime he had acquired the small farm of Dolcniw in his native valley in Cardiganshire and he returned as soon as he could to farm it. I loved to hear his tales of working underground. I fear I was an assiduous and sometimes exasperating cross-examiner of his work as a miner. I learned that small boys of thirteen were valuable to their fathers in the allocation of drams – wheeled vehicles on the tramlines – to carry all the coal they could hew. Together they would get more drams than one man on his own.

After his return to the county he played a prominent part in Cardiganshire Liberal politics. He was very much a 'King and country, *Daily Mail* reader' who was immersed in farming politics in the NFU, organising his local agricultural show and prominent in fundraising in the Second World War. I well remember the Red Cross fundraising campaigns, 'Wings for Victory' and others. Our country was fighting for its life and all, however small a cog, had their part to play.

My grandmother, Mary Anne Edwards, was an equally prominent Liberal and I am fairly sure also an active local suffragette judging by a photograph I have seen recently, taken before the 1914–18 war.

In 1921 there was a bitterly contested by-election in Cardiganshire between two Liberal candidates – one being David Lloyd George's private secretary, the other, deeply opposed to Lloyd George, was a QC and leader of the South Wales circuit. My grandmother chaired the village meeting at Penllwyn for the Prime Minister's wife, Mrs Margaret Lloyd George, who was speaking in support of their candidate. She had a full schedule of village meetings for many nights throughout the county, while her husband governed the country in London or from Versailles.

My grandmother had received a grammar-school education in the Rhondda around 1870, rather unusual at that time for a girl. She was a redoubtable mathematician, and taught me algebra in her seventies until her health failed her. She was one of the founders of the County Nursing Association which involved fundraising with the aim of training girls to be nurses, of which my mother was one. During World War Two she chaired a local tribunal deciding which women should be called up to serve in the forces. She was deeply affected by her role and one day after such a tribunal she suffered a severe stroke, which left her speechless for the rest of her life.

Sending young girls away from home to work in factories or forces in distant parts of the country was not her only worry. One of her daughters had graduated in German and married a German banker who, I believe, was in the enemy forces. Her eldest son, also a banker, with the Chartered Bank in the Far East, was on a ship sunk by the Germans between Australia and India. He was handed over to be a prisoner of the Japanese and believed to be dead for some years. My grandfather, in the absence of firm news, refused to have a memorial service for him. How right he turned out to be when his son returned home, although a mere six stone in weight after his incarceration.

This was the home where I spent the school week, with some of the passions and strains of war reflected daily in our living room. It was here I began to know a little of the world outside our small community, and followed avidly the to and fro of Rommel and Montgomery's battles in North Africa. It was of immense interest for me to visit Benghazi, Tripoli and Alamein as a defence minister in the late 1960s. It brought back to me my real fears, when chapel finished early on 3 September 1939 and we had gone home to hear Neville Chamberlain's broadcast announcing war.

Until I recently read the life of Saunders Lewis, one of the founders of the Welsh Nationalist Party, later Plaid Cymru, I had forgotten a local incident involving an attempt to reject the incoming child evacuees, mainly from Liverpool. A meeting was called in my village to vent opposition to the incoming evacuees, which my grandfather and the local county councillor opposed vehemently. The evacuees were welcomed by the village with open arms!

The Nationalist Party, concerned about the effect alien English influence might have on our own genuinely Welsh culture, damaged itself considerably at this time by both its pacifist and anti-English attitude. Some recent historians have tried to whitewash the nationalist stance, but it was a political mistake for which they paid severely for many years. In fairness, it would be absurd to argue that today's nationalist leaders would embark on such views. Their attitude reflected the brilliance of Saunders Lewis, who even his great admirers would concede was not always a consistent politician.

Such was the cauldron of emotions in which I grew up as a small boy. Contrary to some of my young friends, and with an early and deep interest in politics, I was never inclined to Nationalist Party politics. Apparently my form teacher recalls me saying at around the age of twelve that I wanted to be a barrister and an MP. It seems I was rather precocious.

But everything Welsh dominated the rest of my upbringing. I would be approaching seven before I could read a little English. I was a slow reader in any event, perhaps because I had started school later than my contemporaries, who outshone me at the village school that my mother and grandfather had gone to, to be followed much later by my nieces and nephews.

Although I spent most of my school years in my grandfather's home, within cycling distance of the university, there was little contact between town and gown so far as our village was concerned, apart from the extra-mural classes in the village, which I attended. The society I was brought up in was essentially an agricultural one and it was the problems of farming that dominated our lives. It was known that at harvest time my grandfather would collect all the available labour from the village to help on his farms in the hills; at school I would frequently be asked by the boys when their fathers would be needed. Obviously it was an event they looked forward to and my grandfather was known to be generous in his hospitality.

My grandfather's house had quite a well-stocked library. All the Dickens novels were there as well as more modern authors. My favourite reading, particularly if I was home from school with a bad cold, was the four volumes of the life of David Lloyd George, my hero. I studied the great man's life closely. The books of Owen M. Edwards were there too and some children's novels and we waited anxiously for the annual production of Rowland Hughes's novels. We also had *Cymru'r Plant* and our denominational children's magazine, *Trysorfa'r Plant*, and the children's section of the *Christian Herald*. On a Sunday night in the winter we would all as a family read in turn from the chosen chapter of the Bible, and have it explained to us. The book of Esther remains vividly in my memory.

Local *eisteddfodau* – competitive literary and musical events in our villages – played a huge part in our lives. My mother was most disappointed that I was an unsuccessful competitor – my uncle had won the prize for recitation in the National Eisteddfod, as did my younger sister many years later. As I found difficulty in pronouncing the letter 'R', I was a no-hoper at reciting poetry. My stepfather, however, was quite successful locally and on Good Friday, when I would accompany him, he would sometimes compete in two or even three events on the same evening, racing like others from one village to another. Many other evenings after the milking he would compete in a village event and we boys would frequently go with him. In wartime, Cardiganshire local *eisteddfodau* dominated our lives. The chapels of the area also gave me opportunities to speak and my first-ever speech was reading a paper at a meeting of the local Presbyterian circuit at Trisant, near Devil's Bridge.

The Young Farmers' Club movement was particularly important for my brothers, and I was roped in to take part in public-speaking competitions, even when I was in the army in Brecon. My stepfather would fetch me and I would change from uniform in the car. He would then drive me back to Brecon to be ready for parade the following morning. I shall always be grateful to my youthful contemporaries for the opportunity and encouragement I had. It was a movement that provided so much opportunity for the young in the countryside, and did so much to stretch their skills, giving confidence to many, including myself. It still plays a vital role in enhancing countryside life for young people.

My paternal grandfather, also John Morris, died before my birth. I wish I had known him. One of the reasons for writing this is so that my grandchildren have some more knowledge of me. He was originally from the north Cardiganshire village of Llanilar, and had gone with his young brothers to London, like dozens of other Cardiganshire folk, to sell milk. Gillian, Lady Rees-Mogg, is a distant cousin and descendant of one of his brothers. The farms were too small to support the large families and it was either the mines in the Rhondda or the milk trade in London for some of the children. He was successful in developing this trade and later an animal cereal business in the East End of London.

Many years later, when I frequently drove through Mansel Street in the City on my way to the north London courts in the mornings, I regretted he had not passed on the freehold of his premises. Had he done so, none of his descendants need have worked.

The Morrises kept their cattle in underground premises around Aldgate, sold the milk on the spot and on their rounds. The young brothers must have been Welsh-speaking monoglots when they first came to London, but John Morris became a deacon at the Stepney Presbyterian Chapel. Apparently when there was a rumour that the rail underground being developed might affect their premises, the brothers donned their top hats and went down to Parliament to ascertain first-hand the progress of the Private Railway Bill.

My grandfather must have done very well. In 1879 he was one of the five or six major donors to the rebuilding of his father's – another John Morris – chapel, Carmel, Llanilar. He gave seventy pounds, which in today's terms is worth £3,381.70 according to the historical currency converter of the National Archives. I have seen the silver trowel given to him to commemorate his gift, which is treasured by one of my cousins. About this time he bought land at Penywern, near Borth and elsewhere in the area, when freehold land was difficult to acquire; it was well before the great estates started breaking up. According to one of my uncles he built the substantial farmhouse to impress his girlfriend from the next farm at Cerrig Carannau. My grandfather, his father, also John, and his grandfather David, who appears on the records as both a farmer and carpenter, were all born on their farm, Ty'n y Fron, Llanilar – David in about 1780–90. When I was a small boy I remember visiting it with my father to inspect damage to trees after a great storm. It was then owned by one of my father's uncles in London and my father was his land agent.

My grandfather would travel down from London at the weekends to supervise the building of his future home – the trains must have been faster in those days. Eventually he took his bride to their new home, my first home too. The blankets were made from his own wool at a mill in Talybont and I remember some of them still being used in my childhood. According to the customary framed testimonial of the period from his fellow deacons of his chapel, 'he had been leaning towards the country for some time.'

He quickly, almost overnight it seems, stood for the first Cardiganshire County Council in 1888 and was elected as a Liberal by sixteen votes. After his first period in office he did not stand again, but played a leading role, with his brother-in-law James Jenkins, in breeding Welsh stock. Like my father after him, he was now a deacon at his chapel in Taliesin. Some of the brothers retired to the area too, to Borth and Llandre; they would meet on the Monday market day in Aberystwyth and walk down the main high street together, each with his walking stick.

The known ancestry of my paternal grandmother, Mary Morris, who I just about remember making shadows in the candlelight with her fingers to amuse me, is much older. From 1625 to 1875 her family were tenants on the Earl of Lisburne's estate at Trawscoed. This makes it easier to trace her lineage, which would be almost impossible otherwise for ordinary people – y werin bobl.

'Morgan' farmed at Cwm Meurig Uchaf, Ystrad Meurig, Cardiganshire, in about 1625 on the large Lisburne estate. The rent was three pounds five shillings, six chickens, two hens and forty eggs, a heriot of forty shillings and a suit at Rhydfendigaid Mill. His son, Jenkin Morgan, was born in 1650 and the second name and first name alternated from generation to generation following the Welsh patronymic system until Morgan Jenkin (1775–1838), when the name settled down to Jenkins, which they have retained to this day, breeding as their forbears did outstanding, prize-winning Welsh black cattle. Including my nephew, eleven known generations have farmed in the same county.

During the period a great many tenant farmers were ejected from their farms for various reasons. Such was the problem that a Royal Commission was appointed to inquire into the situation entitled, 'On Land in Wales and Monmouthshire'. My ancestor, David Jenkins, gave evidence through an interpreter on 28 April, 1894, and he testified that his father and grand-father went several times to the agent and the landlord to be allowed to continue on the farm. They were compelled to leave the following autumn for having trapped hares and rabbits that were eating their swedes. 'The sin of shooting hares was an unpardonable one, being the offence against one of the most sacred laws of the estate,' he said. He ended his evidence calling for a Land Act 'which will deal justly with landlord and tenant, will provide fair rent, security of tenure and compensation for improvements to the tenant'. Generations later these measures would be embodied in war-time agricultural legislation, particularly the Agricultural Holdings Act of 1948. He was a far-sighted man.

Having farmed for more than 250 years at Cwm Meurig Uchaf, the fam-ily was peremptorily ejected in 1875. Fortunately they acquired another farm a considerable distance away in Talybont, hence the union of the two families, and the Morrises and Jenkins continue to breed and exhibit Welsh stock to this day.

My grandmother's brother, Llewelyn Jenkins, was the first member of the family to go to university, shortly before the start of the twentieth cen-tury. He would tell me that as a graduate of Aberystwyth, he was a benefi-ciary of my great-grandfather's prescience in giving five shillings towards founding the new university in 1875. The gift is recorded in his diary, now kept in our National Library. It brought to life for me what my history books had taught me at school: that the new university had been built from the pennies of the miners, quarrymen and farmers of Wales. He gave the money four weeks after his ejection and move to the new farm, to me a mark of some resilience.

Llewelyn Jenkins became an education officer in Cardiff and cam-paigned for many years for capital status for the city of which he became deputy lord mayor. He was closely associated with Professor W. J. Gruffydd's campaign when the professor stood as a Liberal against Saunders Lewis in the bitter wartime by-election for the University of Wales's Parliamentary seat. I dimly remember as a very small child enjoying giving out leaflets at the National Eisteddfod in Machynlleth in 1937, advertising next year's Cardiff Eisteddfod, of which he was honorary secretary.

Such are my beginnings and despite the fact that, according to my mother, my father voted for the Conservative candidate, supporting the national government in the 1930s, I am not surprised on which side of the political fence I have played a small part for more than fifty years.

Schooldays at the excellent grammar school of Ardwyn in Aberystwyth, were happy ones. Together with my lifelong friend (Lord) Elystan Morgan, we founded the school debating society and fought each other at rowdy elections and mock trials. The headmaster, Colonel David Lewis, must have had immense patience with both of us. Then it was on to my first university in the town at seventeen, graduating at twenty, having been president of the college debating society. The student population was divided between school-leavers like myself and war veterans, with sometimes up to ten years' age difference between them and us. For the first time I met young men and women from outside my small community, many of them from South Wales. During my association with them I believe I matured quickly; politically and geographically there was a world outside the Rheidol, Ystwyth and Eleri Rivers and the social and political experiences of my new friends were so different from mine.

Then, like many others before me, I moved on from the Aberystwyth Law Faculty to Gonville and Caius College, Cambridge to read for a post-graduate degree. Cambridge was another world to me. I had never lived in college before. I had spent three years in hard academic slog at Aberystwyth and I was determined to use my time at Cambridge to broaden my horizons. Unfortunately I had very little money and this limited my interests.

I joined the university Labour club as soon as I got to Cambridge – I was still twenty – and threw myself into Labour club and Cambridge Union affairs. I spoke as a proposer or seconder in debates in the Union against Tam Dalyell and Giles Shaw, both MPs of the future – one Labour and one Conservative. Tam Dalyell was then chairman of the Cambridge University Conservative Association. I became international secretary of the Labour club, which involved sandwich-making for the club's Sunday afternoon meetings, my principal duty and my first step on the ladder! Eventually I was appointed membership secretary-elect, a key position, had I returned the following year.

Cambridge matured me a lot and helped to prepare me for responsibility for younger men when I joined the army. Again I was mixing with much older students, with wider horizons than mine. Among other things,

I went on one occasion to the English Society to hear a poet hitherto unknown to me – Dylan Thomas. The meeting was in one of the rooms at the Cambridge Union. I formed the view that Dylan was a master of words, although he babbled on sometimes inconsequentially. The Welsh Society was the *Mabinogion*, and I attended its meetings and some of the Welsh services on Sunday. I remember a don, Moelwyn Hughes, a scientist, preaching on nature.

Many years later, I was particularly delighted and grateful to become an Honorary Fellow of both institutions as well as the University College of Wales at Swansea, Trinity in Carmarthen and Lampeter.

two
FORMATIVE YEARS

A S PART OF MY POLITICAL EVOLUTION, my interest in devolution was formed during my years at my university in Aberystwyth. I don't think the word 'devolution' was then used. I had been brought up in an active Liberal household, but my political activities in the Liberal cause ceased between the elections of 1950 and 1951. I was nineteen years old and decided that I would join the Labour Party. I did not understand what the liberalism preached in Cardiganshire was about. Their politics were quite reactionary and had little relationship with the material in the *News Chronicle* that I was then reading occasionally. I delayed a little as I had been elected president of the College Joint Debating Union and during my election to that office I had received considerable support from my fellow Liberal-minded students. I thought it would hardly be right to ditch them so soon afterwards.

The two matters uppermost in my mind were the need to strive for equality of opportunity for the individual, and better and more democratic government in Wales. From the very beginning I was conscious of the need for all-Wales institutions if we were to be effective as a nation. I was to be consistent in this throughout my political life. I have never had a reputation for philosophical pronouncements, so I hope this short statement will suffice to explain my start line. These aims were to remain my two compasses throughout my political life.

It would take time for me to work out precisely the kind of governing institution that I believed Wales should have. I knew it would only be the Labour Party that could deliver whatever form of democratic accountability was necessary for Wales. I was to have the privilege of spending a good part of my life in seeking this, and ultimately seeing it achieved when I attended the opening ceremony of the National Assembly for Wales in 1999.

I asked for details of Labour Party membership from the Party's Welsh Secretary, Cliff Protheroe, in July 1952 and I was invited to meet the secretary of the Cardiganshire Labour Party, Tyssul Lewis. I went to his home in Llanbadarn, Aberystwyth, the next month. A local party member, Dr Clapham, a university lecturer and an Englishman I believe, was also present. I was put through my paces by the two of them for a good hour. Joining the Labour Party, even then, was not a simple matter. They had to scrutinise the genuineness of my application but despite coming from an unusual background, I was told that my membership would be accepted. In some of our urban wards it was said at the time that it was easier to become a freemason than to join the Labour Party. The Party sometimes paid a huge price for this when active opposition on some local issue emerged, particularly where personalities were involved: the price of not having a fairly broad membership was, and I suspect still is, rottenness in local decision making. The local accountability of a broad membership is of vital importance. I am heartbroken these days when I hear of the size of ward and management committee attendances. Cardiganshire, with a sparse membership, could not afford to be fussy, yet they were careful.

I told Tyssul and Clapham that I would join the Party on my twenty-first birthday, which would be in about three months' time. I did.

It was at this time, when I came home on holiday from Cambridge, that I began to call on a person who was to become a lifelong friend and adviser, Gwilym Prys-Davies, now Lord Prys-Davies. Recently married, he and Llinos had a flat in Aberystwyth where he was reading for his articles to become a solicitor. On reflection I must have been a nuisance, calling on the young couple on a Saturday night to discuss the future government of Wales. And none of the issues we discussed would have been remotely acceptable then to the Welsh Labour Party.

The first battle within the Party was for a Secretary of State for Wales. Scotland had had theirs since the end of the nineteenth century. There was considerable, but not a unanimous, feeling that Wales should have one too. Jim Griffiths battled hard within the Labour Party as a former Cabinet minister for the colonies and the creator of modern National Insurance, and with the prestige of being the deputy leader of the Parliamentary Labour Party, to get the adoption of a Secretary of State for Wales as policy. Nye Bevan was at last persuaded in the period before 1959. He had argued against it for many years, visualising a Welsh Office as a mere 'post office' for passing down the policies of other government departments into Wales. In some ways it was, at the beginning.

It is my personal belief that the Bevanite wing in the Welsh Labour Party was crucially influential with him. I also believe that Nye's near political neighbour, Tudor Watkins, MP for Brecon and Radnor, played a key role.

Nye eventually gave way to Jim Griffiths's campaign, to my great joy, and I was able to put a commitment to a Welsh Secretary in my personal manifesto, as stated in my election addresses of 1959 and 1964.

The second battle within the Labour Party was the question of an elected body for the whole of Wales. This had not at this stage become a live issue. Ideas had not been properly thought out, or indeed thought out at all.

It is important to remember that, short of some form of 'independence' for Wales, there had always been a step-by-step approach in the Labour Party to the development of practical ideas for bringing government closer to the people, and it was painfully slow at times. Independence is still, whatever some may say publicly, the nationalists' real aim. It may be variously dressed up in more acceptable ways, but in all honesty that is the only conclusion that I and, I think, many reasonable people would come to. That is the fundamental difference between the nationalists and the Labour approach to Wales – one minimising their aims for presentational purposes and the other, pragmatically building a consensus both within and outside the Party and trying to bridge serious divisions. But the disagreements on devolution within the Labour Party were manifest throughout my time in the Commons, and regrettably have still not been put to rest.

There were three important figures in the Welsh Labour Party who either were, or were to become, major advocates of Devolution. Jim Griffiths, Goronwy Roberts and Cledwyn Hughes all shared the conviction that the aim of devolution should be pursued because it represented what they thought was the right principle. Within the United Kingdom we were a nation, albeit a small one. All nations had the right to be part of a decision-making process. How far they could go with it, and what machinery would be used, was a matter for exploring and, inevitably, for argument.

Before I entered Parliament, Goronwy Roberts wrote to both myself and Gwilym Prys-Davies with ideas for some kind of conference to explore the issue, but regrettably after I became an MP he did not pursue it.

Jim Griffiths was trying to find a way forward. In the absence of any significant written work within the Party he turned to Gwilym and invited him to write a substantive paper on an elected Council for Wales. Jim was seeking a way to crystallise some of the ideas that might be suitable. The paper was eventually published as a pamphlet by the non-political body *Undeb Cymru Fydd*.

The pamphlet was a first and important stage in practical thinking, putting something down on paper with a view to a model policy for Wales which was not prejudiced by outworn and dead slogans, and it was decades overdue.

I was quite fascinated by this. It was a beginning and in accord with what I intended to study academically, if not politically, when I could develop my own ideas. There were, inevitably, long and earnest discussions until I disappeared into the night to cycle the eight miles to our farm up the valley.

Basically what we were doing, very pragmatically so far as I was concerned, was seeking a way forward. The aim was clear: democratic decision making for Wales, taken in Wales. This was to be my paramount aim and I would seek to develop the principle. I was learning all the time and I hope we both benefited from our discussions. Today's generation, or at least the majority of them, would not lift an eyebrow. But policies in so many fields, then radical and adventurous, later became commonplace and reasonable. What has not been understood is the cold climate in which we were then working.

I went to the Young Farmers' County Rally in June 1953. I had come down on the overnight train, having completed the exact number of term days necessary in residence in Cambridge, and one of the stalwarts of the county Labour Party, Mr R. Llewelyn Jones, an astute elderly council road worker who had served his county in many fields, came up to me with a startling proposition. He had founded, in particularly difficult times for any trade unionist in a rural area, the first branch of the Agricultural Workers' Union in the county. To my astonishment, he invited me to be nominated by the Agricultural Workers' Union as the county Labour candidate for the next election. I was twenty-one. I was duly nominated and made my speech in Aberaeron on the 'Development of Mid Wales', seizing on a phrase in a recently published report by the non-elected Council for Wales and Monmouthshire, the government's standing advisory board on Welsh affairs, which stated that 'rural depopulation was a form of economic adjustment'. When I told the selection committee that I intended to start my National Service soon, my defeat by a much older and more experienced person, a director of education, who was also born in the county, was inevitable. The experience from my audacity in standing was invaluable later.

I did not return to Cambridge after June 1953. I had passed my postgraduate LLB exams, since relabelled an LLM degree and granted to me as such. As an external graduate – it did not apply to their own graduates – I was expected to spend part of the following year writing a short thesis. I had intended to pursue my interests in devolution by preparing mine partly under the supervision of a distinguished Belfast professor, Professor Calvert who, not unexpectedly, was the great authority on the Stormont Parliament. This model had been working since the early 1920s and, whatever its problems, I believed it was worth studying as a working model of government devolved from Westminster. I wanted to develop my political ideas academically by looking in some depth at an experiment which had been an attempt to remedy some of the democratic deficit in the Province. I was determined to know all about the practicalities of this kind of devolution.

However I felt that I had strained the resources of my parents more than enough and in the end I decided not to pursue the idea of writing the thesis. There were six younger children to be educated or set up as farmers. There were no grants for a second university. The second year would have been a disproportionate luxury financially and would have used up a whole year of my life! Such was the viewpoint of a young man in a hurry. Having prepared for the bar exams over the 1953 summer recess – they did not seem particularly difficult compared with university exams – I reported for my two-year National Service. It was important to me that I served with other young Welshmen, so I opted to enlist with the Royal Welch Fusiliers.

I bought the *Liverpool Daily Post* to read the bar final exam results in late October 1953, in the cookhouse of the Royal Welch Fusiliers' Hightown Barracks in Wrexham, where I was square-bashing. I must have scraped through my Bar finals and my commission was later granted at Eaton Hall.

My parents and sister came to my passing-out parade. There were many different infantry regiments' uniforms on show. The Scots were in their kilts and trews. I wore my black flash, the memento granted to the RWF for not implementing the order to cut their powdered long hair when abroad. Someone in the crowd said that I must be the padre cadet, the nearest I have ever got to ecclesiastical preferment!

Two long years in Germany and Wales followed. In the Cold War as a young officer, this occasionally meant guarding the train from Hanover to Berlin through the Russian sector with a section of men and the blinds drawn down all the way, patrolling the frontier and peering at the various *volkspolitzei* on the other side, and being a junior umpire in battle exercises on the German plains and at Gatow Airport, Berlin. One thing I learned was the uselessness and extreme danger of tactical nuclear weapons, despite the exhortations of the senior general – one Richard 'Windy' Gale. The more he talked the more convinced I was of the dangers of any escalation of such weapons.

Then I was transferred to Pembrokeshire, for some of the time as assistant adjutant on the tank range in Castlemartin, undoubtedly the best part of my military service. I would draw on this experience as a young MP, when there was considerable controversy over the proposal for the German army to train at Castlemartin, a very daring scheme at the time – only a short time earlier we had had a policy of non-fraternisation in Germany.

Like many young men and women I was troubled as to how I would find sufficient resources to start at the Bar. I toyed with the idea of working in the Far East as some of my family had done, in my case I could work as a lawyer. A few months before I completed my service, I was accepted by a firm with a mixed barrister/solicitor practice in Singapore. I then had cold feet and politely rejected the offer. How different things could have been.

The overwhelming fascination of following a political/legal career at home had proved too much. I was determined, come what may, to both practise at the bar and become an MP in Wales.

When I completed my National Service in October 1955, I had the good fortune to join the Chambers of Mars-Jones (later Sir William Mars-Jones, a high court judge) at Farrar's Building in the Temple as a pupil.

three
FORMING A FARMERS' UNION

WHEN I CAME HOME for Christmas in 1955, all hell had broken loose in the agricultural community. The National Farmers' Union in Wales had split and a small but vociferous minority in Carmarthenshire and Cardiganshire had broken away. I went with my stepfather to a meeting of farmers in the Lion Royal Hotel in Aberystwyth where the case for the breakaway was put. My YFC credentials and street credibility were still very strong.

The upshot was that after the meeting I was asked by one of the chief rebels, D. J. Davies, a substantial and innovative farmer, to come and join the Farmers' Union of Wales as its legal adviser. He also happened to be president of the Cardiganshire Labour Party, where two-and-a-half years earlier I had lost the nomination to be the county Labour candidate.

I was taken to a small smoke-filled room in Carmarthen where I was presented to the leaders of the breakaway union and duly became deputy general secretary, the legal adviser of the new union and deputy to a staunch Tory, Mr J. B. Evans, who taught me more about real politics so far as dealing with people was concerned, than any other person. The Conservative Party in Wales missed out in not providing this great Welshman with a role appropriate to his talents. There followed two of the most demanding years of my life. The intention was to resume my pupillage at the Bar as soon as possible. I promised to stay in Wales for three months. Three months became a year, and a year became two.

The new union, the FUW as it became known – *Undeb Amaethwyr Cymru* – had no resources and no connections outside its two original counties of Carmarthen and Cardigan. It was formed because of deep anger and disappointment with the parent body in London. The main grievance was that the NFU had not treated Wales properly and had not given national recognition to the NFU Welsh Council. The catalyst seemed to be that they had spent a great deal on substantial and expensive new headquarters in Knightsbridge – they were on a different planet from the struggling seventy-to-eighty-acre man in Wales. Of greater importance perhaps was the complaint that they had not been sufficiently strong advocates for the small farmer at the annual agriculture price reviews. Also they had not campaigned for enough agricultural research facilities in Wales, and so on. There was a package of grievances. It is almost forgotten now how important that annual review was to farmers. A few pence per gallon on the price of milk and the like were crucial to their monthly milk cheques.

My heart had warmed to this new cause; I had gambled a great deal in taking up this job, and I suspected there would be problems about returning to my old pupillage. There were: when I made inquiries during my first year away, my mentor, Mars-Jones had taken silk, and could no longer take a pupil. But the job was not without its advantages. I would be paid a reasonable salary. I would become known throughout Wales – I could save, and would have resources to start at the bar at a time when reasonably paid legal aid had not yet fully developed.

We had a small office in Carmarthen, and an insurance company, the National Employers' Mutual, helped to finance new county offices and a Wales office in Aberystwyth. I would be saved the ninety-mile-a-day round journey from my home to Carmarthen.

Despite my inexperience, my job was to provide legal advice to farmers in each county and to campaign for membership at the same time, basically to try to set up the union as a national Welsh body. The executive council felt that we had to open up a North Wales office as soon as possible as it was thought to be fertile territory for new membership. I was sent on a rather lonely but adventurous mission to see Mr Tom Jones, secretary of the farmers' marts in Merionethshire and a particularly prominent Welsh nationalist in the area. We had absolutely no other line to pursue and depended on this one being fruitful. Otherwise we would only be a minority body operating in two counties, which was certainly not the aim of the founding fathers.

When I got to Dolgellau, Mr Jones made it clear I was not welcome, declining to give any help. The impression I had was that the sooner I was out of his town the better. He was just about courteous, but for such an assertive man, quite nervous. It was clear that he thought that the less he said the better. He had obviously weighed up the importance of his loyalty to his former employers. Like J. B. Evans he, too, was a former county secretary of the NFU. That was where his paramount interest and loyalty lay; whatever his political views a national body to represent Welsh farmers was not on his radar screen. I understood his point of view, but it was one of my immense disappointments in life at the time. My mission seemed to have been shattered.

I telephoned Carmarthen from a phone box and was immediately instructed to abandon Merionethshire for the time being and to go on to Caernarfon and find an office there to open up business. This I did. I had no contacts, but I suppose the enthusiasm and intrepidness of youth carried me forward. In retrospect, I was quite mad. I had no intention of failing, but where to start? I later wondered whether subliminally what I had learnt as a junior umpire in mock battles on the German plains was influencing me – opening up one front and coming right up against insurmountable obstacles and then diverting around it. This is hindsight – I am trying to explain my perseverance.

Having taken some very small and rather peculiar premises in a main street in Caernarfon, I called a press conference – a two-man band – issued a statement and my first contact followed, from a Mr O. T. Ll. Huws, a charming, determined farmer from Anglesey. He was sometimes unrealistic because of his optimism, but a tower of strength. He lavished encouragement on me.

I organised a series of public meetings to publicise the union, first in Caernarfonshire and then in Anglesey. I might have made a good double-glazing salesman, such was my intrepid cold-calling. It was winter then, before the lambing, and fortunately there was not so much to do on the land once the milking was over.

Caernarfonshire proved a hard nut to crack. Farms were relatively small and times were quite hard, and the smaller farmer was loath to jump to our camp. After all, the security of association with his friends and equals and a sound insurance company like the NFU Mutual were important to him. Who were we? Missionary south Walians whom he didn't know, indeed had hardly heard of! Yet his problems were at the heart of the breakaway. He had nothing in common with the barley barons of England, whom it was felt wielded too much influence at price review negotiations.

Anglesey proved easier, and in both counties there was a better chance, which sounds incongruous, to recruit from the larger farms. Many of them did come over. I was encouraged when a farmer of a distinguished lineage, Mr John Williams of Brynsiencyn, joined, and a particularly substantial farmer, a Mr Rowlands from the Bangor area, became very active and supportive. Mr Glyngwyn Roberts from Anglesey became a tough convert and savaged a retired – I hope he was retired – bank manager in Llanerchymedd who advised caution at a public meeting. Glyngwyn was later to become a distinguished president of the union.

Every night a team of speakers would come up from Carmarthenshire and Cardiganshire to meetings I had organised. Sometimes they would stay for one or two nights, or even occasionally return that very night, a round journey of 150 miles or so. After all, the milking had to be done. Hundreds gathered for a huge debate at Chwilog Market. I was proud to have organised it; it was like a revival meeting of old.

When one thinks of the distances involved and the claims for attention from their own fairly small farms, I can only marvel at the effort these farming men selflessly put into the campaign, and at the help they got from their families. I must say – and it is difficult now fully to unwind the film reel of the past – the bitterness of the campaign was more than I was ever to experience in my later political life. The great strength of the founding leaders was that they had individual allegiances to all political parties and to none. Despite this, we were maligned as 'nationalists' and 'conscientious objectors' – the latter a very much vituperative term of the period – 'preachers' and 'unemployed taxi drivers'. The union was given three months to live.

It gave me a lot of pleasure to attend the fifty years celebrations at Newtown in 2005, a rather longer life than the three months envisaged in 1955. But there would be a long wait before the prized official recognition was obtained.

My time at the FUW was a hard two years involving an immense amount of driving. I had offices for farmers to consult me at Llangefni, Caernarfon, Dolgellau, Aberystwyth and Carmarthen. We later opened an office in Bridgend. On my way home from weekly visits to Dolgellau on mart days I would stop off in Staylittle to give a WEA lecture on agricultural law. It was a long day, leaving home well before 8.30 a.m. and returning about 10.30 p.m., if I did not stay the night. Hardly a normal day for anyone, but I fear a pattern of activity that I have continued all my life. I was helping to form my first all-Wales institution. I have, over a very long period of time, paid for this frenetic activity, when eating was only an occasional and erratic indulgence. My poor stomach paid the price for a lifetime.

It was my task to prepare policy papers for the union, particularly at the time of the price review. Our members wanted to know where we stood and, with the executive's approval, they were forwarded to the ministry's Welsh Agricultural Office. Its secretary seemed rather shy of associating with us. We had a considerable presence at major agricultural shows and the National Eisteddfod. I founded the Union's newspaper, Y Tir ('The Land') and was its editor and sole contributor. It survives fifty years later.

I represented individual farmers at various tribunals and gained valuable experience. One of my most interesting was representing our members at the Tryweryn Defence Committee to try to thwart the plans of Liverpool

Corporation to drown a Welsh valley by damming the Tryweryn River. It was to no avail, despite the opposition of most Welsh MPs and indeed so many others throughout the whole of Wales. Gwynfor Evans, Plaid Cymru's President, was also on the committee. He seemed very distant and hardly spoke to me. I had never met him before. He certainly knew who I was but he made no attempt to find common ground before or after the meetings.

Jumping ahead, the time came to leave the union when I was chosen as the Labour candidate for Aberavon. I had real hopes of becoming an MP and needed to resume my training to become a practising barrister. I left the union in good heart with a strong and growing membership in most parts of Wales. I had played a small part in setting up an all-Wales institution which had all the marks of enduring.

I decided that a pupillage in Swansea would be much more convenient than London. I would be able to hone my professional skills and nurse my constituency at the same time. I was immensely fortunate in becoming a pupil of one of Wales's leading personal injury barristers, Alun Talfan Davies (later Sir), who had wide experience of the problems of workers in the steel and coal industries. This kind of work was to enhance my awareness of the problems of my future constituents, experience I badly needed.

four
MY SEARCH FOR
A PARLIAMENTARY SEAT

DESPITE THE HEAVY DEMAND from my union workload, I had
kept my eyes open for political opportunities. Together with
Geraint Howells, I became a member of the general management
committee of the Cardiganshire Labour Party. By-elections in Pontypool
and Newport were well outside my reach. In the autumn of 1956 Britain
invaded Suez and I was invited to speak at a Labour Party protest meeting in Carmarthenshire. The Labour theme, emphasising that all necessary
steps should be taken by the UN and only through the UN, was 'law not
war'. I think the audience approved of me despite – or was it because of –
my youth. The local Member of Parliament for Carmarthen West was the
elderly Sir Rhys Hopkin Morris QC, Deputy Speaker of the House of Commons and much respected, despite his rather austere views. He was an
established Liberal of the old school, almost of a Victorian, certainly of an
Edwardian vintage. However, he had Conservative support at elections;
Carmarthen elections were usually a two-horse race. This was the seat
that I thought was both winnable and suitable for me. There were then
6,000 registered milk producers in Carmarthenshire and having been
brought up on a dairy farm, I understood their problems.

In fact, I could see no other seat in Wales that was suitable for me
and that I could win. I knew nothing about industry. I was, as Leo Abse
MP was later to write in *The Spectator*, 'the product of a rural sub-culture'.
I was rather proud of this, despite his total lack of comradely feelings when
he wrote it, which was not unusual. The whole tone of his paragraph was
quite malicious.

To my dismay, Hopkin Morris died quite suddenly. The by-election
would be a by-election to outclass all others, or so we thought; I suppose

everybody does the first time they stand. This was a winnable seat, with the ability to deliver a massive vote of censure on the government's illegal frolicking in Suez. They needed the best candidate possible. My hat was already in the ring and I had some connections with part of the Gwendraeth Valley and Llandybie in particular. I decided to seek the nomination.

My good friends in the Agricultural Workers' Union came to my aid and I went round some of the miners' lodges in the then flourishing coalfield and gathered nominations from the Great Mountain Pit, Blaenhirwaun, and one or two others, but not Cross Hands Pit. My failure there turned out to be crucial. I believe some nominations came from the Ammanford area too.

Some of the rail union branches were helpful, particularly from Whitland, and I had a nomination from the Felindre Party in the Teifi Valley, from a most friendly stonemason known colloquially as 'John y Gwas' (John the servant). I was recently told he was so called because he gave assistance to everyone, particularly in the filling of forms – he was, in fact, the people's servant. The candidate favoured by the party nationally was to be Lady Megan Lloyd George who was recently, after years of hesitation, a recruit to the Labour Party, although it seems that her support in the lobby was assured some time before she lost her Anglesey seat in 1951 where she had been the Liberal MP since before the war. She had been in the political wilderness so far as the House of Commons was concerned since then, although prominent in the cross-party Parliament for Wales Campaign. I believe I was away in the army at the time and took no part in it.

The National Executive of the Labour Party did not actually nominate a candidate as technically they could for a by-election. In Carmarthenshire they preferred to gather local support and this tactic proved the best. That did not stop the Welsh regional office from giving what encouragement they could to Lady Megan. It was not an entirely level playing field. I gather that my candidature was regarded as outrageous: experience, age, political standing, they all counted against me. My pluses were limited. I understand everything possible was done to shake the apples off the tree in the form of nominations for Lady Megan.

The big day came. My stepfather, ever willing, although it was a field completely outside his experience, drove me down to Carmarthen for the selection meeting. We picked up three or four agricultural workers on the way; cars and transport in the country were in short supply. Agricultural workers were low paid and the battered old banger, if they had one, was a vital artery to one's place of work. When I became a transport minister I was to discover that Powys had one of the highest ratios of car owners in the land. It was a necessity, not a luxury and I did not forget this in discussions on road taxing policy.

A black cat tried to pass in front of us. My stepfather, like many, if not most, people, did not give way to the cat. It had to wait. I thought this a bad omen.

The choosing of the candidate was at St Peter's Church Hall, Carmarthen, and the place was packed. A miner, the well-regarded Islwyn Thomas, was in the chair. The regional organiser, Cliff Protheroe, was at his side. I had never met Megan before and she oozed charm. I can't remember who spoke first, Megan or myself. I can't have done so badly, a mere boy compared with her, the most experienced of politicians. I lost 45–46. Afterwards, I was told I should have demanded a recount. I still wonder why, but I have always discounted any errors in arithmetic. I should have had them checked again to make sure. With more experience this would have been the obvious course. But at the time I was not going to be a bad loser.

Megan told me on a later occasion that her father, 'the old man', David Lloyd George, always prepared two speeches for an election count – one for winning and one for losing. Despite his long tenure of Carnarvon boroughs, he had some results too close for comfort.

I pledged myself publicly and immediately to support Megan. At that point it was the blackest day of my life. Where else could I aspire to a Welsh seat suited to whatever talents I had? In the next few months, I was offered nominations by the national agent, Sara Barker, in part of the Wirral, West Derby and Bradford West. I declined them all as I had no interest in an English seat, although I noted later all these were to be won by Labour from time to time. This was a reward for my immediate and continuing support.

My next job was to fulfil my promise of supporting Megan. Those were the days of four or five meetings each evening, the candidate arriving later and later as the night wore on. Every Welsh MP, including Aneurin Bevan, who delivered a terrific speech to a packed meeting of hundreds, if not thousands in the Market Hall, Carmarthen, was drafted in. How he revelled in the hecklers. Today our party leaders have ticket-only audiences and fail to excite them as did the extempore passages from speeches by the likes of Nye.

I played my part and was delighted to open the campaign at a meeting in Penygroes with Clement Attlee, probably his last by-election campaign. Clem spoke briefly and almost sharply. The message was clear. It was quite contrary to the UN charter for the government to have invaded Egypt. It was illegal.

There was considerable agricultural discontent during the election – hardly noticed by the national papers. The price of milk had fallen by four or five pence a gallon and this was very damaging to the industry. County Councillor J. S. Davies of Llanybri, a prominent milk producer, provided a photograph of himself on his farm to be printed on one of Megan's leaflets. My union became quite unhappy as Mr Davies was one of the eight founder members, and I was out speaking at Labour Party meetings most nights, when I was not speaking at union meetings in other parts of Wales. The Liberal candidate, with Conservative support, was Mr Morgan Davies, a man with a sound agricultural and local background. As a former Welsh secretary of the NFU and the principal of an agricultural college in the north of England, he turned out to be rather an ineffective politician. There were no other candidates.

The unhappiness of my union expressed itself in a strong letter of protest from my president, Mr Ivor Davies, forbidding me from taking any further part in the election campaign. It could not have been more firmly put. With the recklessness of youth, I sent an equally firm and hopefully courteous reply declining to accept his order.

Nothing happened. We all carried on as before. My gamble had paid off. I was not in an immediate hurry to leave the union, as I had not then explored the possibilities of another pupillage.

Election day was in March 1957 and Megan won by 3,069 votes. I was overjoyed. Justice was done nationally. I fortunately did not suffer from any self-pity. I got on with my union work and Westminster seemed further away than ever. It was only a dream.

Would I have won the seat? I have always been clear in my own mind that I would not. Megan was an outstanding candidate, the best we could have had: she had the illustrious name, the charm and immense political skills. Whatever attractions I may have had, the downside would have been considerably heavier than the upside. However, had I won it, I doubt very much that I would have lost it later. From my later experience, I would have nursed the constituency to whatever lengths necessary to ensure retention. We can always wonder what might have happened, but if I am right Mr Gwynfor Evans, President of Plaid Cymru, would never have become Member for Carmarthen, and that part of Welsh history would have been rather different.

My personal life, aiming to practise and to hold a precarious seat at all times would have been very different too. Practising at the Bar would not have been possible. My number one priority would have been holding the seat in all weathers. I would, however, have been much better placed to be a minister of agriculture. Certainly in those days Labour MPs thoroughly versed in the problems of agriculture were not too plentiful.

At that stage it was my burning ambition. I never attained it. I felt I could have done justice to agriculture, to farmers and the rural community from whence I came. I would also have killed cries in the Labour Party to nationalise land. There was quite a demand for this in the Party and it came to the surface frequently.

I became active in the Socialist Agricultural Society and travelled up to its meetings with D. J. Davies, where I came to know some of its leaders like Harry (later Lord) Walston and John Mackie, who were very big farmers. John Mackie was later to become a junior minister of agriculture. We represented small Welsh farmers; they were successful big farmers. We got on well. We all wanted a prosperous industry and memories of food shortages during the war were still strong. Economic self-production was very much in all our thoughts.

Suddenly, another door opened. It was announced in the summer of 1957 that W. G. Cove, veteran member for Aberavon since 1929, was to retire, and nominations were invited for the next general election.

Should I or should I not throw my hat into the ring for this, for me, seemingly impossible Labour seat, with a 16,000 plus majority? A constituency dominated by the steel industry at Port Talbot – an industry of which I knew nothing. My lack of connections reminded me of my lonely foray to North Wales on behalf of the FUW. The experience stood me in good stead; it was another mountain to climb.

I consulted with D. J. Davies, my long-standing friend, who was still president of the Cardiganshire Labour Party and with Tyssul Lewis, its secretary. They enthusiastically prompted me to stand. How to make contact? D. J. Davies agreed to write an introductory letter to anyone we could think of. Tyssul Lewis's wife kindly typed the letter, on the basic typewriter of the day, and many copies – they had to be originals.

I asked the Aberavon agent, Billy Vaughan, for a list of delegates to the General Management Committee. This was refused, but Billy did send a copy of the Aberavon constituency party's annual report, with a list of quite a few of the delegates nominated to serve on the executive. Our methods were primitive compared to today's practices, but we had nothing else to go on. I had to conjure up vague addresses of delegates based on their wards. The Post Office seems to have delivered in more cases than I could have hoped.

Some responses came and I was invited to speak in the Cornelly Ward. Questions on the steel industry were bound to test me. I had a good reception at the meeting and survived the key question. Mr Ted Davies, an AEU foreman fitter at the works, who later became chairman of Mid Glamorgan County Council, asked me what I knew about the steel industry? 'Nothing,' I said, 'but I am willing to learn.' I told him I was a trained barrister and hoped I had the facility to master a brief quickly. He recounted this episode when he took part in a Welsh TV film on my life, by then he was well over ninety! He was also kind enough to say he had never known me to quarrel with anyone in more than forty years representing my constituency.

Surprisingly the reply went down well. I got my first nomination, and struck up a friendship with 'Ginger' Waters, a quarryman, who was the ward secretary. Ginger was an ex-serviceman, from one of the guards' regiments I believe. He suffered from a terrible stutter and had been threatened with disciplinary action when taking a message as the platoon runner to a young officer during the war. Unfortunately the officer had a bad stutter too, and thought that Ginger, who had never met him, was taking the mickey. He loved to tell this story.

In the company of the almost inarticulate Ginger, I was taken into the steelworks to meet shop stewards. Access was easy in those days. More than 16,000 workers came and went each day. We went up the Afan Valley to the mining village of Glyncorrwg and met an elderly but impressive councillor, Jenkin Thomas, who was working on the side of the road as a stonemason. Two nominations followed. Kenfig Hill unexpectedly nominated me. This was a strong, almost independent ward with a broad cross section of very articulate members. I had four nominations in all.

The key meeting was calling one Sunday afternoon at the home of County Councillor Rees Matthews. He was a senior steelworkers' representative and drove a crane, stoking the furnace in the steelworks. He gave nothing away, but I believe the impression I made was crucial.

There was no doubt among the press, cognoscenti and councillors in South Wales that there was only one candidate. It would be a shoe-in for Alderman Llew Heycock, the progressive chairman of Glamorgan Education Committee, an engine driver and the constituency treasurer, who had worked man and boy for the party and the people of Port Talbot. To many, the education committee was the only hope of a better life for their children.

The general secretary of the Aberavon Labour Party was W. H. Vaughan, a small man physically but in no other respect. He worked for British Railways as a station yard manager. He lived in the same ward as Heycock and was determined to play by the rules, seeking detailed guidance from time to time from the national agent. Writing on 10 June 1957, in response to Ginger Waters, who had requested a list of affiliated organisations, he stated:

> The executive is determined to show utmost impartiality in the selection of the parliamentary candidate . . . I hope, therefore, that you will appreciate that we must not . . . leave ourselves open to attack for having given any one candidate for selection an advantage over another.

There must have been a great deal of controversy and forecasting in the constituency, because a press statement was issued with the names of the nominated candidates which said:

> No one person can decide, no group of persons can decide, no single organisation can decide. It is the whole party which decides the issue. No one has any special claim to the candidature. He or she must take their chance and abide by the wish of the conference acting collectively.

This was signed by Vaughan and county councillor Gwyn Davies, president of the Aberavon Constituency Party. Vaughan also wrote a firm letter in the same vein to J. Campbell, the general secretary of the NUR, saying that sponsorship by any organisation would not be revealed to the GMC when the candidate was selected. Heycock was a prominent NUR member locally.

The nominations came in and eventually the selection conference was fixed for 23 June 1957. Heycock had thirty-two nominations. Nothing had been left to chance. Mr Emlyn Emmanuel had thirteen. They were all from British Iron and Steel and Kindred Trades' Association branches. County Councillor Jenkin John from just outside the constituency, the favourite son of the miners, had five. Trevor Williams, born locally and an able *Daily Herald* journalist, had eight. Ray Fletcher, a Labour lecturer, had three. I had only four nominations. I have forgotten how many nominations County Councillor D. H. Davies had, two or three. The executive chose the shortlist and the order of speaking: Fletcher, myself, Williams, D. H. Davies and Heycock.

I understood that there was intense dissatisfaction among the steel unions that Emmanuel, who had the second highest number of nominations, had been left out. He was a very respected councillor from Neath, worked in the steelworks and was prominent in steel union affairs. Jenkin John, the miners' candidate, was also left out. An appeal to the National Executive was unsuccessful. I think that Fletcher, Davies and I were put in to make up the numbers. We were harmless. Not for the first time in the history of the Labour Party, two of the most serious contenders against the favourite, Heycock, had been left out. The steelworkers had forty-nine possible delegates and the miners twenty-eight.

We spoke as agreed and answered preselected questions. I spoke in the ten minutes allotted to me on the dangers of the hydrogen bomb. In our absence, the meeting went on to vote. On the first vote, Davies ten, Fletcher twenty-eight, Heycock sixty, myself forty-two, and Williams thirty-eight.

I had come second on the first ballot. In the next three ballots I picked up a further fifty-eight votes, making it one hundred. Heycock was only able to add a further fifteen, making his total seventy-five. I had won a totally unexpected and stunning victory. I shall never forget being summoned from the room I sat in to be welcomed as the candidate. The party had by then given me the traditional unanimous vote.

We all made short speeches. My only recollection was that I thanked all who had taken part, and felt very honoured to be chosen as the Party's candidate for Aberavon. I promised to do my best to serve the constituency. The chairman had been slightly put out when Protheroe had asked him, in the middle of the voting, to tell the meeting to exercise its vote carefully and responsibly, whatever that meant. It was certainly not an encouragement to vote for a mere stripling like me. In later years, he told me many times that he regretted listening to Protheroe. He had interpreted it as an indication to vote for Heycock; this interpretation was not necessarily correct, but he took it as such. Why the advice was given I do not know. I had riled Protheroe more than once by making what he thought were radically Welsh speeches at Wales Labour Party conferences, and coming so near in Carmarthen was the last straw. We were never close thereafter.

Vaughan very wisely advised me to go home – it would be better for me, he said. I took his advice and rang my mother on the way. She could hardly believe the news, neither could I. It more than made up for Carmarthen.

In the first vote, both the steelworkers and, I suspect, the miners swung behind me. Matthews and an even more influential steelworker, Dai 'Banky' Thomas, a member of the Steelworkers National Executive, also from Heycock's ward, had sent in a branch nomination on behalf of Emmanuel and gave every encouragement (that is a three-line whip) to their fellow delegates, of whom they had a potential forty-nine, to attend. In those days they actually turned up, and I believe they did that night. I was to work closely with the steelworkers for very nearly forty-two years.

The fact that I had done well against Lady Megan, and being a young and enthusiastic man had helped, but a much more important reason for my success was the vote of the angry steelworkers who had been denied their candidate. Every man swung to me. I owed it to them thereafter to make steel and jobs in Port Talbot and South Wales my top priority. I tried my best. It dominated my life, and I kept a close eye on whatever happened at Port Talbot Steel.

Shortly afterwards I first met Margaret at the National Eisteddfod in Llangefni where Gomerian Press, which her father chaired, had a stand. Her brother John was a contemporary in Cambridge and he, Roland Moyle, later to be a minister of state in Northern Ireland, and Gareth Jones, later to be vice master of Trinity and myself, would go from the Squire Law Library for tea.

When Margaret returned from a three week holiday in Germany I took her out. Very shortly afterwards I asked her to marry me and she said yes. We got engaged at Christmas time, when I fetched her from Oxford where she taught small children. A year later we were married and settled for the time being in Swansea. Although she knew she was marrying a prospective MP, neither she nor I any idea what that was to entail.

Margaret has always been there, encouraging and advising and sharing it all, the ups and the downs. Far too often she has brought up our girls almost single-handed. It is difficult to convey adequately the pressures on the wife or husband of a busy MP.

For more than two years I nursed the constituency. The election was a long time coming and I left the FUW. After my pupillage with Alun Talfan Davies, I became one of his devils, which meant that I worked on his legal papers, while we lived in Swansea and Margaret did supply teaching. It was a happy period.

We waited anxiously for the election which never seemed to come, but it gave me a wonderful opportunity to get to know my constituents as thoroughly as I could, and the few miles between Swansea and Port Talbot made it so much easier. Alun became a lifelong friend and he and Lynn were very kind to Margaret and myself. On the first occasion that Margaret came down to stay the weekend with Alun and Lynn I met her at Swansea station wearing the bowler hat that most barristers then wore. She jokes that she nearly turned back.

I acquired considerable expertise in driving Alun's Armstrong Siddeley – mustard-coloured with black mudguards – from one end of Wales to the other, and I picked up some of his work in appearing for local authorities in opposing bus fare increases. It was very lucrative. He was the Liberal candidate for Carmarthen at the time and he had wide interests. I was there at the founding of *Barn*, his Welsh language *New Statesman* as he called it. His company HTV later captured the ITV licence for Wales. In my time he had joined with my father-in-law in publishing a massive Welsh-language dictionary. It was his idea, but too big for him to handle alone. At the time it was a substantial enterprise and Alun put a great deal of his resources behind it. My father-in-law was both a publisher (Gomerian Press) and printer and it made sense for them to handle it jointly.

Before, during and after a case the practical policies for so many aspects of Welsh language development became the meat and drink of our conversations. We discussed every aspect of Welsh life. He knew cultural and industrial Wales well. I learnt a great deal from him. He was later to devote much of his time and energy to the Aberfan Disaster Fund. How he found time for these interests with a huge junior practice, I will never know. His own Welsh publishing business, Gwasg y Dryw, Llandybïe, took up a lot of his time, worries and money. I listened to one or two other schemes which did not take off. Alun was never put off; his enthusiasm never dimmed.

five
ELECTED MP FOR ABERAVON

MY PREDECESSOR, BILLY COVE, generally referred to as Mr Cove, had held the Aberavon seat from 1929, but he was not sufficiently well to come to Aberavon in the two years or more that I was the prospective candidate. He clung on. There was no proper pension as of right in those days, only a means-tested allowance. This was a deplorable way of treating Members of Parliament, who had devoted themselves for such a long time, for not very generous remuneration, to serving their communities. (Like Mr Cove, I was usually addressed as Mr Morris and I valued the respect it showed. I was so pleased when, after I had been retired for some years and was standing at a bus stop near Port Talbot station, a lady came up to me and enquired if I was Mr Morris.)

When I became an MP on 8 October 1959, the salary was a magnificent – to me – sum of £1,750 a year. There was no parliamentary money for secretarial assistance so Margaret did the lot unpaid for years, including managing my diary and telephone calls. MPs paid their own postage and all telephone calls outside London – they had a monthly bill from the House. Car mileage was not yet thought of, but fortunately a pension came in only a few years later, paid after ten years service. Such was my concern for my family that I rang up the Fees Office on my tenth anniversary to check my entitlement, to their great surprise. I did not want to find myself in the position of my predecessor.

The only perk was free train travel, including a night sleeper to or from your constituency to Westminster. The poor MPs living far from London used to catch the sleeper on a Thursday night to their homes in order to save a night in a hotel. What is the right amount to pay a public representative will always be argued about. All I can be sure of is our remuneration in my young days was totally inappropriate. Those were the conditions in the House of Commons that I enthusiastically entered.

The first question we had to decide was where we would live. Despite our new love for Swansea and its people, the company of all my professional friends and our proximity to Port Talbot, Margaret and I came to believe quite quickly that the pluses of living together and seeing my small family as they would grow up, demanded that we should move to London. My main role was to be on the floor of the House.

I had commuted from Westminster to Swansea on a weekly basis for more than a year, but by then my daughter, Nia, had been born and when I left for London on a Monday, Margaret would return to her parents' home until Friday. By early December 1960 we had bought a small home in Chislehurst, which was convenient for London. To have a reasonable standard of life, and hopefully in due course buy an additional home in Wales for the parliamentary recesses, which was for both of us a high priority, I needed to continue practising at the Bar. There was no housing or living allowance in any shape or form.

In any event, even in those days, my ambition was to be a law officer, and with one or two exceptions in recent times, I do not know of any law officer who has not had considerable and current experience of practising. It is an essential prerequisite – the job cannot be done in any other way. This is why Prime Ministers have been compelled to appoint law officers from the House of Lords, when qualified and suitable candidates from the House of Commons have been difficult to find.

I believe, and it is generally accepted, that it is a fantasy to be a law officer without some standing at the Bar and the ability and experience to give legal advice to the government of the day on a wide range of matters. I suppose a junior law officer can cruise the country, visiting the Crown Prosecution Service and putting the spotlight on such issues as gender and racial problems. In my view that is mainly a political rather than a legal job. They can be dressed up as silks by making them QCs, but even with such an honorific title, without proper legal experience or acknowledged legal academic expertise, how can they write a decent legal opinion?

It was my aim to be as proficient as I could in my chosen profession and I was determined from the beginning to be properly prepared for the role of a law officer if I was ever called on. However I also intended my whole future to be focussed on politics and to practise as much of the law as I could without detracting from my political career. To be a good MP, serving my constituents to the best of my ability was my clear aim. To be a competent and experienced lawyer at the same time would be a challenge.

Before my arrival, Aberavon had taken the view that such a safe seat should be offered as a platform to a politician who could play a major part on the national stage. Hence, I was told, there had been some feeling that Michael Foot, who was then without a seat, should be offered it. I believe that such an offer was made informally. Michael declined as he wished to fight Plymouth again and again. I was the beneficiary of his loyalty to Plymouth.

According to David Marquand's book on Ramsay MacDonald, who was my predecessor but one, there was some local discontent about MacDonald's absences from the constituency. He was, after all, Labour's first Prime Minister, but Labour constituencies in general had not really taken on board the intense demands of ministerial office on their local MP's time and the time available had to be shared. We were in Parliament as Labour MPs to bring about a Labour government and to be effective ministers, if the electorate at large permitted it. You had to find the time to be both an overworked minister and a good constituency MP. At any rate, by my time the lesson had been learned: although Cove never held office in his very long period of service, I was not aware of even a murmur of discontent such as that from which MacDonald had suffered. Whenever I got a ministerial post, Aberavon shared in my success and was generous in its congratulations.

What I did, so far as Aberavon was concerned, was to introduce the concept of regular constituency surgeries. It sounds incredible but Cove, like some other MPs, did not hold a surgery in his thirty years as an MP. Constituency cases, other than by correspondence, were dealt with by his admirable agent, Billy Vaughan.

I took the view that since I did not live in the constituency, and indeed had never been asked to do so, I should always be available, if necessary, seven days a week. There were quite a few occasions when I had to catch an overnight train to deal with a problem: a flood, the closing of a factory, or trouble at the steelworks. There never was an occasion when anyone had to ask, 'Where is the MP?' He was always there when wanted.

Industrial trouble, in particular union issues, was rife in my early days. It was the era of unofficial strikes. Pits closed, small factories became redundant. I was able to give whatever help or assistance was required within days and I was seen to be immediately doing my best. There is nothing worse than allowing a situation to fester over the weekend and the chatter to grow in the clubs, chapels, rugby matches or wherever people met, blaming the MP for the problem and inability to solve it.

My speedy arrival was often quite a surprise. On one occasion I had a telegram from Cymmer requesting my immediate presence involving a pit. The message went back by return, 'Call a meeting for Friday!'

Coupled with surgeries every few weeks I tried to do what was necessary. We had no Labour headquarters in the constituency, and although my

Labour club gave me a warm welcome and the use of part of its premises for election times for many years, I was determined not to hold my surgeries there. I needed neutral ground, and many of my constituents had never been in a club in their life. I was not an MP for those who had voted for me only. I asked the town clerk, Mr King-Davies, whether I could hold my surgeries in the council offices. I had the council's cordial agreement and I could always meet my constituents on this neutral ground. I think this approach was welcomed by all.

These days there is an expectation that the MP should live in his or her constituency and I understand it. Ministers in my time, in fact, were obliged to have a home in London, the system was geared to that requirement and I hoped to be a minister.

We were home in my wife's village of Llandysul during most recesses, which was convenient for the constituency, until my growing family became too much of a burden for my mother-in-law, despite her ready willingness to accommodate us. The time had come for us to acquire a home in Wales, and I could now afford it. There was no second home allowance. A family home became available in my wife's village. Margaret had come enthusiastically with me to London, and I owed it to her that when I bought a home in Wales, it should be in her village. It took exactly an hour, when eventually most of the M4 motorway was built, to get from Llandysul to Port Talbot, which was sometimes quicker than going from one end of my constituency to the other. It was joked that my determination to complete a great deal of the M4 came from wanting to get home quicker.

Aberavon had been first won for Labour by Ramsay MacDonald in 1924 and has been held by the party ever since. Billy Cove's last majority, in May 1955, was 16,297 and mine in October 1959 was 17,638. My mother and stepfather came down to hear the result. Given the difficulties that she had triumphed over in life, she was understandably a proud mother. I was to fight eleven elections in all and apart from the 1983 election under Michael Foot's leadership, when our manifesto was described by a member of the Shadow Cabinet as the 'longest suicide note in history', I was to enjoy a 20,000 majority, more or less, on all occasions. My last majority was 21,571, giving me 71.32 per cent of the poll.

My first Conservative opponent in 1959 was a respected local boy, Geoffrey Howe, who had also stood in 1954. It was a courteous and tenaciously fought campaign. Many members of the Conservative Bow Group came to assist him, including the late lamented Ian Gow, who was murdered by the IRA. As some admitted to me years later, their 'away days' in Aberavon were quite an experience for them. My task was to establish my status as a newcomer from West Wales, as Aberavon's 'Labour' candidate.

My Labour constituents had, by and large, made a habit of voting, 'Cove, Labour'. On my posters, I emphasised that Morris was the Labour candidate. They read, 'Vote Labour, Vote Morris'. It worked.

In 1959 Parliament had gone on to the bitter end. We started hard campaigning in August 1959. I was persuaded to go from door to door and speak, sometimes at length, to every constituent in Glyncorrwg, at the top end of the Afan Valley, then an active mining village. The sun was hot and although I was young and fit, the intensity of campaigning nearly broke me and I was useless for the next two days.

Some other method was necessary if I was to last the course. So we arranged to go to each ward in turn with a team of helpers in cars, and developed street-by-street canvassing. I soon found speeches on the loudspeaker, time after time, for eight to ten hours a day, also too demanding, such was my inexperience. Instead I taped short party messages, played by a member of my team sitting in a car, which supplemented my short speeches. In between, County Councillor Cyril Lewis, one of my close friends, could go on all day – he had taken voice training in his youth as an aspiring boy soprano. Meanwhile, I made myself known by getting out of the car and actually meeting hundreds of constituents at the same time. If they were out, or working on shift, it soon got around that I had been in their street.

The tapes saved me an awful lot of energy and I was as fresh as paint at the end of the day, which meant I could spend more time talking to people. Even then in 1959 and the 1960s, the two or three times a night meetings were attracting fewer and fewer people. I insisted for quite a time on eve of poll meetings, talking in the main to party supporters. Much as I enjoyed it, it was no substitute for street contact with hundreds, if not thousands, of constituents who could discuss their problems and question me; any lengthy problem was given an appointment at my surgery after the election. The same pattern was followed for each of my elections, although as time went by other demands, such as radio and TV across Wales, forcibly shortened the available number of days. I missed the personal contact and I never took my constituents' support for granted.

The really exhausting time was when we had two elections within months in 1974 and I had, as secretary of state, to lead the campaign in Wales for the second election, including personally writing the Welsh Labour manifesto. It was agreed to without amendment by the Welsh Labour Council. Some Welsh Office work continued to polling day.

The Labour Chancellor Hugh Dalton once remarked that an MP only met a handful of constituents, about twenty I think and the same ones, in an average year. That may have been true of him but not me. Through canvassing, meetings and my surgery I learnt more than in any other way where the shoe was pinching for my constituents. However high and busy my office, with a total of seven to eight years in Cabinet rank, nothing was more satisfying than leaving Cabinet on a Thursday, coming down to Wales on a Friday and trying to solve individuals' problems. Regrettably, I was an absent member of the family for most weekends.

Just before my first election I received a shattering blow. Billy Vaughan, the constituency party secretary and agent to be – in the Labour Party the appointment of the agent is theoretically a personal one – died at Paddington Station on his way home from a meeting in London. He had personally run the constituency for many years. Cove was our man at Westminster but Vaughan was Mr Labour in Aberavon. It was to him you went with your problems. He was a JP and an OBE.

The loss seemed irreparable. Fortunately, the Party moved quickly to appoint Harry Williams, Secretary of the Trades and Labour Council, who had considerable trade union connections as a staff worker at the steel-works. I was told that in those frantic days before the election, his wife, Mair, who taught Welsh among other things in a local school, would spend hours mugging up election rules and responsibilities in bed, so that she could safeguard Harry. She was always well armed and very protective of both of us. I could not have been better served by these two and their hospitality was boundless.

When Harry died the same succession system operated and Malcolm Gullam, a very active trade unionist, became my agent, probably the senior lay agent in Wales. I don't think I can remember a more professional one.

I was again excellently served: Malcom was my shield and had close contacts and vital links with the steelworks. He could use both the shield and sword on my behalf and needed no encouragement to use either. Beryl, his wife, bore the brunt of constituents' telephone calls and her role was not always made easy by the impatience of a few anxious to express their grievances to her. Two or three times a week he would ring me up before 9 a.m. and update me and no week went by without a detailed report when we agreed on the action to be taken. As an important member of the works council, there was not much he didn't know. I am eternally grateful to Malcolm and Beryl for the years that they looked after me and for their service to the constituency, to the Party in Wales and Malcolm to trade unionism.

The importance of my relationships with both Harry and Malcolm was that they were steelworkers and respected trade unionists. They kept me in daily touch with the problems at Port Talbot Steel, where most of my constituents worked. They ensured that the trade unions and I worked closely together.

My agents all believed that all my constituents had the right to personal access to their MP. I agreed and however busy I was with affairs of state, I saw them all myself. There were no such people as 'case workers' – other than ringing up a local government officer, which he sometimes did, and arranging my list, I had no help other than my agent. He was the known point of call and councillors and everyone in a position to help knew how to contact him.

When I became secretary of state, it seemed the whole of South Wales sometimes wanted to see me on a Saturday morning. I maintained a firm rule that I did not take in the washing of other MPs, although it would have been so easy not to divert them all, to the disadvantage of my patient constituents. When the Welsh Assembly came into existence, my correspondence and surgery halved.

Harry Williams had warned me that there were two things I should avoid at all costs. The first was not to get involved in trade union problems; the second was not to interfere in the borough council's problems. At election time I would, in the course of campaigning, pick up details of constituents with local council problems. The formula I adopted, whether it was housing repairs or any other local problem was to pass on the question by letter to the council officials, requesting information. This would then be passed on to my constituents, being extremely careful not to take any credit for a satisfactory answer, otherwise I might be inundated with similar problems at the expense of the local councillor, whose job it was to handle it. The same procedure applied to problems raised at my surgeries. It was a satisfactory method and local government officials were quick to respond to my inquiries. Constituents were happy that their queries had been promptly dealt with and that they had an answer from the responsible authority.

six
ENTERING THE
HOUSE OF COMMONS

AFTER THE GENERAL ELECTION on 8 October 1959, Margaret and I returned to my parents-in-law for the night, the result having been declared around midday. Margaret was pregnant but had been at my side throughout the campaign. We decided that the new MP and his wife should have a couple of days off in Tintern. I regret to say the fact that, under Hugh Gaitskill, we had lost the election badly did not sink in properly with me. More important I fear was that I had won my seat and increased the inherited majority from 16,297 to 17,638. Such is the self-interest of a winning candidate.

Some two weeks or more went by before we were summoned to the new Parliament and the taking of the Oath. (A few years later, I was to draft the Oath of Allegiance in Welsh for the use of Members. It never occurred to me at this stage.) There were three new Labour Members from Wales: Ifor Davies (Gower), Elfed Davies (Rhondda East) and myself. Ifor, much older, and I would travel up together from Swansea by train. We were taken under the wing of the Reverend Llewelyn Williams, MP for Abertillery; a gregarious man, very funny and conscientious. Llew, Ifor and myself became a band of brothers and sat together in the House on the third bench behind our front bench. We were all embarrassed, particularly Llew, when Leo Abse MP, all dressed up in his preposterous Budget day finery with stovepipe hat and lace cuffs, came and sat next to him. The eyes of the whole House were upon our row.

One of the first things Llew told me was never to say anything about another MP, because it will get back to the person concerned within half an hour. Never gossip. How right he was. Margaret never knew the trivia in the House until she read about them in the papers. Her opening question later would be, 'Did I know . . .?' I believe it was the poet, W. H. Davies who said, 'Nothing so dwarfs the mind as the constant dwelling on trivial things.' It was advice that stood me in good stead over the years.

It was curious how little guidance an MP had when entering the House. It was only a kind telephone call from Desmond Donnelly, MP (Pembrokeshire), who had been so encouraging to me when I was seeking a seat in Parliament, which gave me any help at all on the practicalities of getting to Westminster and in the essentials thereafter. He sent me a rail warrant so that I could buy a ticket to London.

I threw myself into the affairs of the House with great urgency. Within days I decided to make my maiden speech in the debate on the Queen's Speech. I telephoned the town clerk of Port Talbot requesting a brief on the need for a bypass, east to west traffic was strangled at the busy railway crossing by the frequent opening and shutting of the railway gates that crossed South Wales's main artery. It had been one of the questions raised at my selection conference. The deputy town clerk, Emrys Griffiths, who later became a lifelong friend and fellow Freeman of Port Talbot, delivered the goods by return – a well-polished brief from a locally born council official. The bypass was opened in 1967.

I delivered my maiden speech without showing any sign of nervousness. I was, however, a little nervous. It was Lloyd George, I believe, who said: 'Unless you have butterflies in your stomach as you approach making a speech in the House of Commons, the speech is probably not worth making.' Although it did not set the Thames on fire, it was a huge relief. I was a proper Member of Parliament!

Looking back on my activities in the first years, I was an assiduous questioner, mainly on agriculture, steel and local problems. I made fifteen speeches in my first year on subjects as varied as the Iron and Steel Bill, agriculture, horticulture and the fall-out of nuclear dust in the Welsh hills – I secured a special adjournment debate on the dangers of a nuclear fall-out of Strontium 90; the problems were to be repeated many years later after the Chernobyl disaster. The fare was similar in my second year: I raised the issue of the Welsh language in census forms and many problems concerning steel at Port Talbot.

I had the good fortune to succeed in the ballot for a debate on the Welsh Books Grant on 2 May 1961. It was the usual half-hour debate, but on this occasion it started at 3.39 a.m. Henry Brooke, the minister for housing and local government, also had the portfolio of being minister for Welsh affairs, and since he did not have a junior minister for this part of his responsibilities, he had to come down to the House himself at this early hour to reply. He must have been cursing this upstart MP but he graciously did not show it. He and I were the only Members in the chamber. It was the first time the issue had been debated in the House.

I began my speech, 'We in Wales have to fight to preserve our own nationhood . . . unless we have a living language, literature cannot survive' . . . .

The following year I kept up the same kind of contributions. After only two years in the House I was asked by the Shadow Cabinet to speak on two occasions from the Front Bench. The first one was a debate on the steel industry, and the second agriculture. One debate was on a Friday when nobody wanted to be there! But I was tickled pink, particularly to speak in a steel debate which I knew would be appreciated by my constituents. I had only been in the House about three and a half years when I received an invitation from Hugh Gaitskell, the Party Leader, to be a junior defence spokesman for the army. From March 1963, I replied for the Opposition to the annual debate on the army estimates, and sat on the Front Bench during defence questions. I was to sit on the Front Bench from about 1962 until Michael Foot sacked me in 1982. There had been considerable controversy about allowing German tank troops to train at the Castlemartin Tank Range; it was an emotive and sensitive issue at the time. I got up after only a short period in Parliament to speak in the party meeting and helped to calm some of the hostility and gave my assessment of the views of the locality. I used my knowledge, having been the assistant adjutant there. Hugh Gaitskell and Patrick Gordon Walker, Labour's defence spokesman, had noticed it and, with good luck, it paid off.

In 1963 I drew a place in the ballot for a debate on the need for a Welsh Agricultural College. I had been putting down questions on it for some time, as the FUW had agitated for this. When it was eventually built many years later, it gave me totally unexpected pleasure that my brother, Dei, was appointed its first Principal. Following on from the formation of the FUW it was the second all-Wales institution that I had played a very small part in creating. It was to be the story of my life.

When I had been in the House three and a half years, the Labour Opposition suffered a double tragedy in the deaths of two men who had grown into leadership – Labour Leader Hugh Gaitskell and Shadow Foreign Secretary Aneurin Bevan. Hugh Gaitskell was a dedicated and clever man and his death was a great shock. He was building a considerable reputation in welding together a divided Party. Aneurin Bevan had reclaimed the traditional stance of the Labour Party in defence and foreign affairs, but he too was prematurely struck down.

Harold Wilson, George Brown and Jim Callaghan stood for the leadership. I voted for Callaghan as I was always to do. In this particular contest there were still repercussions within the party from Harold Wilson's resignation from the Board of Trade Presidency. There were anxieties about his ability to unite the party. I felt that Callaghan was a more consensual figure. Callaghan was very much a third on the ballot, but a respectable third. George Brown was a man in whom I had no confidence; I deemed that he would be unreliable as a national leader. I decided to switch my vote to Wilson and rang him to tell him on a Sunday morning, when he had just returned on the sleeper from Liverpool. He was undoubtedly pleased and, I presume, was counting the switchers. Wilson won the contest and was elected Leader of the Opposition on 14 February 1963. It was the beginning of a strong association with Wilson and I grew to admire him. He was to say much later that as a minister I was a 'safe pair of hands'.

Not long after this Wilson was travelling by train to speak in Cardiff. I had arranged to travel with him as he had wanted to talk about problems at Port Talbot. In those days the trains had compartments and you could speak in comparative privacy. After disposing of our business concerning Port Talbot he asked me who I thought he should appoint as the first Welsh Secretary. This was in 1963 and the General Election, if not imminent, was approaching. I was only a young MP and delighted to have been asked. I was quite forthcoming, 'There is only one man,' I said, 'Jim Griffiths.' He raised an eyebrow. 'He'll talk too much in Cabinet,' he said. Jim did have a reputation for putting his hand on his heart and occasionally speaking with a great deal of emotion. I stood my ground and explained he was the only man who could appeal to the whole of Wales and the Welsh Labour Group. 'What about Ness Edwards?' he asked. I fear I was adamant in my strong preference for Jim. I was sure, despite my inexperience, that I was right.

My first Parliament was coming to an end. I was immensely active in the House and I was steadily building a sound junior practice at the Bar. Part of the weekend I would be speaking in my constituency or across a wide area of Wales wherever the Party wanted me. I paid my own expenses. There was intense political activity in anticipation of the approaching election and I spent part of most Sunday mornings translating my speeches into Welsh for the Welsh-language newspapers. I fear my family saw little of me for much of the weekend at this time. Meetings were still immensely popular and I was in demand in many parts of Wales, in addition to Aberavon.

What weighs down many urban MPs, particularly in London, is the sheer weight of constituency work. Today it is even worse, with the development of emails and the expectation of immediate action. I kept my work down while sticking to my rule to see everyone who wished to see me personally. I was a counsel of last resort when more local avenues had failed.

Nowhere was too far to go, from debating the Common Market with Tony Crosland in Coleg Harlech, to a Sunday afternoon seminar in Birmingham or explaining devolution to young Fabians in London. The advent of twenty-four hour media coverage has, I fear, undermined the advantages, forgetting the personal disadvantages, of the personal appearance of an MP in distant parts of the country. Looking back, I marvel as to how I kept up the pace.

For some time I had no union sponsorship and had to fund my own election campaigns. Years later, after the death of Ifor Davies, I obtained the sponsorship of APEX, the Clerical and Administrative Workers' Union. My debt to Graham Saunders, the union's South Wales and the West organiser, was immense. He would drive me, usually accompanied by Margaret, on our general election campaigns in constituencies all over Wales. He was also a non-executive member of the Milk Marketing Board. On one occasion, in my absence, he ran into a cow. Fortunately the press did not get hold of the story.

seven
WORKING WITH
MY FELLOW WELSH MPS

THE WELSH MPS were a varied and interesting group, as a body both loyal and conscientious. Most were former manual workers with little higher education other than at the Central Labour College. They made up for this by their grasp of the essentials of political advocacy. I just missed Dai Grenfell (MP for Gower) and father of the House. It was said that he spoke five languages, I suspect all self-taught. To these MPs the 1930s were still a living experience which they were determined not to repeat. The advent of the National Coal Board and the National Health Service were markers of major fulfilment for them. They had all given enormous service to their constituencies and enjoyed majorities of the same order as mine. None of them had any problems with security of tenure. They generally came to the House a little late in life when they had won their spurs locally.

They were, at first, a little suspicious of me. I was a young Welsh-speaker from mid Wales. They had fully expected a man they knew well – Llew Heycock, to join them. I had been a lawyer for a breakaway farmers' union and was probably thought to be some kind of nationalist infiltrator.

Steel and coal were major interests for me and the other South Wales MPs. Since some did not speak often in the chamber, they saw me as a reinforcement. I was drawing on my short professional experience and they were impressed by my interventions and questions on pneumoconiosis, mining hazards and sickness benefits. Hansard is full of my interventions in this early period. Most of the Welsh MPs had been there a long time and many occupied the Welsh table in the tea room most of the day. They were teased that once seated they were afraid to leave because the moment they did so the characters of the leavers might be ripped to ribbons by those remaining. I think they enjoyed the joke, although there was an element of truth in it. They enjoyed each other's company and were generally a temperate lot. Jim Griffiths had warned me soon after my arrival to keep clear of the bars. Unfortunately after I had been in the House quite a few years I took a delegation of my local councillors for a drink. The barman asked me if I was a member – I'm not sure what impression this made on them.

Some Welsh MPs hardly spoke in the House, although most of them jostled for a slot on the annual Welsh Day Debate. They enjoyed the esteem of their constituents for their application to individuals' problems. The great expert on compensation was Harold Finch MP (Bedwellty), who later became an under-secretary at the Welsh Office. He was a former NUM South Wales compensation secretary. After he retired I was delighted as secretary of state to put him forward for a knighthood. He never expected it.

George Thomas looked on all his colleagues with suspicion. I don't think he made life easy for his fellow Cardiff MP, Jim Callaghan. George was always in the Cardiff newspapers, and was the unchallenged 'Mr Leasehold Reform' – his great success. I suspect he measured his column inches in the *Western Mail* daily. He was a great friend of Dai Rosser, the *Western Mail's* indefatigable political editor. Dai would ring around his favourite Welsh MPs on a Sunday night asking for copy and most of us obliged. Jim Callaghan, on the other hand, was on the Opposition front bench; George never got there during this period. Although they had both been elected in 1945, Jim was Shadow Colonial Secretary, and suffered in Cardiff from the story that he had more Africans at his dining table than Welshmen. The contrast did not help when he had a difficult election in Cardiff against a well-known English cricketer, Ted Dexter. The Tory candidate had been specially brought in because of his sporting popularity. Jim saw him off with a modest majority.

I had immediately warmed to Jim. In an apparently more leisurely age he spent time taking Margaret and myself around Blackheath, where he lived, in our quest for a house. He was really a Cardiff member and at the time had only a limited knowledge of the rest of Wales. Over the years he repaired this omission to some extent. He was astute and ambitious and usually tried to make progress by consensus. He did not really ally himself to the left or the right. As the son of a chief petty officer on the Royal Yacht *Britannia*, and a former naval officer himself he was, not unexpectedly, firm and consistent on defence, and paid for it. I was close to his way of thinking on most issues throughout my political life.

Both Leo Abse and Desmond Donnelly (Pembrokeshire) had sparks of genius, and flaws as well. To me it is a matter of regret that their talents were not usefully employed by Harold Wilson when he formed his first government. The busy bee of the Welsh MPs was Tudor Watkins (Brecon and

Radnor); he was secretary of both the Welsh Labour Group and the All-Party Welsh Parliamentary Party, then still of some importance. His first language was Welsh. He was one of my mentors; he gave me innumerable tasks and made me chairman of the Rural Affairs Sub-Committee of the Welsh Labour Group – my first little job in Parliament.

The north Walians, I felt, were a little distant. The encouragement they gave was limited and when I opposed local option for the Licensing Bill – I was instead advocating an all-Wales solution to the problem – Goronwy Roberts was quite unhappy. He had met me before I came to the House and he had been helpful. But he seemed to me to be indecisive and I had further experience of this when we were both new ministers. He was a little too grand for me, however he had shown many leadership qualities in the 1950s and he had a fine command of English and Welsh. Goronwy Roberts and Ness Edwards successfully put forward a proposal for a Welsh Grand Committee. They came to it from opposing ends of the Labour Welsh political cal scene. I was not aware of any consultation with anyone else. It was a purely private enterprise.

My relations with Cledwyn Hughes (Anglesey) were always good. He was a rising force on the Opposition front bench, a hard worker and he got things done. One could write a book about T. W. Jones MP (Merioneth), who was so much more vocal than his brother Idwal Jones, MP (Wrexham). On a Thursday night, T. W., Idwal, Cledwyn and Tudor would gather in one of the downstairs rooms. T. W. was a lay preacher with the Scotch Baptist Church. He would go through his sermon for the following Sunday with his colleagues, seeking their approval. I was never invited to these little congregations.

I was a little afraid of the Welsh whips. I soon got over this and whenever I had real difficulty in a conflict with my professional work I would go to the Chief Whip, a Cardiffian – Herbert Bowden MP. He was a man with a stern countenance but a heart of gold so far as my pleas were concerned. Another whip, Arthur Pearson (Pontypridd), the tall Vice-Chamberlain of the Household and a Welsh guardsman, lost a great deal of face when he prohibited his Welsh colleagues from going home on a Thursday. They ignored him because as cash-strapped MPs they could avoid paying one night in a hotel by availing themselves of the free train sleeper, one of the very few 'perks' of those days. When Pearson turned up at the platform in Paddington, also going home, all was lost for him. What was remarkable was that whatever the majority the government had he did not have a telephone!

Aneurin Bevan (Ebbw Vale) was a distant figure whom I had admired very much; I watched him in his last few years in the House before illness cruelly struck him down. I had heard him speak in the Carmarthen by-election in the packed Market Hall with hundreds, if not thousands of people all standing and enjoying his repartee. I heard his great speech in Scarborough about a British Foreign Secretary going naked into the councils of the world – without a nuclear bomb. His new vision did not endear him to his supporters. But his reconciliation with Gaitskell made the Labour Party electable. He would have made the best Labour Foreign Secretary since Ernest Bevin, one of the architects of NATO. He had a rather flat voice, slightly nasal perhaps. But he was certainly not the most popular with many of the old-guard Welsh MPs. Their test was frequently how many years one had worked underground.

Bevan was as sharp in private conversation as on the public platform. When Desmond Donnelly MP deserted him – and probably as a journalist wrote paid articles decrying him – he offered to buy Bevan a drink at a Labour Party Conference, to which Bevan replied, 'and what will you buy it with, thirty pieces of silver?'

The outstanding Member for Wales was, of course, Jim Griffiths (Llanelli), a former President of the South Wales Miners' Federation. He had been, as the National Insurance minister, one of the founders of the modern welfare state, and a distinguished Colonial Secretary who had overseen the bringing of peace to Malaya in a long drawn-out war.

Jim was fond of recalling that when he went to school in Betws, Ammanford, as a five year old, his mother told him, in Welsh, to be kind to one little boy who had problems, adding, 'were it not for all sorts, there would not be the likes of us'. It had helped to guide Jim's life in the need for care for others.

He also told me that as a constituency MP he had gone to see R. A. Butler, then minister for education, to try to get D. J. Williams, one of the convicted Lleyn Bombers, re-instated as a teacher. Whether anyone knew of his actions, I don't know. Jim added, rather sadly, 'It was never acknowledged.'

He was my principal mentor. He had also encouraged Gwilym Prys-Davies in his work on an elected body for Wales, which today might be seen as the green shoots of devolution. He had fought since the 1930s for a Welsh secretary of state. He later recognised that the appointment of a Welsh Secretary was not a long-term solution. He was feeling his way, and building pragmatically on what he read and the need he recognised. This is why it was of enormous significance when he turned to Gwilym for proposals. He knew his nationalist background, but trusted him to develop proposals for Welsh Labour. The two worked well together.

I once discussed Gwilym's contribution and background with Morgan Phillips, the powerful general secretary of the Labour Party, when he came to speak at a Labour Party rally in Aberystwyth. He raised no objection to what was being done, which was significant since he was the epitome of the South Wales band of leaders who were mainly products of the Central Labour College, but he added, 'I fear that Gwilym will not last,' suggesting things would be too difficult for him in the Labour Party. He was wrong as it turned out.

There is no doubt in my mind that Jim Griffiths is the father of Welsh devolution, based on this and his personal encouragement to me at a time when it was politically very lonely to be a devolutionist in the Labour Party in Wales. He was the political compass which was to guide me for the future, and there was no doubt that he was one of the outstanding South Wales industrial MPs, sharing all our interests.

Where does he rank against Aneurin Bevan, whom I admired too? Jim had his roots in the radicalism of semi-rural, Welsh-speaking West Wales. Bevan had his roots in the syndicalism of the mining valleys of Gwent. He never ceased to remind us of the appalling miseries of the 1930s. His rebelliousness was tamed by the opportunity for achievement. During his ministerial office, he turned out to be a skilled negotiator whilst maintaining his aims. Nevertheless rebelliousness did break out again and as I entered the House the Bevanites were becoming more and more aware that office would elude us until the electorate was prepared to believe that Labour could unite to deliver. We were just getting over the misery of a fractured party.

Jim had achieved a great deal as the pioneer of National Insurance. He once came to Port Talbot to speak to a Saturday afternoon Labour educational gathering to explain the principles of equality of benefits 'from the duke to the dustman'. He said that everyone should draw the same benefits as there would be no stigma if benefits were universally paid. Taxation would deal with excessive payments. He abhorred the means test. Pensions should be sufficiently high that extra payments would only have to be paid to a small minority for whom the safety net was not strong enough.

He was a successful Cabinet minister, at the cutting edge of policymaking and implementation. As deputy Leader of the Party he was wise, conciliatory and far-sighted in his approach to Europe, towards which I was lukewarm to say the least. He had been imbued with the internationalism of the Central Labour College in London, but unlike some of his colleagues had not thrown overboard his Welsh language inheritance. He looked at politics from the viewpoint of two tragic world wars. He 'primed the pump' in policymaking for Wales and wished to learn pragmatically how Wales could be better governed; the fact that he made few great pronouncements should not belittle that he came to understand where we should get to on devolution, and how.

I remember him saying: 'What you say and do in a particular ministerial post in the first five days will mark you for the rest of your time in that post.'

When I entered Parliament, one of my first tasks was to write a report for the Welsh Parliamentary Party, following a letter from the National Union of Teachers of Wales (UCAC) to the minister for Welsh affairs requesting that 'the Welsh language be given the status of an official language'. This 1961 letter was to be a catalyst for new thinking on the language and would lead to significant changes in both its status and use.

The report on the legal position of the Welsh language was to have been prepared by myself and the other, much more senior Welsh lawyer, Roderic Bowen, QC, the Member for Cardiganshire. Regrettably, he took no action. In my report I reviewed The Act of Union 1536 and the Welsh Courts Act 1942. The 1942 Act repealed the relevant section of the Act of Union prohibiting the use of Welsh. I gave examples of the growing practice of using Welsh in government publications. At the time there was litigation in the High Court about the use of a Welsh nomination form in an election in Carmarthenshire. Leaving this on one side, I concluded that in general, with the repeal of Section 17 of the Act of Union 1536, there was nothing to prohibit the use of Welsh in any form. I concluded that 'for the further removal of doubt' the Welsh Parliamentary Party should approach the Home Secretary, the minister for Welsh affairs, to request a bill, in the nature of an interpretation act, which would merely state that 'any form, minute or document, written in the Welsh language would have equal validity as if it were written in the English language'.

So far as I know, this was the first time that the phrase 'equal validity' was used in a memorandum for government consideration, although I am sure I was not the only one to express sentiments of the same kind. It was to have great consequences.

I added:

But I must stress that legislation would not of itself do a great deal. What is needed is a great administrative drive to use Welsh, not merely as an administrative convenience but rather as a national alternative language to a bilingual nation with a majority of English-speaking monoglots.

My 1962 report was accepted by the (All-Party) Welsh Parliamentary Party which decided to ask the Home Secretary and minister for Welsh affairs, Sir Keith Joseph, to receive a delegation from the group on 6 November 1962. It was led by Lady Megan Lloyd George, its chairman, accompanied by Arthur

Probert, Tudor Watkins, Roderic Bowen QC, Goronwy Roberts and myself. They decided to try to persuade the minister to set up an inquiry into the status of the Welsh language. They also agreed to my suggestion that Sir David Hughes Parry, a distinguished academic lawyer, should chair it.

Lady Megan invited me to open the discussion. I am recorded as saying:

> There is a general anxiety as to the status of the language and doubts exist which should be resolved.

I went on to point out that the Welsh Courts Act 1942 had itself been passed to remove doubt but had only limited application. A further Act appeared to be required. Sir Keith expressed considerable sympathy, but he was not committed to change if the government embarked on this kind of working party. My report was given to the senior civil servant present, and a copy sent to an official at the Home Office as the documents at Kew show. Clearly the government was fully aware of my report which would inevitably have been made available to the working party. Sir David Hughes Parry was eventually appointed as chairman and the terms of reference of the working party were 'to clarify the legal status of the Welsh language and to consider whether any changes in the law ought to be made'.

They concluded that 'there should be a clear, positive legislative declaration of general application to the effect that any act, writing or thing done in Welsh in Wales or Monmouthshire should have like legal force as if it had been done in English. The effect of such a declaration would, of course, be to raise the status of the Welsh language in Wales to one of equality with that of English . . . Of those with whom we discussed the subject we found an overwhelming majority in favour of applying the principle of equal validity.'

The words of their conclusions echoed those in my memorandum. In retrospect, there was not an ounce of an objection from anyone in the Parliamentary Party. At the time it was only a small feather in my cap as a young MP. But it was to begin a course of history for the Welsh language that still has not reached its end, beginning with the Welsh Language Acts 1967 and 1993.

From the inquiry's report came the Welsh Language Act 1967 which declared that:

> Anything done (in a document) . . . in Welsh shall have like effect as if done in English.

In a small way I believe I can claim to be one of the many people who paved the way to the 1967 Act. I had set down, in a lawyer's way, concrete proposals consolidating aspirations into an easily understood formula – 'equal validity'. Dr Gwynedd Parry, in his masterly book *David Hughes Parry: A Jurist in Society* referred to the expression 'equal footing' being used in the 1930s. It comes very near, but it could be said that it lacks legal conciseness. In any event, I was not aware of it.

One of the secretaries of the Welsh Language Society, Cymdeithas yr Iaith Gymraeg, Mr E. G. Millward, wrote to me in 1962 stating the Society had been founded to inquire into the status of the Welsh language in different government departments and to seek some place for it in those circles. He added:

> We heard with great joy of the intention of the Welsh Parliamentary Party to bring the matter before the government and it would be good if you could tell us what the opinion of the Parliamentary Party is on this very important issue. Nothing would be better than if the Society disappeared if status for the language was achieved and that would be a matter of particular praise if the Parliamentary Party could achieve this.

On my understanding of the aims of the society I enquired about membership. However, by 7 February 1963 they had moved forwards to civil disobedience. In another letter Mr Millward said, 'By now you will know that the aim of the society is to break the law in small innocent ways to bring attention to the lack of status for the language.'

It was acknowledged that my interest in membership had not been replied to because, Mr Millward said, he was fairly sure that I would not agree with the methods that the society was intending to adopt. It was emphasised that they were not intending on this course for action for its own sake, but for publicity for their cause. He ended his letter of explanation by saying they all 'glorified' in my efforts for the language and my promise to provide details of developments. It is interesting to look back nearly fifty years on how the society developed and how my interest in supporting Welsh institutions could not find an outlet in this particular new movement for the obvious reasons they rightly point out. I fear their successors were not as complimentary to me for my efforts when I became secretary of state.

It was around this time that the Wales TUC was formed. The Welsh Labour MPs were pretty lukewarm, if not antagonistic. Some of the Welsh mining MPs had form; they had been traditionally opposed to local district agreements from a long way back. They feared possible trouble in the future if the Wales TUC went its own way.

I sent a telegram of good wishes to the organisers of the conference at Aberystwyth. To me it was another all-Wales organisation to add to the far too few we had, namely the University of Wales, the Welsh Joint Education Committee and later the Welsh Board of Health, the Welsh Hospital Board. The National Museum, National Library, National Eisteddfod and the Royal Welsh Show were, of course, non-statutory bodies. For this reason I supported Alun Talfan Davies and others at the time in opposing the break-up of the University of Wales.

eight
THE STEELWORKS

EIGHT YEARS AFTER my first election campaign I had to prove that I had succeeded in my stated aim of learning about the steel industry. To jump ahead for a moment, as a junior minister at the Department of Power, I was charged with supervising our first white paper on the nationalisation of the steel industry.

Port Talbot Steelworks dominated the Aberavon constituency. Sixteen thousand steelworkers went through the gates during the week. There was hardly anyone in the area who did not work there, or had some close relative on its payroll. Workers came from miles around. So strong was the link with the community that the company gave a year's paid leave of absence whenever one of its workers became mayor of the town, which happened quite frequently. Magistrates were paid during their absence from work, I believe on the basis that the chairman of the company was a magistrate too and did not lose any of his salary!

It was, of course, the Steel Company of Wales then. I was taken along by Billy Vaughan to have lunch with the bosses soon after I got the nomination. There was a mutual interest. They wanted to find out who the new Member might be; after all, steel nationalisation was in the Party's election manifesto. I wanted to see the colour of their eyes too. The chairman, the managing director and the finance director, were all there. It was a tough audience for a young man. They made no attempt to influence me. I enjoyed a good and fruitful working relationship with the works, both management and men, whether the industry was publicly or privately owned. I was always told what was happening and when there was hardly a cloud on the horizon, the Managing Director, Fred Cartwright, had me to lunch in London to warn me that so far as staffing was concerned, future years would become very difficult indeed. He had plans for cushioning the blow; he was a man with great foresight.

Port Talbot and its tinplate satellites were the products of an earlier period of contractions and amalgamations. The huge works had been built to serve the post-war need. Workers came in from everywhere, including a strong Welsh-speaking contingent from works in West Wales.

King George VI was invited to open it in 1949, but by the appointed day he was too ill to do so and the minister of fuel and power, Hugh Gaitskell, officiated in his place. That gives some indication of the importance of the plant. The jobs were well paid and it was sometimes known locally as 'Treasure Island'. Because of the need to operate this huge investment to its maximum capacity, the demand for labour drawn from all parts of the kingdom was considerable. It was undoubtedly overmanned, but this was a result of a deliberate policy not to leaving staffing to chance. The wheels had to turn quickly and the furnaces had to stay lit at all times. There had to be plenty of fully trained workers right round the clock, working on a continental shift system, to justify the investment.

We paid for it much later, in the thousands of human problems arising from the shrinking need for labour. Through wise trade-union leadership at the plant we got through. I was on almost permanent call in those days, and cannot count the number of meetings and telephone calls I had with both sides.

The Conservative minister Peter Walker had grandiose plans for doubling capacity in the 1980s. They fell by the wayside and some who should have known better tried to put part of the blame on me. Instead, the problems of redundancy dominated the following years. There was an overwhelming local wisdom that desired, above all other things, for the works to survive, and siren calls from outside for industrial action were rejected. I was not popular with everyone in South Wales for doing what I could to achieve this aim. Going out on strike would have meant thousands going on an ego trip and possibly ending all hope of the works surviving. I, too, was terribly disappointed and had, when expansion was envisaged, pressed and pressed management time after time for news of contracts being signed. But they never were.

As MP, and particularly as secretary of state, I enjoyed the closest contact with management. I always had access to them and access to ministers, from Labour Prime Ministers down. I was taken into their confidence and they listened, at least, to my concerns. This meant I was able to bring practical help and influence at crucial moments.

My connections with the unions were self-evident. They had put me there and, as is said in diplomatic communiqués, there were occasionally 'full and frank exchanges of views'. I cannot understate the quality of union leadership at the works, coupled with wise management led by Peter Allen, later tragically killed in a train accident, and Sir Brian Moffat. They strove for far more flexible working practices. It was easy to talk about the need for efficiency, but flexibility was not always easy to achieve.

The works were quite traditional and not always responsive to change. In my early days, I heard the odd and fortunately rare tale of resistance, even to the wearing of safety boots. In this and other fields, only far-sighted action by the Works Safety Council and management achieved progress and greater efficiency. I was told once of disparaging remarks about the future of Port Talbot, apparently made by Bob Scholey, then Chairman of British Steel. My own ministerial colleagues were not always enthusiastic about Port Talbot due to its history of industrial problems which was sometimes thrown in my face. It was said that Denis Healey as Chancellor was not a fan, but I found no basis for that. I was able to argue with colleagues that industrial problems were things of the past when I was a young MP, but memories regrettably lingered on.

We had to prove our case to justify investment and this was my main task. Anyone who thinks it would have come in any event would be foolhardy. At least that is my perhaps biased perception. Like Sisyphus in the Greek fables, I endeavoured over the years to push the stone up the hill so far as investment was concerned, and happily with more success. I had a forewarning of the problems that might face us when, as a young minister, Harold Wilson unexpectedly asked me to visit Italy in 1965 to learn what was being done industrially there. We were a three-man team, David Ennals MP (Dover), shortly to be a junior minister and Peter Shore MP (West Ham), his PPS. We were all young and eager to learn, and we seized the opportunity.

Mussolini, whatever his many faults, had pioneered a government body to invest in industry and try to alleviate unemployment. As I remember it, this body invested right across the board, in particular industries and infrastructure. Eventually our government would set up something similar with powers to invest.

We visited the Taranto Steelworks near the heel of Italy which I understood had been sited here as part of the attack on the appalling problems of unemployment in southern Italy – the *Mezzogiorno*. The steelworks were of considerable size and provided steel for the industrial plants of northern Italy. As we moved around the works it was quite a shock to find hardly a workman in sight. I was used to seeing the immense human activity in Port Talbot Steel but there was nothing of the kind here. Their workforce by this stage, if not at inception, was the slimmest possible. We asked a great many questions on this and I quickly realised there might be unwelcome precedents here for us at Port Talbot. I took it as a clear warning of what might be in store.

Inter-union problems had been rife in my earlier days – tension between the craft and production workers, with their ingrained practices. The worst times of all were when we had unofficial strikes. I tried very hard to maintain Harry Williams's precept of not getting involved in union affairs, despite the many calls for me to intervene. However, things got desperate sometimes as the weeks of a long strike went by with nobody to talk to – officially. 'Why does the MP not do something?' would be the cry in the clubs and the town. Where was my magic wand?

I remember going to see the Parliamentary secretary for Labour, Willie Whitelaw, one Christmas Eve, around 1963, to try and get some government action. In those days, the ministry of labour was quite a power house in industrial disputes but no one was prepared to do anything.

When I left the minister I was very upset and felt for my constituents as the strike was dragging on. Christmas was going to be a limited festive occasion for all of us. We were in the process of buying a bigger house in Chislehurst, now that we had three girls. I had agreed the price, and the contract was to be signed just after Christmas but I felt I could not go through with it, with so much despair in my constituency and I withdrew from the purchase. No one ever knew, certainly not in Port Talbot. Silly perhaps? Overreaction? Probably, but I had reacted instinctively. I could not proceed, given the uncertainly which my constituents were facing. I have no regrets. Fortunately when one door closed another opened.

Port Talbot Works had curious negotiating practices. Neither men nor management were part of the national negotiating machinery. They negotiated locally with each other on their own. Trade unions nationally and employers' organisations were very unhappy about this. I well remember Johnny Boyd, then assistant general secretary of the AEU, coming down to the Wales Labour Party conference in Swansea during an unofficial strike and meeting with me and representatives of the unofficial strikers from his union on the margins. I could do this in his presence and not upset anyone. He began the meeting by greeting his members, 'Well, half-brothers'. It summed it all up.

What is always frightening when speaking of Port Talbot Steelworks are the huge, mind-boggling figures involved. All that investment has to earn its keep. It has to compete in the global world. The world did not owe Port Talbot a living. It would have made life much easier if it did. Every penny had to be fought for.

nine
MY FIRST JUNIOR OFFICE
AT THE MINISTRY OF POWER

THE LONG-AWAITED GENERAL ELECTION came in October 1964, Labour just scraping a majority. I had no expectation of office – I had only been in the House five years and I surmised that those with experience of the 1950–1 Parliament would lead the procession to Number 10.

I intended to return to the Bar, which I had neglected for some months and rang up Stanley, my clerk. I had a warm welcome and prepared to go and see him in chambers. I knew from the level of work I had been doing before, that the briefs would quickly start to flow once again. Chambers were concentrating more on crime, and had become almost a 'crime factory'. It is always much easier to restart at a junior level. But before I got to chambers Stanley rang back and said he had news for me. I was to be Parliamentary Private Secretary (PPS) to Sir Dingle Foot, QC, MP, the new Solicitor General. I was rather pleased because I had known the great man through his friendship with Megan Lloyd George. He had also led me at the Old Bailey. But another call came through shortly after, inviting me to go to Number 10. There could only be one reason – I would be in the government.

I went to see the Prime Minister, Harold Wilson. After some small talk about his not having worn a morning coat to Buckingham Palace, but a black jacket and striped trousers – fortunately, I was not wearing the barrister's rig-out that day – I don't think I ever did to go to court in it – he offered me a junior post at the Ministry of Power. 'I am offering you this,' he said, 'because of your great interest in steel, which I have noted. I know you have campaigned on steel nationalisation and have asked many questions over the years. Mind you,' he added, 'you've got the poisoned chalice.' I did not quite understand this at the time, but after I got home it dawned on me that with a tiny majority and two rebellious members, including my friend

Donnelly, our chances of getting the legislation through were not high. I hardly gave this a thought; my job was to get on with it. I was elated and so pleased that my first ministry was so close to the interests of so many of my constituents.

I had to ring my clerk to say that I was, for the time being, leaving the Bar and would not be Dingle Foot's PPS after all. Whether Dingle actually knew that I had been his PPS for about an hour, I never knew. He never mentioned it.

My first job was to prepare a white paper on the public ownership of the steel industry. My boss, Fred Lee, was not particularly knowledgeable as to how we were to set about it. We had all campaigned on a slogan, and it was amazing that not much thought had been given to how to turn it into reality.

As well as steel my responsibilities, under my boss, included coal, gas, electricity, nuclear power, oil and clean air. I believed, and continue to believe, that such a fundamental industry as steel should, as one of the commanding heights of the economy, be one way or another within the responsibility of the state. I regret that we have not found a way to ensure that such a basic industry does not fall into foreign hands. In my view this applies also to gas, electricity and, particularly, water.

On the first weekend in my constituency after the election the local press, including some national press stringers, came to see me. I stated the obvious that, as the manifesto said, we planned to nationalise steel. This had an immediate effect on the Stock Exchange the following Monday. I learned to keep my cards closer to my chest in the future.

It was not that many years since 1957, when I had told the ward meeting in Cornelly that I knew nothing about steel, but I would learn about it. In my five years in the House I had left no stone unturned. I had talked to and lunched with Sir Henry Spencer, the boss of Llanwern RTB steelworks, to the unions, and regularly to an ex-civil servant, Mr De Peyer, from the Ministry of Power, who fed me with questions and material. Given my amateur status, I was as well informed as anyone could be.

The permanent secretary seemed to be semi-retired and retreated when he could to the South of France. The department was run by the deputy secretary, Matthew Stevenson, a hard-nosed, tough Glaswegian. He came and saw me and explained that the department was fully geared to meet our wishes, whatever they were. He had the right people in position to work out plans for the steel industry. He himself, as a young man at the ministry, had helped to plan for the nationalisation of steel. A few years later, more senior by this time, and at the Treasury, he had helped to plan denationalisation. Now, more senior still, he was ready to plan the industry's renationalisation. The saga was the finest tribute to the impartiality of the Civil Service that

I know, and Mat Stevenson proved it by his work. He delivered and put flesh on the bones of our slogans.

We got on with it: I co-ordinated much of the material for my boss; it was my first job as a minister, and the white paper was approved by Cabinet and Parliament. Getting a bill through the Commons was another matter. The two rebels, Donnelly and Woodrow Wyatt, came to see us and tried to bully us. Wyatt claimed we could never get the bill through the House. Looking Fred Lee in the eye, he said, 'Fred, it's like what we did as children, playing last across the road.' It would need some imagination to believe that Wyatt was ever a child – a mischievous but clever little man in a bow tie would be a better description. He ended up in the Conservative Party.

Two trade unionists also came to see us attempting to stop us bringing the industry into public ownership, the general secretary of the Iron and Steel Trades Confederation (the ISTC), Harry Douglas, and the Secretary of the Boilermakers' Union, Ted Hill. The first was known for his right-wing views, but Ted Hill was an avowed left-winger. It was a sad meeting, but equally a dangerous one. To have two leaders of some of the most important unions in the industry against us was very unwelcome. I could not understand how Ted Hill had come to the meeting at all. Fred had only to listen. Steel nationalisation was in the manifesto.

The oil industry was also within my brief. The North Sea was about to be developed. Incredible as it seems now, there was a doubt then as to whether the North Sea was capable of economic development. If my recollection is accurate, it certainly was not seen as a field of activity in which the government should participate. It was felt government money should not be invested in such a gamble. I fear, apparently because of commercial considerations, the circulation of papers was very limited. The decision was taken, I suspect at Cabinet level, that there would be no governmental involvement in North Sea exploration. The civil servants kept all of the information close to their chests, particularly the allocating of zones. There was no role for a parliamentary secretary.

Looking back, it was a remarkable decision. I surmise a cost benefit analysis or something like it had been done. My later experience in the Celtic Sea shows that one can drill dry boreholes, and I suspect that the mandarins took this view about the North Sea. The oil industry did not have any such inhibitions and invested its money. It would be argued that as a country we would benefit from taxation, and we did, which was very fortunate. Nevertheless the oil industry and the mandarins had agreed that the state had no direct role. The government machine and the oil industry seemed very close, perhaps too close. Regrettably I had no experience in this field and had no input.

Among my responsibilities was touring the country meeting all the gas and electricity boards and appointing their part-time non-executive members. I ate more smoked salmon at lunch than at any time in my life. In fact, I acquired a taste for it. At that time we did not eat smoked salmon in Cardiganshire.

I insisted on shortlists of two or three candidates. I was not going to be a rubber-stamper. Some board members had been in post since the Nationalisation Acts of the 1940s, and had long ceased to be useful. I invented the maximum of ten years in post, three terms of three years each and a final year. The preference was for two periods of three years. Non-executive board members became too cosy and changing them was quite a radical view in this field at the time. Progress was steady but slow.

My real problem was with the coal industry. Monthly meetings with the chairman of the Gas Council and his equivalent chairman of the Electricity Council were easy. Coal was quite a different matter. The chairman of the National Coal Board, Lord Robens, gave the impression of resenting my boss's accession to office and looked down on him. Before he left the Commons, Alf Robens had been deputy leader of the Party. I think he may have regretted leaving the Commons, and losing the opportunity for high office again. Perhaps he had expected a summons to return. I could only guess.

Monthly meetings with him and his deputy chairman, Sir Humphrey Browne, could be very difficult, with much symbolic banging on tables on Alf's part. He wanted a substantial run down of the coal industry to balance his books. When he went out he would tell the press that it was the minister who wanted to run down the industry, not him.

We were putting proposals forward for a rational restructuring of the coal industry, with investment for alternative employment when there was a pit closure. I knew the problems too well; I had pits in my constituency, in difficult areas. Alf was distinctly unhappy with government support for alternative employment, saying he would lose all his men as they might prefer to work in factories. Years earlier Nye Bevan had prophesied a time when this might happen, and no one would have to go down the pit.

Alf's versions of our monthly dialogues were regrettably a distortion of reality. He was covering himself by ensuring the press thought that the pressure for closures came from the ministry and not from himself. He was able to preserve the image of a man of the people and defender of the miners. I fear that sources emanating from the Coal Board blamed Stevenson for planning colliery closures. Wild newspaper stories were particularly painful for him, but he survived to become a very impressive permanent secretary.

The practice developed of the deputy chairman inviting me after the monthly meetings to dinner in the Stafford Hotel so that he could explain the Board's real views, with the intention of helping to oil the ministry/Board machinery and make the reality behind our dialogues workable.

One of my unhappiest experiences was to be summoned to go down to South Wales with Jim Griffiths, the Welsh Secretary, to visit a village where there had been a pit disaster, at the Cambrian Colliery in the Rhondda. The old man, deeply moved as an ex-miner himself, and myself too, visited a schoolroom where there were thirty-one coffins laid out, one of them being that of the under-manager. Thirteen men were also injured. I had never been down a pit, but I soon remedied this, and went down Brynlliw, near Swansea. It was the first of many pits I visited. Dai Francis, Secretary of the South Wales NUM wrote at the time: 'I never thought that in 1965 we should be faced with a tragedy such as this.' Disasters on this scale were thought to be a thing of the past.

I had moved on, fortunately, from the Ministry of Power, by the time of the Aberfan Disaster, when the lives of so many children were lost, tragic victims of the moving tip. Lord Robens did not distinguish himself by his delay in visiting the disaster. Everyone else had done so before him, including the Prince of Wales and the then secretary of state, George Thomas. His reason was that his visit might impede the rescue operation – and in any event, he was receiving an honorary degree that day at Sussex University. His photograph in the dailies the following day in cap and gown did not go down well. At the subsequent public inquiry under Lord Justice Edmund Davies, the defensive attitude of the Coal Board came under severe criticism.

I built up a sound relationship with the NUM in South Wales. I was the first minister to visit the headquarters of the NUM in South Wales and they honoured me by presenting me with a miniature Davy's miner's lamp. My grandfather would have been particularly pleased. There are always changes in an extractive industry and coal was no different. What I wanted was proper consultation in South Wales for a managed run-down over the years. If it was done in this way, I felt we could control the injection of alternative employment to run parallel with it.

It was during this time that the Ministry of Transport, with our support at the Ministry of Power as the sponsoring department for the steel industry, took the decision to build the new harbour at Port Talbot to import iron ore.

There were many claimants for this major facility. Jim Callaghan wanted it built at Cardiff, halfway between Port Talbot and Newport. It would underpin his GKN Steelworks at Cardiff. Sir Frank Soskice, QC, MP canvassed for Newport (his constituency), to help Llanwern. Without a suitable harbour for massive iron ore ships, Llanwern would become an inland steelworks, a recipe for eventual disaster. Swansea was also keen on developing its port, and Donnelly actively canvassed to develop the unique facilities at Milford Haven.

The existing port facilities at Port Talbot were very basic. It could only berth ships of 10,000 tons on a good tide. The monster ore ships of the time were well over 100,000 tons and bound to become much bigger. My case spoke for itself and I could really have let it run its course, but I took a very close interest in the developing story and saw the steady flow of papers. Both ministries were content when Tom Fraser the transport minister, to my intense joy, took the decision to build at Port Talbot and the Cabinet approved it. He had my strong support, and his decision was eventually to save Port Talbot. Had it gone the other way, the history of Port Talbot and steelmaking would have been grim. My good friend, Jim Callaghan hardly spoke to me for some months; he got over his disappointment in time. There were other problems where I had a role in conquering. It turned out that the Crown owned the foreshore, and I was told that since the rating of the harbour would be based on profit, we would be rated more than the London docks. Dick Crossman's Department challenged me that the Local Authority would not forego a rating bonanza!' The Town Clerk called a meeting of the 'city fathers' that afternoon and the message was loud and clear: 'If there was no harbour there would be no bonanza. This was local government at its best and I was able to trump Crossman!

The grand scale of the facility entitled it to being eventually opened by Her Majesty the Queen. I was present at the opening as a proud local MP and a junior minister in a government that had taken the right decision, one which would bring immeasurable benefit to my constituents for decades. I was lucky to be in the right place at the right time – in fact in the two relevant ministries. The industrial future of Port Talbot for many years was settled at this time.

I had begun on what was a steep learning curve – 'how to be a minister'. Looking back I fault myself that I did not take an even more innovative and enterprising role. I was always the youngest at the Cabinet committee meetings, and tended to rest on my laurels – being just a little too pleased I had arrived there. Most of us were new and inexperienced – I had soon got over my awe of the mandarins. I remember discussing with Peter Shore on our visit to Italy in 1966, that having the experience of one ministry behind us, it would not be a bad thing to have a general post of junior ministers – a wide reshuffle, so that we could start afresh. Whether this comment was conveyed to his boss I do not know, but within months I was no longer at the Ministry of Power.

TOM AND JOHN MORRIS WITH COUSINS, SOME FROM GERMANY
AND CHINA, ON THE EVE OF WAR, AUGUST 1939
Back row (left to right): Olwen (Morris) Lewis, Dei Morris, Gwyneth
Winkler, Eddie Winkler (seated on Gwyneth Winkler's lap), Rosemarie
Winkler, Dot Edwards, Gareth Edwards (baby seated on Dot Edwards's lap),
Peggy Davies-Edwards, Rhiannon Davies-Edwards.
Front row (left to right): Tom Morris and John Morris.

IN GERMANY AS A YOUNG OFFICER (newspaper cutting), 1954

AS DEPUTY GENERAL SECRETARY AND LEGAL ADVISER, MEETING
MEMBERS OF THE FARMERS' UNION OF WALES IN 1955

TRAVELLING WITH HAROLD WILSON BY TRAIN TO CARDIFF, SHORTLY
AFTER WILSON'S ELECTION AS LEADER OF THE LABOUR PARTY,
FEBRUARY 1963

ABERAVON
PARLIAMENTARY DIVISION

GENERAL ELECTION

THURSDAY
MARCH 31st, 1966

7 a.m. to 9 p.m.

If you are a Supporter of Labour, please exhibit
this photograph in your window. It will save your
time—and the time of our Canvassers.

JOHN
MORRIS

THE
LABOUR
CANDIDATE

VOTE MORRIS X

Top left: SPEAKING AT KENFIG HILL, 1964

Bottom left: THE ALL-PARTY WELSH MPs, 1964

Above: ELECTION ADDRESS LEAFLET, 1966

Top left: WITH THREE WELSH MPs AT INDUCTION TO THE GORSEDD OF BARDS AT NEWTOWN EISTEDDFOD, 1965

Bottom left: AS DEFENCE MINISTER, TESTING EQUIPMENT ON CAIRNGORMS, 1969

Above: AS DEFENCE MINISTER, WITH INDIRA GANDHI AT THE LAUNCH OF INDIAN FRIGATE *NILGRI*, MUMBAI, 1969

LAUNCH OF HMS *COURAGEOUS* BY MARGARET AT BARROW-IN-FURNESS, 1970, WITH OUR DAUGHTERS NIA, NON AND ELINOR

ten
MINISTRY OF TRANSPORT
(1966–1968)

I HAD ONLY BEEN FIFTEEN MONTHS in the Ministry of Power when the call came to move on. There had been a ministerial hiccup at the Ministry of Transport involving Tom Fraser. Tom was a delightful man, whom I suspect would have made an ideal secretary of state for Scotland – the job he wanted. He had no interest in transport and after more than a year had failed to deliver a policy. It was not wholly his fault. He had, I believe, been put in the wrong job, and the department could have been more helpful. News of my move came on 10 January 1966, our wedding anniversary. My boss, Fred Lee, first heard about it on the radio. It was a discourtesy uncharacteristic of the period.

Barbara Castle, a successful minister at overseas development, had proved that she was much more than a political demagogue. In those days able and clever women reached the top of the Labour Party without social engineering; they were successful and distinguished politicians. The fault was that they were few in number, both in the lower grades of achievement and as MPs. In Wales there were only two at the time, out of thirty-six. We had leading lights in the Party in Barbara, Alice Bacon, Margaret Herbison, Edith Summerskill, Eirene White and Megan Lloyd George, to name but a few – all doughty fighters in their own right, and more than a match for their male contemporaries. They were outstanding women who took no prisoners, very controversial at times but all deeply respected for getting things done.

Harold Wilson drafted Barbara to Transport. She had two parliamentary secretaries. One was Stephen Swingler, son of a senior clergyman, very left wing and anti nuclear weapons, though he proved that he was a doer. Before becoming a minister he had never sat at a desk, he said. His fellow parliamentary secretary had held more than one junior post in the 1945–51 government and was due for retirement. He enjoyed sitting in the magistrates' court on a Friday in Welwyn Garden City or somewhere like that. Since his colleague was in the Lords, Stephen had to shoulder the burden of all the Commons work, and transport was a very 'sexy' subject at the time, with rail closures still happening all over the country – the aftermath of Beeching, which had been enthusiastically implemented by Ernest Marples, the previous Tory transport minister. Marples was a go-getter in many ways, and operated on the curious philosophy that the time required for him to be at his ministry desk was one day a week. If his civil servants wanted to see him at other times they had to come to him in his home around Eaton Square. I presume he varied this principle when he was at his vineyard in France.

Transport badly needed a new approach. The railways were the poor relation, not well run and lacking in investment. Road building was the department's priority and apparently very little else. When offered this prized office Barbara demanded one of her parliamentary secretaries be replaced. She wanted the best, or so it was said. Harold offered her a choice of three. In a long life in government I have not heard anything like it. Sometimes senior ministers use a right of objection, which is listened to but no more. The three names offered were Judith Hart, a prominent left winger, Bruce Millan and myself. With barely a year's track record to judge us on, the talent scouts must have done their work well as all of us, in due course, became Cabinet ministers. When I heard the tale years later I was very flattered.

When I was parachuted in to work under Barbara, we were poles apart politically. How she reached her decision in choosing me I do not know, but it began the most exciting, rewarding and politically educational period of my political career. Barbara was to reach her top form at this time. She was constantly in the public eye and developed the concept of the photo opportunity into a fine art. She got on with it, but she made enormous demands on everyone.

In her autobiography, she says I told her she had all the qualities for becoming Prime Minister, but I would never want to marry her. She was much amused. Barbara had a good sense of humour and did not mind having her leg pulled. She, Stephen and I were very close and the press described us as the 'Transport Tricycle'. I was the only car driver, although Stephen had driven a tank in the army.

In the evening I would man the tea room in the House while Stephen held the bar, constantly fielding the many questions and grumbles from colleagues. If we or Barbara wanted a word we would jump into her car and travel with her to wherever she was going in Westminster to check on her viewpoint. It was almost a day and night ministry, long before the development of twenty-four-hour media awareness. When I subsequently went to the Ministry of Defence I was shattered to discover that no one took much political interest in me. I only saw my boss, Denis Healey, from time to time, with gaps of many weeks. If I wanted to discuss my work generally it was by appointment, usually about once a month. Meetings on specific topics, of course, were more frequent, but it was leadership by remote control. Denis just let you get on with it. In the House no one was interested in accosting me with a complaint. It was a metamorphosis.

Barbara had no faith in her department. She regarded her permanent secretary, Sir Thomas Padmore, who had had a very distinguished career previously, with distaste. He and the department had let down Tom Fraser, and there was no forgiveness from a fellow politician, even a beneficiary. It seemed, and I may be wrong, that Sir Thomas's absences in Liverpool playing his violin were not unwelcome. The impression I have is that he was not often present at ministerial meetings. Whether he had tête-à-têtes with his minister I do not know. I never heard of them. I hardly ever saw him. I suppose in his eyes there was no need to waste time on parliamentary secretaries, and I do not recall any conversation with him.

Before my arrival the pace of Stephen's parliamentary work was phenomenal. I believe he handled about forty-five adjournment debates in fifteen months, and they could take place in those days at any hour of the night. After I arrived we shared them according to our responsibilities. As some indication of the pressure, we shared a total of six adjournment debates one night alone before the Easter Recess. British Rail kindly hired a room for me at the Charing Cross Hotel – I lived in Chislehurst – and I would be summoned down as and when my subjects were called during the long night and the following morning until the debate petered out about lunchtime.

The most adventurous thing Barbara did was to bring in an academic economist, Chris Foster, later Sir Christopher, as her special adviser, with the rank of deputy secretary. He virtually ran the department for her so far as policy was concerned. Contrary to popular belief, Barbara was a good listener, and her policy meetings were huge. Anyone was welcome to chip in regardless of rank, but every participant had to be prepared to fight their corner.

My brief was the railways, a mountain of a task, road safety and the waterways. We came to the conclusion that things were not good at British Rail. They seemed to be sucking in an enormous amount of good Treasury money, with very little to show for it. Their only efficiency strategy was to follow Beeching and continue to cut down the railway system. This caused immense public unpopularity, although the public in turn were not particularly keen to avail themselves of the railways. It was said that Marples once commented it would be cheaper to close the mid-Wales railway line from Swansea to Shrewsbury, pay for a taxi for each passenger and give them a bottle of whisky to console themselves on the long journeys through mid Wales where sheep outnumbered people.

When George Thomas became the Welsh Secretary, after my time at transport, he apparently opposed the closure of this line in Cabinet, on the grounds that it went through five marginal constituencies: such were the pressures we worked under. The line is still running.

I was entrusted with the chairmanship of a joint inquiry into British Rail's finances and management. Half of the committee's members were from British Rail, including its vice chairman and there was one trade unionist, from ASLEF. The NUR, much greater in size, was not very pleased that I had chosen a trade unionist from one of the smaller unions. The other half was made up of industrialists with considerable experience, and departmental officials. They included a former chairman of Shell and the future chairman of 3i.

It was quite a team for a thirty-five year old to handle. We met, I believe, once a fortnight. There was a constant flow of papers from the rail board and the department. After more than a year we reported to Parliament that the main problem of the railways was not their length but their breadth. A great deal of fat could be trimmed by reducing the number of parallel lines. This capacity was undoubtedly excessive and far from fully used. We proposed slimming the railways as opposed to cutting off the ends. We also proposed relieving British Rail of many of its historical financial burdens such as pensions, museums and so on. We hoped these reforms would bring financial respectability.

I don't think the much later Conservative formula for the railways, splitting off ownership of the track from services, was ever considered. No one thought of separating the track from the wheel. It would, I suspect, have been regarded at the time as a Mad Hatter's tea party, and no one can say it has shone as a formula, and it is probably one of the low points of John Major's premiership.

Barbara presented the White Paper to Parliament. After she reported to Cabinet, Harold Wilson sent me a note of thanks and congratulation. I was over the moon. The report was the basis of much of the Transport Act 1968 – the bill being, at the time, one of the largest ever, if not the largest.

I regard my committee's report as the most satisfying thing I did as a junior minister. I had the amazing opportunity to chair a committee, and the rejuvenated Department of Transport, rose to the occasion. Our deep involvement in running the railways breached every concept of the Morrisonian doctrine of nationalisation, but there was no alternative.

As Barbara's representative I had to get stuck in and, in the face of the palsied leadership of the board and its senior officers, get heavily involved in micro-management with all its perils; even the plans for the reconstruction of New Street Station in Birmingham were crawled over by myself and my advisers. Every proposal for rail closure was examined minutely by me and new ones would be put forward in voluminous files with great frequency.

Together we took the Bill through the House. Barbara would not have a guillotine. The opposition membership had possibly more potential for ministerial distinction than any other standing committee – Michael Heseltine, David Webster, Peter Walker, future Speaker Bernard Weatherill, and others of obvious talent and potential. We were fully tested day after day, night after night and right through the night.

The pressure was such that the Prime Minister appointed an additional parliamentary secretary to take over many of my day-to-day duties. I relied absolutely on my private secretary to agree the contents of my letters which I duly signed in the corridors of the House in the late hours of the night and the early hours of the morning. My constituency hardly saw me for weeks, and my family were people I occasionally had breakfast with.

During my period at the department, we also took two breathalyser bills through the house. One was lost because an election was called half-way through. We dropped random testing from the second bill.

One of our triumphs was breaking the NUR's opposition to railway liner trains. Container traffic was in its infancy and Marples had invested a substantial sum in encouraging the building of liner terminals, but the railwaymen would not have them. The NUR executive was composed of members who could not be re-elected without a gap of three years in their membership. The result was that they tended to spend their gap three years outdoing their rivals in militancy. Sid Greene, the NUR general secretary was powerless.

I had the bright idea we should try to out-talk them. I persuaded Barbara that we would go along to their headquarters to meet their executive and talk on the issue for as long as it took, just her and me; no officials. It would be a marathon if necessary. She agreed to my suggestion as there were no other ideas as to how to break the deadlock.

Unfortunately the night before we began I had two engagements. The first was at the London Holloway Road Welsh Presbyterian Chapel's St David's Day supper where I had to make a speech. Margaret and I then left, I changed into a dinner jacket and we attended Elizabeth Taylor's fortieth birthday party at the Dorchester. Richard Burton was from an old family in my constituency and the Jenkins family, Richard's original name, were friends and supporters. We got there before midnight and danced away. Princes Margaret and Rudolph Nureyev were among the guests. The Jenkinses invited us to meet 'their Elizabeth'. We dutifully did and this beautiful lady with lovely eyes smiled at us. There were a lot of young Jenkins nieces there and they were as smart as the numerous starlets present. It felt like I was at the ball on the eve of Waterloo. It must have been well past 3 a.m. when we made our way home. We had not been able to see the film premier (it was rumoured that Richard had given a 0.5 per cent of the film's profits to the family) due to my duties at Holloway Road. It was some evening.

Before 10 a.m. the next morning Barbara and I met outside Unity House, the NUR headquarters in Euston. The talks began. Every imaginable objection to railway liner trains was canvassed. There was no shortage of subjects to talk about and at the end of the day victory was not in sight. Day two followed in the same vein. The union feared competition from Tartan Arrow, a road haulage firm. When the chairman of the nationalised road transport company was summoned off a golf course and ordered to buy the company, which he did, the union saw we meant business. It was our luck that we had no ministerial advisers!

Day three and more talking. Barbara was not exactly a Trappist nun, but even she must have found it difficult to match the wide-ranging political philosophising of some of these hard-line and erudite railwaymen. Railway signallers tended to be the most argumentative and knowledgeable of railwaymen. In those days they had time between trains to memorise the rule book and much else. Barbara had sent a plea to Wilson to be excused Cabinet that morning and the PM obliged. In those days one had to have a very good reason indeed to be excused.

In a state of exhaustion on all sides an agreement was in sight. Barbara had an important engagement to accompany her husband, Ted, who was chairman of a London county council committee, to meet the Queen when she came to the South Bank to open their building. A message of apology had to be sent to the Palace. Barbara was rather sore, as it was one of the few occasions in her life she would have been at Ted's side as his consort and not the other way round.

We got the union's agreement about 8 p.m. Barbara retired to change into a long evening dress, after announcing her success to the media. She rushed to the South Bank to be on hand to bid goodnight to Her Majesty and Prince Philip.

What a day! What a three days! But it was a prize worth having and the beginning of liner trains, which could take an unopened container loaded on a ship in Sydney and deliver it to Glasgow later in the year. We believed that much of the future of the railways depended on liner trains. Barbara and I went to open two of the terminals in London and Cardiff. I think I also opened one in Swansea.

Waterways, to coin a phrase, were very much a backwater, unloved, unused and under-invested. Given the congestion on our roads, I believed a limited amount of specialist freight could be sent by water. Of more importance was the possibility of encouraging leisure traffic and solving conflicts between boating interests and fishing, the country's greatest leisure sport.

As part of my duties I went to a conference on waterways in Oxford, to be addressed by a retired four-star General Hughie Stockwell, a former colonel of my Royal Welch Fusilier Regiment, and the commander at Suez. Hughie, who was a canal enthusiast, was commandeering volunteers, and perhaps even those who had been ordered to do community service, to restore the Kennet and Avon Canal. Hughie began by saying, 'I let one canal slip through my fingers, but I'm buggered if I'll let any more.' I thought this was the man for me.

I later attended a dinner of the London Canal Society at Regent's Park Zoo, of all places, addressed by a fellow Welshman from Merthyr Tydfil and one of the leaders of the LCC, Illtyd Harrington. Illtyd made a revivalist speech in every sense. We were back in a nonconformist chapel of yesterday. I persuaded Barbara that here we had two men, so different in every way, but whose talents could be harnessed to put new life into canals.

Barbara agreed that Illtyd should be put on the Waterways Board, which was a pretty moribund organisation, starved of money and talent. His name was put up to Number 10 for approval but rejected. I have no idea how the Labour Party heard about it, but I suspected the National Agent had blocked the appointment. Illtyd some time previously had been refused approval by the National Executive Committee as the Labour Candidate for Dover for his left wing views. Barbara agreed to go to see Harold Wilson at Downing Street to try to change his mind. Very unusually she asked me to accompany her. I was respectable politically and without any tinge of left-wing influence. We got there after the 10 p.m. division. Harold was smoking his pipe and we were offered a brandy. Barbara prompted me to put the case to him. Eventually Harold turned to me with that quizzical look of his and said, 'you can have him'.

Illtyd and Hugh went round England and Wales evangelising the merits of canals, and the combination was a huge success. Some forty years after I had opened locks on the Stour Canal, I was invited back for another celebration. It was a pleasant surprise; there was so much enthusiasm. Seeing the boats gathered together at a canal junction with the crowds of supporters was very impressive. It was a family occasion and I was pleased to have had canals as one of my responsibilities. They had become somewhere that families from the industrial cities through which they flowed could enjoy themselves.

One of my most pleasant tasks while in the transport department, and as it turned out, a particularly rewarding one for South Wales was setting up the Drivers' Vehicle Licensing Agency (DVLA). Over the years governments had inherited a system of local taxation of vehicles, usually carried out by local authorities. The huge escalation in the number of vehicles was dragging the system to a halt. A national agency was thought necessary in order to ensure vehicles could be cross-checked, as the police required. There was little or no experience in the department and from my recollection, the planning was done at middle-ranking level. The papers came to me and the decision was taken to go ahead. With hindsight a great deal of further and more detailed planning was necessary.

Where was it to be sited? Employment considerations and the dispersal of government agencies were vital considerations for the government. For the DVLA it was also a vital requirement to have a turn round of postal applications within five days, which limited possible sites. Three or four towns were considered. Swansea was a strong candidate, but the civil service had submitted that the area was not very attractive to dispersed civil servants. I was rather irritated and marked the file, 'Have you not heard of the Gower Peninsula?' This clinched it and the Swansea area then became a frontrunner. I forget who actually took the decision, either Barbara or, as was the procedure in those days, a Cabinet committee.

I was sent down to choose the actual site. There were two sites in Swansea – one near the sea and the other in Morriston. There was a further site in Neath and another in Port Talbot. Fortunately Port Talbot had a question mark against it, because of the deep excavation necessary for a building of this size. It would have been most embarrassing to choose my own constituency.

One Easter Monday Margaret and I drove down unaccompanied to visit the sites. Morriston was a clear winner for me, as it could serve a wide area with good transport access. It would help employment in the western valleys as well. I was confident of my recommendation to Barbara, which was accepted.

The huge building, with employment prospects for up to 4,000 staff, was quickly built. Regrettably there followed many years on a particularly painful learning curve. The centre just did not deliver. I saw the problems in those years from the standpoint of the courts, which grew more and more exasperated, but it eventually settled down to give the kind of service it does today.

The first lesson I learned was that in the face of such a huge changeover from a local to a national service, we should not have attempted to locate the new centre on one spot. We should have tested it out in one region first. My reasoning could apply to other government agencies as well. The second lesson was that the particular part of the civil service I was responsible for was just not capable of handling such a huge project. Whether those lessons have been learnt now, I cannot say. What I am sure of is that nearly forty years' employment has been provided in an area that badly needed it.

While we were still taking the Transport Bill through the Commons, Barbara was summoned to be Secretary of State for Employment, an even more important post charged with reforming the trade union movement. I was in Port Talbot attending to my constituents in my surgery at the council offices. When she was told that Harold Wilson the Prime Minister wanted to speak to me, the telephone operator thought it was a hoax and put the phone down. The Number 10 telephone exchange was, as always, up to this task, I was eventually connected, and Harold told me I was going to defence as a senior minister of state in charge of procurement. The pay was significantly more than an ordinary minister of state as we had inherited the mantles of the old political heads of each of the three services. It was the only time in my ministerial career that I was reasonably well paid.

Harold Wilson, in his book *The Labour Government 1964–70*, wrote: 'John Morris . . . who has distinguished himself as Chairman of an inquiry into the finances of British Rail, succeeded Roy Mason at Defence' (p. 523).

It was quite daring of Harold to transfer two key ministers before a flagship bill was completed. Barbara was elated. My pleasure was similar. She had put in more than just a good word for me. Margaret went out and bought Barbara a huge bouquet of roses exactly the colour of her hair, and she was photographed besides these flowers for all the morning papers.

In the course of our discussions on the railways, we had to retire the chairman, deputy chairman and half the board. I went to Montreal to interview the chairman of the Canadian National Railways and came back overnight with the bad news that he was not interested in the chairmanship of British Rail. Harold, unbeknown to me, canvassed the idea that I should be chairman. Barbara rightly blocked it on the grounds that I lacked business experience. Only a few years later a Tory successor but one appointed Dick Marsh, now Lord Marsh, who had followed her as minister, to be chairman. So I suppose it was not such a strange suggestion by Harold after all. Having been a very young President of the Board of Trade himself, Harold was not afraid of appointing the young.

It had been a particularly fruitful ministerial period for me. We had introduced the breathalyser, seat belts, and I took the seventy mph speed limit through Cabinet committee in the absence of Barbara, who was speaking at a trade union conference. Roy Jenkins as Home Secretary gave the impression that he was dying to do battle with the Ministry of Transport, but after a lot of questions he bottled out. He knew that if we lost, she would have taken it to Cabinet.

My enthusiasm for the breathalyser was based on shocking accident rates from the Road Research Authority, particularly after closing times at the pubs, and also from my experience in drink driving cases when I had seen many police surgeons crucified in court giving evidence. My regret was that the statute made proving the offence so complicated by creating so many hurdles to jump – proving that the test was carried out by a policeman in uniform and so on. We unfortunately built a cottage industry of litigation for many years to come. Unhappily in my very first sitting as an assistant recorder in Cardiff I had to try a breathalyser case. The issue that was argued was novel and apparently complicated. After discussing the matter with the recorder, over dinner and a great deal of wrestling with the issue, I was satisfied that what I would determine on the morrow would be sound law. Despite my anguish of the night before, this is how it turned out – the defence did not appeal.

They were years of intense ministerial activity. I was fortunate in the opportunity that Harold Wilson gave me, and the trust Barbara had in my judgment. Barbara was a marvellous person to work for. Every morning she arrived with the briefs for our meetings carefully annotated and her questions underlined. I have tried to follow her example; I had learnt so much. Man management is one of the keys to a successful career within the ministry and in my two ministers I had learnt a great deal of the craft. You have to try to get the best from the material you have.

eleven
THE MINISTRY OF DEFENCE (1968–1970)

IN MY VIEW being the minister of state in charge of defence procurement – my official title was 'Minister of Defence (Equipment)' – was the best job in government. At my level, there was no day-to-day politicking. You talked to the military, to shipbuilders, to aircraft and tank builders and the like. You supervised defence sales. Cynics called you the 'Merchant of Death'. You met soldiers, sailors and airmen every day of the week.

Selling arms overseas did not cause me too many problems in principle, provided you controlled both the type of armaments and the recipients tightly. The old argument 'if we don't do it, someone else will' had considerable force, but only up to a point. I was very conscious of industrial jobs in Britain, after all I represented a steelmaking constituency. Countries who wished to buy weapons and vehicles to keep down their own population were very unwelcome and we had various levers which could be quite useful like export credit guarantees – meaning the government effectively guaranteed the price to the manufacturer. Most doubtful customers went elsewhere. They did not get the equipment, but it needed a ministerial decision to stop them. That was why political control was so important.

Where I was able to exercise real influence was in stopping sales of mixed-use equipment to South Africa. So many things, from computers down, have such a dual use. Borderline cases went to a Cabinet committee made up in the main of appointed life peers from other departments. I was a constituency MP representing concerned real people. I think I had a substantial influence on the committee and from memory most of those sales did not take place. I was quite pleased with our control machinery.

I had the room of the First Lord of the Admiralty and, it was rumoured, Churchill's blue leather furniture. There was a mark on one of the grand bureau bookcases. Whether there was any basis to the story that it was the result of an exasperated Churchillian kick I do not know, but it was shown to foreign visitors as such nevertheless. They usually took a keen interest.

I arrived at the ministry so physically shattered by my time in the Department of Transport that I announced that since I thought I was going blind, I could not read any papers. This was a distinct disadvantage so I was promptly sent to west London to see the top naval oculist – an admiral of some sort. He spent a good part of a morning deciding whether I was fit for duty and eventually, after exhaustive tests, determined that I was only tired and there was nothing else wrong with me. In life, however tired I have been from exhaustion occasionally, and I do become extraordinarily tired, I have been fortunate to recover very swiftly, and so it turned out on this occasion. I set out to enjoy my office.

My fellow minister of state was Gerry Reynolds, a dedicated defence politician, who through uncertain health had, it seems, never done his National Service, and he was determined to make up for it. Denis Healey, our boss, was away in some distant part of the world discussing nuclear problems at one parliamentary question time. As we waited behind the Speaker's chair together, Gerry turned to me and said, 'I'm going to die in six weeks'. I have never dared to read Hansard for my parliamentary replies that day. He steamed on as if nothing of the kind was to happen. Regrettably he did die shortly afterwards and I went to his funeral in the Guards' Chapel. Roy Hattersley then joined me as my fellow minister of state. I continued to look after procurement; Roy looked after personnel – the armed forces.

As the inheritors of the high offices of secretaries of state for war, air and the board of the admiralty, we deputised for the secretary of state in chairing the service boards from time to time, including sitting at Nelson's table while presiding at the admiralty board. It was great experience to develop the art of getting on with people in the well-oiled machinery of the military. Everything was done to a high standard, and when I eventually went to the Welsh Office I took my experience with me, which I hope was not unhelpful to a young department.

It was interesting to watch the rivalry of the three services in their fight for money from the centre. It appeared the navy did not want to be Whitehall warriors at all and did not always field the best people for the ministry. It was a handicap to them in the fight for resources.

The ministry had been struggling to produce a new torpedo for about twenty years. Whether they achieved it I do not know. The money just poured out and there was not much to show for it. I once said it would be in the national interest to retire a good part of the government scientific civil service and give each a £100,000 to open a tea shop in Brighton. There seemed to be no procedure to retire scientists whose skills were exhausted and to replace them with those who had new expertise.

Denis was the most intellectual boss I ever had. He had a double first from Balliol and possessed a wide cultural hinterland. He was the Prime Minister we never had. It was a great loss to the country. Unfortunately he did not suffer fools gladly. Harold Wilson had put one of his best men in at the Ministry of Defence. It has not always been so. He did the job for six years and since the normal period of appointment of servicemen and senior civil servants to a particular job was three years; by the time he left office he was on his second or third adviser. I wish there was this continuity now. I sometimes wonder how many more recent Labour ministers are in the same league as Denis. I fear not many.

Denis told me that one of my jobs was to tell the military designers, who strove to do what they could to meet operational requirements, when to stop. The military had one major fault – they always wanted 'all-singing, all-dancing' machines. If they went on unchecked we would not have produced anything. The danger was that when you did stop you could be immediately out of date. There always seemed to be a new unsatisfied requirement. I did my best to understand operational requirements and I was very conscious of the time between conception and delivery. I put in project managers on each weapon in development. I suppose my predecessors and successors did something similar. They all reported to me through the chief scientist. I was determined to satisfy military requirements and at the same time get value for money. From recent reports, particularly the Gray Report, it seems the problems I had remain. The military's role should be that of advisers and customers. Regrettably that report, advocating a new approach on their involvement, was rejected in the main at the time.

Long before my time the decision had been taken to put Rolls Royce engines into American Phantom aircraft. As with our purchases of nuclear arms, contracts with our American allies could be difficult to interpret. We and the Americans both thought we spoke the same language: hence the difficulty. Sometimes English in one country meant a different thing in another, which could be of vital importance in a contract. From time to time I went to the United States to try to reach a better understanding.

One of my great pleasures was to attend ship launches, including nuclear powered submarines. Before I left the ministry, Margaret was greatly honoured to name the *Courageous* in Barrow. The bottle of home-produced country wine, as is the Vickers tradition, was well and truly smashed, to the relief of the crew, whom it is said can be superstitious about this. In her speech she was able to refer to her long ancestry of merchant navy sea captains from Newquay, Cardiganshire, who would traverse the oceans in the tall ships – the Cape Horners. A captain of an earlier *Courageous*, an aircraft carrier which had been sunk at the beginning of the 1939–45 war, came from the village of Rhydlewis, just up the road from where we lived.

This began a great association between the *Courageous* and Margaret. She kept in close touch with the captains and wrote to each one in turn so that her good wishes and interest could be conveyed to the crew. To her surprise, when she was once invited to go on board on a 'families' day' the ship submerged and she was asked, properly shepherded, to bring it up to the surface, which she did successfully. Margaret became very concerned when the *Courageous* was seen on television emerging in the waters of the Falkland Islands during the Falklands War, but the submarine suffered no casualties and was unscathed. Eventually, still in pristine condition, she had to be de-commissioned. She had no role in the post Cold War period. We were allowed, within reason, to choose the date for the ceremony in Plymouth. The date I chose turned out to be the day after the 1992 general election. After the count in Aberavon we slept for a few hours in a motorway motel and I raced to Plymouth. The adrenalin kept us going. After the festivities we slept for a few hours in a motorway lay-by, absolutely exhausted and made our way back to London to pick up the pieces once again after an electoral defeat.

Recently, nearly forty years later, we were invited to Plymouth to see the hulk that was once the great *Courageous* stripped of most of her fittings, and open to visitors. I thought it was a pity that the defence ministry could no longer afford to keep her in a condition and in an appropriate place so that she could be seen by visitors. Defence secretary Browne turned down my plea but recently the *Courageous* has been moved and made fit for visitors through enormous voluntary effort. Margaret gave practical help in the production of a book, *Submarine Courageous, Cold War Warrior*, and we went to Devonport on 6 March 2010 for what was described as a 're-launch'. Many of her captains, now retired, were present.

Defence sales were also my responsibility. One of our big deals was to sell Chieftain Tanks to Libya – it was before the revolution, when King Idris ruled. I made quite a few visits as it was important to us to have their currency and provide good employment at home. On one visit during a gap in negotiations, I was travelling in the company of the Ambassador, Sir Donald Maitland, to Sabratha to see the Roman amphitheatre. I was accompanied by motorcycle outriders and any other traveller was swept off the road. Unfortunately one of those was Margaret, travelling in the opposite direction with the Ambassador's lady. My military escort was no respecter of persons and the wives were pushed aside into the sandy gutter.

The Libyans eventually came to London to negotiate the details of the contract, including language and other training. The outstanding matters were comparatively small but negotiations went on and on, and eventually my patience was exhausted. I found out how little was outstanding and decided to give it to them and get the contract signed. I believed production delays and mounting hotel charges were costing more than it was worth. The Libyan negotiating team just did not want to leave London. The deal was done, and contrary to most defence sales they were not covered by export guarantees, which is too close to a 'never-never' purchase, nothing down and years to pay. The Libyans had the money and I ordered a very large deposit to be paid to the ministry account in Liverpool. You do not come from Cardiganshire without having a close interest in money. We have the reputation of casting our bread upon the waters when we know the tide is coming in. My officials were amazed that I drove home the opportunity of substantial cash on the nail. I could control this particular tide.

I was elated as I had put in a lot of personal effort to secure the deal. We seemed then to have a permanent balance of payment crisis and I wanted to do my bit, particularly by ensuring the early payment. In the Commons lobby that night I came across Roy Jenkins, then Chancellor of the Exchequer. When I told him of the deal and the cash down I foolishly thought he would slap me on the back, but I fear the great man looked down his nose and soon found somebody more important to talk to. No wonder there was a distinct limit to his success in the Labour Party so far as MPs were concerned. Welsh MPs in general, with one exception, could not stand him and he did not have much time for them either. It was a huge mistake on his part.

One of our side interests during the negotiations was the suggestion by the Libyans that they were minded to have a royal yacht built by us for King Idris. We took the team out to evaluate their requirements – quite simple really, a yacht larger than the Turkish yacht and a cabin for the King slightly grander than the Queen's. Then the revolution came and the tanks were not delivered and the yacht was not built. I suppose eventually the balance of the money that we were sitting on in Liverpool was repaid – less our expenses.

Margaret was able to come with me on some trips abroad and would visit the troops' wives. They were frequently quite young, some not even twenty, and while the men were on duty they were on their own with their small children, sometimes far away from the main base. She instigated a lot of welfare arrangements, and encouraged clubs for the wives who lived in Holland, quite a few miles from the base in Germany. Her priorities were right – the families were high on her list.

On one occasion we travelled back from Libya via Tobruk, Benghazi and El Adem. In our childhood many of these names loomed large in our thoughts as Rommel and Montgomery battled it out across the North African Desert. Since there was not much else on the map, these 'towns' were writ large. It was a great disappointment to see how small they were. The troops' families lived in huts on mud floors, and little had been spent on their accommodation as we did not anticipate holding on to them.

Recently on a Commonwealth-related visit to Cyprus I found the British forces' accommodation at the Royal Ledra Palace Hotel was worse than at El Adem. A series of parliamentary questions in the Lords eventually put this right, but I was aghast that some months before our visit a minister had actually visited the area. Whatever his efforts, the result by the time we happened to visit was nil. Sewage was coming back in the toilets, electric light plugs hanging out of the walls, and no such thing as air conditioning in a long-established peacetime base in the heart of Nicosia. El Adem was a scandal, but we were pulling out of it. How a minister could visit this type of service accommodation and not explode with indignation baffled me. The President of the Cyprus Senate told us his government had done everything required – it was the responsibility of the UK government. Regardless of our troops' interests they seem not to have exerted themselves. I got a promise for action and work was due to be completed by the end of 2010.

On two occasions I went to India, one of them to see Mrs Ghandi launch the first Indian-built frigate, the *Nilgiri*. Harold Wilson sent for me before I went. He apparently wanted Mrs Ghandi on side in a forthcoming commonwealth conference and I was instructed to deliver a personal letter. My officials were not sure what her attitude would be. In the event she graciously hosted a lunch for me and was charm in itself. She seemed to be glad to talk.

I became deeply concerned about the war in Biafra, as the civil insurrection in Nigeria was called. Civil war is the most anguishing of all wars and my concern deepened by the day as we were supplying mainly small arms and the ammunition usage was on a World War Two scale, to little avail. Most of the bullets, it seemed, were being fired into the bush. I began to question to myself the morality of it all, supplying endless arms, but not being prepared to go for the kill by supplying aircraft and pilots to bring this ghastly war to an end. I was quite prepared to increase the tempo of arms supply, but deeply concerned about the misery caused to ordinary people through a long, drawn-out war.

I went to see Denis Healey who was recovering from a hernia operation in the Chelsea Military Hospital. I put my rather muddled case as best as I could. I hope he understood; it was probably the nearest I ever came to resignation. I decided to soldier on, but after this, since I wanted to ensure my responsibility for authorising particular consignments, I instructed that I was to countersign every despatch of equipment. It was my only really unhappy period in the ministry. Was it the pacifist feeling in me welling up, or was it my passionate concern as an old soldier of a few years' duration only, for deaths of soldiers and civilians? It left a deep mark on me which I have never discussed with anyone.

Looking back, my purpose in the ministry was to get value for money. The *Times* billed my appointment with the headline, a small one, 'Slasher Morris goes to Defence'. It was a period when the government could claim to be spending more on education than on defence and I was proud of that. But once our share of the cake had been determined, I was to do what I could to ensure the money was well spent. One thing I was adamant about was the futility and overwhelming danger of tactical nuclear weapons.

Shortly before the general election I had a letter from the Prime Minister that he was minded to recommend a Privy Councillorship for me. Nothing gave me greater pleasure at the time. I was not yet forty and the announcement came in the Birthday Honours in the middle of the election campaign. I was eventually sworn in, after we lost the 1970 general election, with part of the new Tory cabinet. My only regret was that I did not request a Welsh testament, which is the only token you have marking the office to which you were sworn.

I remember one hot August when I was duty defence minister – we always kept one minister in London in Denis's time. My friend, Elystan Morgan, then a junior minister in the Home Office, and I were walking down a deserted Whitehall to a Cabinet committee which required our presence, when Elystan jokingly observed, 'John, you have the army and I have the police. Shall we take over?' Thank God we did not live in a banana republic.

What did I achieve in defence in those two years? I learnt to work with a boss totally different from Barbara at Transport. In both cases I was entrusted with vast responsibilities – a training I was not to forget, and I never had any disagreement with my superiors – my concern over Biafra stands alone and I am quite proud of it. My personal achievement was to continue to learn how to manage. What effect I actually had on my vast budget it is difficult to say. There is a real problem managing the defence procurement budget which so far does not seem to have been resolved. There needs to be greater continuity of ministers – it is almost a non-political job. The role of the military is important: they are the consumers. But after taking their views into full account, the buck stops with the politician who decides. The armed forces should never be sent into action except in proper numbers, trained for the job and with the necessary equipment.

These seem to be such self-evident propositions that I am dismayed they are too frequently breached.

In conflict it is better to err on the side of over-provisioning than hope under-provisioning will do. In the distant past we seemed to have run out of ammunition rather too frequently, even after D Day, if the author of a recent book is correct.

A second point is that defence is only the handmaiden of foreign policy. Those who decide foreign policy must never forget that defence must be provided with the wherewithal to carry out those policies. If they do not have it, policy should be adapted accordingly.

I strove endlessly to get value for money. If a problem could not be resolved I frequently marked files: 'to be returned for my attention within three or six months'. I carried on the practice in the Welsh Office. The temptation of allowing dust to settle in pigeonholes housing memoranda on seemingly intractable problems had to be closed off.

It was my least frenzied period as a minister and I rather enjoyed it. I had a window of opportunity to see more of my family, and together with Margaret I was able to visit our responsibilities in various parts of the world. Both of us were able to improve a little of the conditions in which our troops and families operated in. In short, I confess it was the happiest period in my ministerial life.

twelve
IDEAS FOR DEVOLUTION (1964–1970)

A JUNIOR MINISTER in a new and innovative government is incredibly busy. The danger is that the problems of the outside world and other government departments wash over your head, until you creep exhausted to bed each evening. I fear I fell into this trap. Nevertheless, although I did not spend much time on the interminable discussions round the Welsh table, I kept an ear open for any developments, although not all cabinet papers came my way. As defence minister, I had appointed Alec Jones MP (Rhondda) as my PPS and that was helpful.

In the 1964–70 government, I followed Welsh Secretary Cledwyn Hughes's proposals for reforming government in Wales. His efforts turned out to be disappointing to him and to all of us. I was present at one of the Cabinet committees when he presented his proposals. As defence minister my department only had a marginal interest, but I had received Cledwyn's paper, which was primarily concerned with local government and quangos.

We had already discussed in his office the opposition of Welsh local government leaders. I suggested selecting one of their number as chairman of his proposed all-Wales authority, and commented that Llew Heycock, as the most powerful force in Glamorgan County Council, would be an admirable choice and should be given a peerage as well. Llew was delighted, particularly with the unexpected offer of a peerage.

However at the Cabinet committee it was obvious that Cledwyn had been unsuccessful in winning friends beforehand. Maybe it wasn't possible; he had ranged against him, as I recollect, both Dick Crossman and Tony Crosland, formidable Cabinet ministers. The argument was that old Whitehall ploy: a bigger and better solution within the framework of local government reform for both England and Wales, and in the meantime his proposals were rejected. This was typical of Crossman's attitude to so many things. He wanted to be a real radical, but seemed to blow hot and cold when suddenly newer arguments proved more attractive.

In his diaries Crossman wrote:

30 November 1966
It made me furious that little Cledwyn wanted to publish his own White Paper on local government reform and even to legislate on it for Wales in this Parliament before our Royal Commission for England and Wales had reported – absolute nonsense.

The superiority of the Wykehamist revealed itself in the nature of his comments. Crossman was determined not to lose his temper again when Cledwyn brought a similar paper back to the Home Affairs Committee.

5 May 1967
A simple solution struck me. Cledwyn Hughes complained he'd had to water down the proposals for a Welsh Regional Council and I thought, that's terrible, they're going to get the worst of both worlds – an antiquated LG reform and a futile Welsh Council. Why not accept this local government reorganisation as a political necessity and then go for a really ambitious plan for a Welsh Council or Parliament? The PM has several times said that the question of decentralisation and regional government – Welsh nationalism and Scottish nationalism – might become an explosive issue at the next election.

The proposals were transferred to the Cabinet's Environmental Planning Committee even though Crossman referred to them as:

. . . a miserable form of local government with an equally miserable recommendation for a co-opted Welsh Council, which so far as I could see would do nothing but supervise tourism.

The matter returned to the devolution Cabinet committee on 20 March 1968, according to the diaries, when Cledwyn brought forward yet another paper and Crossman commented:

Home Rule for Wales based on the Stormont Parliament. But he doesn't want anything like the powers of Stormont . . . it wasn't at all clear what the devil his Welsh Parliament would do.

There appeared to be a lack of consistency in proposals from the Welsh Office and whatever was proposed seemed to run up against intractable opposition from one corner or another.

It was after this time that I wrote to Harold Wilson enclosing a memorandum (19 June 1968). From the Cabinet committee meeting minutes I had seen, and I believe they are reflected in the Crossman Diaries, I had become increasingly concerned at the Welsh Office's failure to win more powers. George Thomas had become Welsh Secretary on 6 April 1968 (the same day I was promoted to the Ministry of Defence). I was sure he would reject any form of parliamentary devolution, but would be more than happy if Welsh Office powers were increased. It seemed to me that even on this the Welsh Office was facing immense opposition from every department that feared losses of its own powers. As a middle-ranking minister in defence I knew any intervention of mine would be most unwelcome, would be verging on the unconstitutional and most of all would be deeply resented by George Thomas. I decided, nevertheless, to take a chance and throw my hat into the ring. I do not think the secretaries in the Ministry of Defence have ever before had to type a letter on constitutional reform to the Prime Minister. I sensed raised eyebrows.

I wrote a long minute to the Prime Minister with a covering letter apologising for my intervention, which could be regarded as improper. But Harold Wilson endorsed my letter in his own hand:

Please re-assure him – unusual. But not in my view at all improper.

I set out the full letter in Appendix 1, but quote here:

In the absence of any machinery for consultation with Welsh MPs who happen to be ministers, I am writing to express my views on the draft conclusions of the Ministerial Committee on Devolution (Second Revise) which I have studied.

This, to say the least, is a sad document, not only for its conclusions, but worse, for its sheer argument on and lack of philosophy. There appear to be colleagues who do not wish to do anything, and others who, when specific proposals are put, be it on functions or decentralisation of administrative centres, if their own departments are affected seek to reject them . . .

It would be a grave error to suppose that present problems are transient. Our aspirations certainly manifest themselves with different force at different periods. But they continue to recur after 500 years. For the purposes of this argument, I have deliberately not canvassed some of the underlying problems, and the need to involve people in decision-making, but I am saddened at the conservatism of the approach of the present document.

As Welsh Secretary, George Thomas had put forward his own proposals for the reform of Welsh local government and a strengthened Council for Wales with executive responsibilities for Welsh tourism and the Welsh Board of Health, coupled with a major strengthening of the Welsh Office.

The Labour Party suffered particularly badly in a by-election in 1967 when Mrs Winnie Ewing won a seat for the SNP in Scotland. In the Rhondda and Caerphilly we managed to hold the seats but lost many votes to the Welsh nationalists. The nationalists had become a looming danger on the political horizon. New thinking was needed for making governmental Wales more democratic and accountable.

In the summer of 1968 there had been some discussions – but ministers seemed to be concentrating on administrative devolution issues and contesting any transfer of functions. Crossman still wanted to wait the Royal Commission Report on Local Government in England (Redcliffe-Maud). Callaghan, as Home Secretary, with the support of the Scottish and Welsh Secretaries, proposed a constitutional commission straight away to consider whether any changes were required in central government functions for different parts of the UK. This commission would be complementary to the Redcliffe-Maud Commission.

At a meeting on 28 October Callaghan said that he saw no alternative to the appointment of a commission, since the government was unable to come forward with proposals of its own and the administrative and parliamentary devolution which had been under discussion were insufficient by themselves. The Prime Minister, summing up the discussions, said that most of the meeting agreed on immediate consultations with a view to establishing a commission, and that this decision should be announced in the Opening Speech later that week.

We were on holiday with Elystan Morgan, and his family in Newquay, Cornwall in August 1968 when he told me, coming up from the beach one day, that he believed the answer to our problems was a Royal Commission for Wales and Scotland. It could consider whether any major changes were desirable for the fundamental reform of government. I immediately warmed to the suggestion, which was completely new to me. Royal Commissions have been derided in the past as 'bodies that take minutes but waste years', or bodies that could be useful for kicking the ball – on particularly contentious subjects – into touch, with the hope that by the time the commission reported, the heat would have gone out of the subject. They were quite popular with many prime ministers, but over recent years have fallen out of favour. I suspect there is greater awareness that eventually someone else, and possibly the incumbent prime minister, will have to pick up the ball again when the commission reports.

Parliament was recalled that summer because the Russians had invaded Czechoslovakia. As we made our way back to London, leaving our young families to their buckets and spades, we pondered further the idea of a commission. In my view it could act as a catalyst for fundamental constitutional changes for Wales that we could hardly dream of. If the evidence went well there could be immense changes. Looking back onto my interest and discussions in the early 1950s, we were now in a new field – or perhaps better expressed, on a 'new planet'. I immediately grasped the significance of an idea that was new to me, as I had not been privy to the Cabinet committee discussions. Here to me was a practical way forward with immense potential.

I don't think Wales, or indeed the Labour Party, had any idea of what could be achieved by a Westminster government determined on change. On the other hand, if the evidence went sour, the clock would be turned back many years. An adverse report would be a major blow, and could turn out to be disastrous. During that train journey and in the following months I realised more and more that if the idea of a commission was adopted, there would be no turning back. With evidence behind us from such a committee of the great and the good, we would be heading for a fundamental change in the constitution.

Our critics in Wales jumped to the conclusion that the Labour Party was merely reacting to current political pressures following bad election results. So it might appear. To me, it was different. Of course there would be much bigger battles ahead for a Labour government – no other government would be interested – trying to work out its reactions to calls for the implementation of any of the commission's proposals. That would be for another day.

Apart from the shock of Winnie Ewing's victory, I fear I was never conscious of any Labour Party pressures in Scotland. It is perhaps one of the weaknesses of the two Celtic countries that it is rare for them to take account of different pressures in the other country; it certainly was at that time. I had very limited knowledge of the political scene in Scotland and occasional discussions with my fellow politicians there, but they did not do a great deal to encourage me. On the contrary, the parliamentary leader of the Scots and his friends were bitter opponents of the kind of constitutional reforms we envisaged, but were quite prepared to swallow a Royal Commission. I sensed that eventually we would have to try to march together. We could never move forward for Wales alone.

The formal consultations with Buckingham Palace having taken place, Harold Wilson, and it is a customary prime ministerial role, announced to the House of Commons the setting up of the Commission in October 1968 under the chairmanship of Lord Crowther, who unfortunately died soon after. His place was taken by Lord Kilbrandon. I had no knowledge of the discussions within the Labour Party or the Welsh Labour Party about evidence to the Commission. I was far too busy ministerially in my own department. Had I known, and particularly if there was even a shred of consultation with people like myself who were ministers of the government, I would have tried to influence the submissions. There was no consultation, and perhaps in the event this was fortunate. I had no political baggage in this respect when a new government returned to the subject.

Harold Wilson enjoyed his summer holidays in his bungalow in the Scilly Isles where I suspect that any unnecessary correspondence did not receive too warm a welcome. Nevertheless, George Thomas wrote to the Prime Minister while he was on holiday on 25 August 1969 setting out his proposals for government evidence to the commission. There is no recorded reply to his letter and I had never heard of it until a recent television programme, which is not surprising. George was seeking to exploit what was understood to be his special relationship with the Prime Minister. He certainly believed that he had such a relationship.

George Thomas's letter to the Prime Minister is reproduced in full in Appendix 2; the following is a short extract:

> If we reject parliamentary devolution, it is the more necessary for us to advance in administrative devolution. I am convinced that an elected or partly elected Welsh Council dealing with administrative functions is both practicable and advisable. The functions of the Welsh Council could be partly executive and party advisory.

He listed eight quangos operating in Wales which could form its remit, along with the health service. His stated aim was to concentrate on administrative devolution, as opposed to Parliamentary devolution. The only reaction from the centre is the record of the minute from the Prime Minister's private secretary on the 3 September 1969 to his counterpart in the Cabinet secretary's office, 'referring to the fact that the Prime Minister has now seen this memorandum and has commented as follows in his own hand':

> Has the Home Secretary not got a coordinating committee on the commission and should this not:

(a) discuss the general question of whether it is right for the government to put forward proposals to the commission at this stage, and

(b) if it decided that government submissions *are* in order, consider the secretary of state's paper and decide whether – or with what amendments – it should be submitted?

HW.

The Cabinet Secretary, Sir Burke Trend, replied magisterially on the 9 September 1969 that:

> The specific suggestions which the secretary of state makes are not, in the main, new. His views on administrative devolution for a partly elected Welsh council were thoroughly canvassed last year ... the committee's conclusions record their views that the proposed council would be an unsatisfactory compromise between local and central government ... If his idea is that separate statutory instruments should normally be made ... in relation to Wales, the proposal seems to encourage variety for variety's sake and might lead to difficulties of financial control.

He goes on to suggest that unless the Prime Minister wished to constitute a special group of ministers, the memo might go to the ministerial committee on the constitution for discussion. Accordingly the Prime Minister suggested this, but it appears that he did not reply to the Welsh Secretary. The Cabinet secretary had formed the view that he was trying to re-run a race that had been lost.

There must have been some very red faces in the Welsh Office. The civil servants did not enjoy a rebuff of this kind. Perhaps sending the letter in the middle of August, when many of the Welsh Secretary's senior staff were on holiday was itself some indication of impetuosity on the part of their master. If they felt rebuffed, how much more galling was it for George Thomas?

In fact the ministerial committee on the constitution was eventually set up on 18 November 1968 and met a month later. The Welsh Secretary's letter does not seem to have been put before it. One suspects that George Thomas had given up by then.

The Royal Commission went on its way gathering evidence across the board, including the Labour Party, but not from the Labour government, which had been voted out of office in 1970. It reported in October 1973. Regrettably there were many divergent views, but the broad thrust was very much in the right direction and was regarded by devolutionists as a positive encouragement for their case. The risk had been worth taking. Of the eleven Commissioners who signed the Majority Report, eight recommended legislative devolution for Scotland and six recommended it for Wales. Three favoured a directly elected Welsh Advisory Council and one favoured a similar scheme for Scotland. Two recommended executive devolution for Scotland and Wales. Two signed a memorandum of dissent, one of them being Lord Crowther-Hunt, later to be adviser to both the PM and to me.

I was asked to comment on the radio and, on the slim basis of the BBC's press summary of its recommendations, I was able to give a warm welcome to its main thrust; it was valuable work on which to build, despite its many divergent views.

Skewen was at that time in the constituency of my neighbour, Don Coleman in Neath. It had a long-established debating circle and the local MP, as its president, would seek a parliamentary figure for one of its monthly meetings about the turn of the year. I had been invited to be the guest speaker on 17 January 1974. I was particularly busy professionally at the time and drove down from Westminster to Port Talbot in a raging gale. I have never known conditions on the Severn Bridge to be so bad, such was the tempest; the authorities must have been within inches of closing the bridge.

My intention, once I got to my agent's house for a cup of tea, was to jot down a few notes for my speech. I had been thinking what to say on the way. It was my normal practice at the time to prepare a carefully worded press statement, although the press did not usually take much interest in what I had to say at local meetings. I had no time on this occasion.

When I got there, John Osmond, the *Western Mail*'s political correspondent was on the phone. He had learnt that I was to address the meeting and was curious as to what I might say.

The *Western Mail* reported the following day:

First Labour MP calls for a legislative assembly: Aberavon's MP

Mr John Morris yesterday became the first Labour member in Wales to make a positive call for an elected assembly with a legislative role. He told a party meeting at Skewen the whole debate over whether an assembly should have legislative or executive power was 'phoney'. He said, 'It is not beyond our wit to fit the Welsh assembly into the legislative process.

'I cannot conceive a worthwhile body being set up without it having the opportunity of expressing its views and influencing the actions of central government on its proposals for Wales.' Mr Morris is the first Welsh Labour MP to depart from an emerging party view that an assembly should have a purely executive role – coordinating local government and carrying out the legislated dictates of Westminster. He agreed that a public impression had been created that Labour was for an executive assembly and Plaid Cymru was pressing for one with legislative powers. 'To some extent I am bridging the gap,' he said last night. But he stressed that essentially the difference between executive and legislative was a matter of words: Plaid was using the issue to conceal its real aim of complete separation. It was allowing the term legislative to be interpreted in a moderate way by a majority of people while reserving its own view of the meaning. But this should not prevent the Labour Party affirming that to a great degree a Welsh assembly was bound to be involved in policymaking.

Mr Morris said it could be involved in the first reading of parliamentary bills relating to Wales and was bound to be consulted on major issues. Even the present nominated Welsh Council prepared a paper on the implications for Wales of our entry into Europe, he said. Asked about some Labour fears that an elected assembly would inevitably grow in the direction that nationalists wanted, Mr Morris said, 'It will grow according to the wishes of Wales.'

The opponents of a worthwhile body are the political legatees of those who opposed setting up the Welsh Office, which has rendered valuable service to Wales.

The Welsh Office began with few powers, against the wishes of the establishment to it being set up at all. Even today, despite its growth, it has not been given the accolade of full Civil Service approval by giving its permanent head the task and pay of a permanent secretary. He soldiers on and the guns he carries in interdepartmental Whitehall discussions are those of a deputy secretary.

Despite the urgency of its proper recognition, the Welsh Office must not become a sort of sacred cow, and neither must the top tier of local government.

Strong Welsh political representation in the cabinet will be necessary, so will effective local government. But it must be clearly understood that if we want to move forward to provide Wales with the kind of government that is required a lot of what we know today must go into the melting pot.

Mr Morris implied two things in his speech. First, reorganised local government in Wales will have to change to fit in with an assembly – the eight new county councils are too big. Secondly, although there will be a minister in the British Cabinet, in Mr Morris's view he should be a representative with political responsibilities rather than administrative – a voice for lobbying rather than decision making.

I have no reason to dissent from the experienced journalist's interpretation of my telephoned comments. I was not quoting from a prepared document as some commentators thought. A great deal of the report was based on my answers to Mr Osmond's questions. What I was doing was making a stab in the right direction. I was finding my way forward, having been disappointed by the variety of views expressed by Kilbrandon's Commission.

The *Western Mail*, in one of its leader articles that day developed its 'interpretation' role. Under the headline 'Choosing his Words' they reported:

Mr John Morris has carried out a useful service in pinpointing, though not necessarily clearing, one of the areas of confusion in the debate within the Labour Party on the Kilbrandon proposals for constitutional reform. Welsh Labour MPs have been debating what functions an elected assembly might be given. The thought of an elected advisory assembly having been instantly dismissed as the intellectual and political absurdity that it is, the choice then lies between legislative and executive functions or a combination of both. Unfortunately, in certain quarters of the Welsh Labour Party the word legislative, in the context of a Welsh assembly, has become a great bogey to be shied away from to the sound of melodramatic utterances about the dreadful constitutional dangers involved. Mr Morris will no doubt now find himself assailed by some of his own colleagues for mentioning the word at all. They will be doing him a disservice by so Pavolvian a reaction, whatever else they may do to themselves.

It is significant that Mr Morris talked about the assembly being fitting into the legislative process. He did not say it should be given legislative powers. The difference is real and fundamental, and makes his views wholly consistent with the evidence submitted to the Commission on the Constitution by the Labour Party in Wales. We agree that it is not a little unreal to envisage a body charged with implementing policy on a wide front having no say in the determination of that policy. The matter can easily be resolved without detracting from Westminster's powers, as was shown by Sir Alec Douglas-Home's Scottish Constitutional Committee which produced a plan for an assembly which did precisely this.

Mr Morris raised another point which demands immediate attention. This involves the continued belittling of the Welsh Office by making its Civil Service head a deputy secretary rather than a full permanent secretary. This standing insult to the department and to the Welsh people has serious practical implications for the influence of the Welsh Office vis-à-vis other government departments as rank assumes such importance in the workings of the Civil Service. It is an issue which should be resolutely pursued now.

There was an element of probing in my remarks, not for the first time in my life – clarity was not a requirement for that purpose. When I got to the House on Monday those of my colleagues who had only read the sub-editor's headlines, inconsistent as they were with the leader-writer's interpretation, gave me quite a difficult time. I had mentioned the 'L' word and to some of my colleagues this was a sin.

Within three months I would be preparing to bring forward proposals for the government of Wales. At that time I was nowhere near working out what they would be and never thought I would have that task. I knew they would have to be acceptable to Parliament, my party and the people of Wales and hopefully provide long-term stability. As it turned out I had, at Skewen, shared some of my thoughts with the people of Wales. But they were still in the early stages.

I was satisfied from the press report that I had kept the door open as to the way my Party should go to create the strongest assembly that they and Parliament would agree to.

thirteen
SECRETARY OF STATE

I SPENT MY TIME IN OPPOSITION between 1970 and 1974 looking after my own constituency and working at the Bar. There was little point in taking part in Welsh politics whilst George Thomas was our shadow spokesman. The only important speech I made was the one I have just referred to at Skewen, and the welcome I had from my colleagues at Westminster was, to say the least, mixed.

I had been very disappointed when we lost the 1970 election. Most elections have some elements of a gamble. There are not many certainties. However, I was inclined to believe that we would win. My wife and I had discussed the possibility of moving to Cardiff if I was offered, and took, a junior post in the Welsh Office. In the event we did not and I was appointed to depute on the front opposition bench for Fred Peart, who had been one of my earliest sponsors in the House. He shouldered the burden of being both defence and agricultural spokesman – hence his description by the press as 'guns and butter'. He was later to be tragically mugged on his own doorstep and never really recovered from his injuries.

Roy Jenkins was deputy leader of the Party for a while. He sent for me, I suspect, so that he could get to know me and others of my generation better, as former junior ministers who might have further prospects. It was the strangest interview of my life. He began by discussing the cars we drove. I said I drove a Rover 2500. He said he did the same so I got some brownie points from this. I was not particularly interested in cars and thought that this was a strange preliminary to what I expected was to be a serious conversation.

He then said that he noted I was a QC and a Privy Counsellor. He asked whether I took the 'Asquithian view' in my silk's practice. I asked what that was. He said that Mr Asquith, after he had been made a Privy Counsellor, would not go into any court unless it was presided over by other

Privy Counsellors in what must have been the Court of Appeal and above. I replied that if I took that view my family might not eat, as I would have little work! The interview came to an end after this. I obviously had not stirred much interest.

This book would have come to a premature end, had not fate dealt me a good hand at this time: I was defending a case in one of the courts opposite the Old Bailey in 1972. James Crespi, who had lectured me on the law for my three years in Aberystwyth, was prosecuting. Suddenly, the court usher interrupted shouting, 'There's a bomb in the Bailey!' Judge and jury leapt off their benches. No one knew the location of the bomb – our courts in the annexe, the main Old Bailey building over the road, or in the street itself, which was also called 'Old Bailey'. Everyone else left the court building at once. I decided to go back first to the small robing room at the back to collect my bag and papers and pack my wig and gown. If the Old Bailey was to go up in smoke, I wanted to leave with all my kit!

While I stood in the lavatory there was a massive explosion; the pane of glass in the window shattered and made a tiny scratch on my hand. I was alone in the building. In the meantime, Crespi had left the court and made his way to the robing room in the main building across the way. He did not know that he was walking straight towards a parked car packed with explosives by the IRA. The massive explosion which followed blew out hundreds of windows in the area. The national newspapers the following day showed Crespi with his head swathed in bandages.

He was a particularly well-built man by then, rather different from the much slimmer lecturer who had taught me years before. He was incapacitated for many months, particularly from the injuries to his eyes from flying glass. He used to joke that his doctors had warned him for many years that he would die because he was too fat, but on this occasion they had assured him that his fat had saved him.

Normally, had I not tarried, I would have been walking back with him as an old friend to share the gossip and compare stories. As I did not have the benefit of Crespi's girth, I could have been in some difficulty. I made my way back to my chambers through empty and silent streets. I was a lucky man.

Ted Heath's government staggered towards defeat, having made major U-turns on economic policy over the years (and plunged the country into the three-day week). Still, I was quite unprepared for victory when it came.

One of the biggest and the most dramatic surprises of my life was to be appointed secretary of state for my own nation – to be Welsh Secretary and a member of the Cabinet. I had watched the campaign to create this office from the sidelines. Scotland had had such a post since 1885. It had been a hard fight to win a similar post for Wales in 1964.

My appointment was a total surprise to me. After the disappointment of losing the 1970 election I had taken very little part in Welsh politics. I had concentrated on my own constituency and rebuilding my legal practice. I had, on advice, applied for silk in 1973 and Lord Hailsham had granted it. My lack of many years sustained experience, coupled with broken service at the Bar during my junior ministerial posts from 1964–70 was against me, but I had powerful supporters in Lord Edmund-Davies and Mr Justice Tasker Watkins, VC.

In the 'lost' weekend in 1974, when Ted Heath tried unsuccessfully to cobble together some arrangement with Jeremy Thorpe, the leader of the then Liberal Party, and failed, Harold Wilson kept quiet. I wrote to him asking for the post of Solicitor General. I had been a senior minister of state and thought this was about my worth.

At that time Cabinet Office, and particularly the Welsh Office, never crossed my mind, and George Thomas was expected to resume the role of Welsh Secretary, which he had filled in the last years of the 1964–70 government. He was also shadow Welsh Secretary from 1970 to 1974 and was very friendly with both Harold and Mary Wilson. Unfortunately, he had set up shop as the principal enemy of devolution and had written a series of quite inflammatory pieces portraying his deep resentment of so many things Welsh in the *Liverpool Daily Post*. He had a considerable bias against the Welsh language and the devolutionists in the Welsh Labour Party were deeply embarrassed by many of his articles.

Personally, I was on quite friendly terms with him. He was friendly with most people provided you did not tread on his toes or his interests, and Wales and Welsh politics was his fiefdom. In fact, he was wary of all Welsh MPs, particularly those he thought might be ambitious. I made it my business to avoid talking about anything of a political nature with him, and I do not recall having any such discussion. I greatly admired the work he did on leasehold reform, a burning topic in my constituency and many others in Wales. In any other matter concerning Wales, I fear I must say the less I had to do with him the better. We were not on the same political planet so far as Welsh affairs were concerned and I have never been one to pick quarrels. What was the point?

I had no idea of what he had been up to. Many, many years later, it came as a total surprise to me that he had lobbied Wilson about Labour's evidence to the Kilbrandon Commission on that Scilly Isles holiday. I am still astonished at this effrontery. Harold, in any event, was fascinated by the machinery of government and took a great personal interest in it. I am glad I did not know of the letter at the time, otherwise I would have been sorely tempted to have joined in.

As soon as the result of the February election was announced, there was a great deal of political excitement as to who would form a government and this continued over the weekend. Out of curiosity I went from our home, then in Kennington, with Margaret and our girls to St James's Park after lunch. On Sundays in those days there was easy access up the steps from Horse Guards Parade to Downing Street, which the girls had never seen. As we climbed the steps, we saw that a small crowd had gathered outside Number 10, which was still occupied by Ted Heath. They were shouting, 'Heath out!' Eventually that afternoon he had to concede defeat and Harold Wilson was invited to form a government.

Wales expected George Thomas to be secretary of state for Wales and both his memoirs and his biography *George* by E. H. Robertson make it clear that he did too. When the call came, late on Sunday evening, he caught a cab and was in Number 10 as Big Ben struck the hour. When Wilson saw him he asked George how he'd like to be Deputy Speaker and Chairman of Ways and Means. According to Robertson, George was astonished and asked: 'Not Secretary of State for Wales?'

It was not in Wilson's gift to promise him the eventual speakership. This came to him on the retirement of Selwyn Lloyd, and he turned out to be an outstanding Speaker.

The call to me came from the Number 10 switchboard at about 12 noon and I hurried over. I saw the new Prime Minister, Harold Wilson. The meeting was quite short. Only adrenalin kept us going, as we were both suffering from post-election tiredness, but he appeared as bright as a button. He told me what my job was, and that I was to bring devolution to Wales: 'How you do it is up to you, but I will be interested in your proposals.' There was no limit, no restrictions, just a plain injunction to get on with it. I was elated that we were being treated on a par with Scotland. I could hardly believe this, as I never thought it would be practicable to deliver devolution to both nations at the same time, having regard to the other priorities for a new Labour government.

This was the fourth job Harold Wilson had given to me since 1964. All our interviews had been quite brief. This one was the same. I did not question his invitation. I knew why I was there. He wanted a devolutionist in the Welsh Office. I was a devolutionist, and he knew that I would give a high priority to devolution. To some extent the life of his government depended on it, as we relied on the support of the minority parties. Labour had only 301 seats, the Conservatives were close behind with 297, the Liberals and the other parties totalled thirty-seven. The Kilbrandon Commission had opened the door to major possibilities for constitutional reform. There had not been such an opportunity since the deeply divided Speaker's conference on devolution in the 1920s.

I had been on this road since the early 1950s and I was determined not to miss the opportunity. It was to be my priority and I was comforted by the fact that circumstances had made it the government's priority too. I was aiming for a body which would exercise national democratic accountability in Cardiff. My fellow Welshmen could then, if they were minded, blame Cardiff and not the 'man in Whitehall' for anything done by 'government'.

Apart from expressing my delight, the only other conversation was my request, as secretary of state, for a permanent secretary. Harold was surprised that we did not have one. I explained that my Civil Service head only had the pay and rations of a deputy secretary. This was because it had been only a small office at the start and had only recently grown through the accumulation of new powers. Like Harold I too was interested in the machinery of government and had asked a series of questions on this point in opposition. Rank in Whitehall terms was important. It was an important machinery-of-government point, about which none of my colleagues had shown an ounce of interest. Harold promised to send the Head of the Civil Service, Sir William Armstrong, down to see me in the next few days. He came to the Welsh Office, I believe, early in my second week of office. It was my first victory.

My meeting with Harold ended by him saying 'Come and meet my kitchen cabinet.' The kitchen cabinet was sitting down to lunch. Afterwards I walked from Number 10 to Gwydir House, the Welsh Office's London headquarters, to meet my new officials. Number 10 must have warned them I was on my way as I was greeted by the private secretary at the door. I walk rather quickly but he was ready for me, and very welcoming. As a good civil servant, he expressed no surprise. I then saw the 'permanent secretary', Hywel Evans, who was as shocked as I was, although he diplomatically did not show it. I had met him once when we had a royal visit to Port Talbot. I was fortunate enough to inherit my predecessor's private secretary, John Lloyd and his deputy, Margaret Evans. They were a wonderful team of protectors for a secretary of state on a steep learning curve and I was to be very indebted to them.

I realised that not only the mandarins, but the whole of Wales was rather taken aback at my appointment. The whole world knew of it, except Margaret. She had been clearing out builders' rubble from our new house in Blackheath all day and there was no telephone there. The election had postponed our move. There was no means of contacting her and I had no idea when she would return. It was only when she returned to our house in Kennington late that afternoon that she answered the first of many telephone calls of congratulations and found out what had happened.

One of my first steps was to send for my old friend, Gwilym Prys-Davies, who had a long time before put on paper some ideas for devolving administration in Wales. This extremely busy solicitor dropped everything and got on the next train to my home in Kennington. In the meantime, I had gone home and shared with Margaret the feeling of not knowing what had hit us. I was relieved that, since I had played so little part in Welsh politics outside the needs of my constituency, I was untainted by the views of others.

Gwilym, Margaret and I went out for dinner in the Festival Hall restaurant overlooking the Thames, which was convenient, and we talked earnestly. We were interrupted when we came home by a visit from my old mentor, Alun Talfan Davies and a friend, who had a senior post involving religious affairs with the BBC. They brought champagne, which we could have done without. We wanted to get on with our plans and their conviviality was not in accord with our need to consider how we would proceed. When they left after a short time, we resumed our conversation. In the precarious political situation in which we found ourselves, we agreed we must act quickly. I recalled Jim Griffiths's advice to a new minister, 'What you do in your first five days of office marks you out for the remainder of your tenure.'

In the circumstances, unusually for a government department, not an ounce of preparatory work on devolution had been done by the Welsh Office. Most government departments, and I have served in five, do what they can to anticipate their new master's needs. My template was the Ministry of Power's preparation for steel nationalisation where even the appropriate Civil Service staffing was in place for our policy. Perhaps they can be forgiven if they thought, like everybody else, that Thomas would be the inevitable choice and therefore any preparations for devolution would be a waste of time. But I am still amazed even now, with long experience of so many departments, that no one had bothered to put pen to paper as to how we should implement our manifesto commitment.

It suited me fine, a blank sheet of paper; I could carry out the Prime Minister's instructions with the freedom I interpreted I had. I decided to announce that we were going ahead with devolution and it was to be my main priority. I did so and restated our commitments to the establishment of an elected body for Wales with executive and administrative responsibilities, and raised the possibility of it being the foundation for a legislative body in advance of consultation with colleagues. I was mapping out the ground, following my instructions from the Prime Minister to bring forward my own proposals.

Unhappily I went down with flu. I tried to keep to my bed, hoping for a speedy recovery. It was extremely inconvenient; I was not able to attend a Cabinet committee, which had been called to settle urgently the Rate Support Grant. Ian Dewar, the under-secretary responsible for finance in my office, battled for me and he was instructed not to give way on anything less than the maximum amount demanded for Wales, an extraordinarily high figure. A veto was put on any other settlement. The result, due to Dewar's advocacy and his firm riding instruction was a fabulous settlement for Wales, well beyond England's. He had done well. It pays sometimes to be absent and almost uncontactable when one's representatives have orders not to concede in negotiations. I have used this tactic occasionally in my political life.

When it came to choosing an official to be in charge of devolution, Dewar, who had proved himself an extraordinarily tenacious fighter, was put forward for the post and I warmly endorsed his nomination. I was tipped off by George Thomas, of all people, to keep a close eye on the contents of the draft Queen's Speech to ensure that Welsh devolution was included. Why he did it I will never know. The fear of being left behind Scotland dominated my thoughts and may have motivated him also. I was holding on with my fingernails for parity and was far from sure I would get it. The worst scenario for me was a bill for Scotland and another bill for Wales. This is why the eventual agreement to have a joint Scotland/Wales bill was so reassuring.

My recollection was that neither country was in the first draft of the Queen's Speech. The Cabinet Office drafters had ignored the realpolitik of a minority government – that it could not afford to ignore Scotland or Wales. Was I overreacting in surmising that the Cabinet Office mindset echoed the lack of preparation in the Welsh Office? I sent over an amendment for Welsh devolution and rose from my sickbed to attend my first Cabinet meeting. With an enthusiastic Prime Minister, the Scottish and Welsh amendments were agreed.

I then went down to meet the Welsh Council of Labour in Cardiff and its secretary, Emrys Jones. I explained that I had not found the Royal Commission's proposals very helpful and that on my appointment the Prime Minister had given me a free hand to bring my own proposals to Cabinet. I explained the direction that I was proposing to go and the need to get Party and Welsh acceptability. I said I was minded to propose some form of executive devolution to my colleagues in Cabinet. It may have been that Emrys Jones was not too happy about this, but I believe that he was so pleased, and not a little surprised, that we were getting on with it that, apart from some minor questioning, neither he nor anyone else raised any objection. After all, we had won the election – although only just.

There was a secretary of state who believed unexpectedly in devolution. There was a Labour Cabinet prepared to act on it. This was a shock in itself.

Devolution, to the bulk of the Cabinet, was not the usual bread-and-butter priority. It was felt round the table in Cardiff that I deserved all the support that I needed. I caught the train back to London knowing they were, whatever doubts Emrys may have privately held, supporting me. Emrys was one of the great architects of turning my party to understand and accept devolution, and his contribution in swinging the Party over from his predecessor Protheroe's reactionary views cannot be underestimated. He was a true devolutionist by conviction. He remains one of the unsung heroes of modern Wales. His quiet earnest approach belied a man of strong beliefs.

The first documents on my desk were tickets for the England Wales game at Twickenham the following Saturday and although there was a change in the personality of the secretary of state, the tickets for this official engagement were inherited by me. My wife, who was, and is, an even keener supporter of rugby than me, decided not unnaturally to go with me. I had not been to Twickenham since the varsity match with Jim Griffiths many years before. As the guests of the English Rugby Union, we sat in the front row of the Royal Box. Elwyn Jones, Lord Chancellor, sat behind me. His brother, Idris, who had been chief scientist of the National Coal Board, had captained Wales and he was always joking that when he went home he was known as the former captain's brother. When he was on leave of absence from Cabinet, to attend some of Llanelli RFC's Centenary celebrations, Harold Wilson used to moan, half-jokingly, about the duration of Llanelli's celebrations.

The band struck up *God save the Queen* which was dutifully and enthusiastically sung. There was no singing of the Welsh national anthem – *Hen Wlad Fy Nhadau*. It was embarrassing – the band sloped off and the crowd in our immediate vicinity remained standing and looked at me in the royal box. They began singing the Welsh anthem and I took an instant but correct decision – I'm not sure what my hosts thought but I and my wife stood up and sang with the crowd. The singing spread. Elwyn Jones followed me, and whatever the quality of our voices we had done the right thing. I sensed a degree of embarrassment among my hosts and the other guests who remained seated. But what did I care! I was there as the senior representative of government in Wales and invited as such. I understand that it began a pattern of our anthem being sung at Twickenham whenever Wales played. I had broken new ground. Harold Wilson enjoyed coming to the Arms Park for matches in my time as Welsh Secretary. We were frequently on the winning side in that golden era.

Why did I, a devolutionist, really get the job? Willie Ross, the Secretary of State for Scotland, was then a vehement opponent of devolution. George Thomas was a bitter foe of so many things Welsh. A Labour government, dependent on support outside its ranks in the House just could not afford to have both Scottish and Welsh Secretaries hostile anti-devolutionists. Willie Ross saw the light during August in the summer recess of 1974, between the two 1974 elections and realised that he had to fight for a devolution bill if he was to survive the groundswell in Scotland. That summer he put his faith in a Scottish development agency with its potential to rebuild the economy of Scotland. Devolution was not his cup of tea, but he did, as I have said, eventually come round to it. As important to him was to deny Wales any similar advance, but it was too late.

I believe, though I have no evidence for it, that Jim Callaghan encouraged my appointment. He had always been one of my mentors. Without his endorsement I find it difficult to believe the Prime Minister would have appointed me. George Thomas in his book, *Mr Speaker*, comments that he bumped into Jim Callaghan in the lobby and asked him if he knew that he was not going back into the Cabinet. 'He gave a brusque, "yes I did".'

George Thomas obviously took no part in our deliberations. The fact that he had put forward his own ideas in opposition many years before no longer registered. Government just does not work like that. You are either in or out. On recent re-reading of the reactions to George Thomas's letter to Harold Wilson in the Scilly Islands, it was clear that the Prime Minister had kicked for touch by referring it to the Cabinet Secretary. The Cabinet Secretary's minute shows how the Civil Service can dig a hole for the tedious repetition of already-canvassed proposals and bury them firmly.

I had, as I have recounted, many contacts with Harold Wilson for a young minister. None of this would explain his sudden surprising decision to appoint me. He knew I was a devolutionist by conviction. He was looking for a devolutionist secretary of state who would deliver the manifesto and to appoint an avowed anti-devolutionist would cause significant difficulties. Not for the first occasion in my political life, the anti-vote against one of the other choices could have been as important as the plus vote for me. I will never know.

fourteen
IN THE WELSH OFFICE

ONCE THE EXCITEMENT of appointment to office, was over, and I had recovered from flu, I had to work out as fast as I could in my own mind what my priorities would be. If Jim Griffiths's advice was correct I had no time to waste. After the Queen's Speech was settled I was able to tell the press that one priority would be, with colleagues, to work on a bill which would bring devolution to Wales.

As with many governments, the tough economic situation, particularly inflation, was the main priority. I was given, as is the custom, a huge tome setting out the department's assessments, my responsibilities as secretary of state, immediate and later problems and the money we had at our disposal in the department. It was too vast to swallow it all at one go.

Ted Rowlands MP (Merthyr), who had been a parliamentary secretary in the Welsh Office for a short period before the 1970 election, was reappointed. Barry Jones MP (Delyn) also joined me. I regarded it as important that I should have a minister from North Wales. I agreed with the department's suggestion for the split of subject responsibilities. I took on the main responsibility for industry, agriculture, constitutional development and the Welsh language.

Work and jobs had dominated my life as a constituency MP – protecting existing employment, constantly searching for new job opportunities and always supporting training and skills initiatives. Now that I had a responsibility for the whole of Wales, I could use this experience. I asked for the figures for unemployment for each area so that I could see, or at least have confirmed, where the main problems were. The inevitable contracting of the coal industry had continued since my time at the Ministry of Power in 1964–6. I surmised that the steel industry would have its own problems too.

I examined the machinery to attract new industry at my disposal and during the summer months of 1974 I became aware of Willie Ross's plan for a statutory development agency for Scotland. I decided that if statutory bodies were being considered for Scotland I would be demanding appropriate provision for Wales. I could see many battles ahead as slots in the valuable legislative process would be particularly scarce in the early years of a new government.

The day-to-day problems of industry were to take a considerable amount of my time, coupled with my long-term strategic plans for employment which hinged on the building of east-to-west road communications in both North and South Wales. I did not believe in plans for their own sake and a grandiose national plan found no favour with me. South and north, east and west had their own different needs. Representing as I did a town, valley communities and a foreshore, I knew that to satisfy one valley might reap very little dividend in the valley next door. We were above all an interventionist government and as I recollect there was a new industrial problem on my desk every week. One part or another of Wales would be clamouring for action. One factory after another was in trouble. When I got my wider industrial powers on 1 July 1975, I had the machinery on the spot to offer assistance. Looking back, if it was possible to measure how I used my time, I think I would be right in saying that industry took the greatest proportion and a great deal of it away from the glare of the press.

In those early weeks I decided on my priorities. It was very much a personal decision. The secretary of state, as a territorial minister, has wide powers – it was 'joined-up government' under one roof long before such a term was being used.

Leaving work on industry to one side, if it were possible, what should be my main public priority? I had been put in the Welsh Office to deliver devolution to Wales. The government needed me there because the voting in the election showed how dependent we were on the minority parties. The government had to prove its intentions and that meant the delivery of devolution if we were to survive. Our support on this issue in the Welsh Parliamentary Party was fragile, and every effort had to be made to satisfy colleagues that if we were bent on delivering devolution, then concern for industrial problems and the delivery of a better infrastructure for enhancing employment was vital. Some of my colleagues did not share my enthusiasm for devolution and many were not interested in the future of the language either. I had to bear this in mind as to what I was seen to be doing.

I was over six years in office. Could I have been re-shuffled? I was virtually unsackable, short of gross inefficiency or misconduct. This was unlikely, although Donoughue, the Prime Minister's political adviser, in his diaries suggests that I and five other Cabinet ministers should go. The fact that the advice was not taken speaks for itself.

The die was cast as to what kind of Welsh Office we would have when Jim Griffiths was appointed as the first Secretary of State for Wales in 1964. I firmly believe the mandarins, under the permanent secretary of the Ministry of Housing and Local Government, Dame Evelyn Sharp, intended the role of the Welsh Office to be not much different from the role of Welsh ministers of state under Conservative governments, staffed by powerful civil servants who were part of Whitehall departments but based in Cardiff with only amateur or part-time ministerial supervision. As I understand it, Jim firmly refused to set up his office in such a way and declined a small office within the Ministry of Housing and Local Government.

He took the fundamentally important step of demanding separate premises and these were found for him near Old Scotland Yard. They seem to have been the former headquarters of various docks in South Wales, including Port Talbot. When I visited it the coat of arms of one of our docks was included in a stained-glass window.

Jim's action went completely across the grain of the wishes and intentions of the Whitehall establishment, but they signified in a crucial way that the Welsh Office was to be a separate department of state, with its own executive powers. I am absolutely confident that if Jim had not had the prestige of a former deputy leader of the Party and had not been an experienced and successful Cabinet minister, the magic moment would have been lost. He was taming the Whitehall establishment in the same way that he had, as Colonial Secretary, helped to pacify the Chinese Malays and the Malaysians.

Jim Griffiths's modest powers were announced by Harold Wilson on 19 November 1964. He was to have oversight over six other departments for the execution of their policies in Wales. This was particularly limited, but it was a start. Under all three subsequent secretaries of state there were further accretions of power. There were some powers over primary and secondary education and under Peter Thomas, health had come over.

I paused and, bearing in mind that I wished my future Assembly to inherit as broad a range of executive functions as possible, I decided on a campaign to win more powers for the Welsh Office across the board. I was continuing the work of decentralisation, but on a much bigger scale and with a greater aim than merely acquiring additional responsibilities for myself.

It is curious that the importance of this has not been recognised by commentators. Without the building bricks of executive powers over as many functions as possible, there would have been no experience of managing them for a Welsh Assembly of the future to exercise. I was determined to besiege each Whitehall department and see what powers I could win.

I had won my first claim to elevate my senior officer to the rank of perma-nent secretary. In due course there flowed from this the appointment of two deputy secretaries, the promotion of Owen Morris – who had once served as a permanent secretary in Nigeria – and the importation of Richard Lloyd Jones (later Sir Richard) from the Ministry of Defence, and Daniel Gruffydd Jones (almost a contemporary at my school in Aberystwyth) also came down from Whitehall. We now had two valuable servants able and ready to shoulder whatever new responsibilities we gained. We were obviously attracting new high flyers as a growing department. This was real politics. Both Richard and Daniel had been the Cabinet Secretary's private secretar-ies, an indication of the status now accorded to the Welsh Office.

My aim was simply to double the size of the department, and should devolution come at least half of it would go to the Assembly, probably much more, because the Welsh Office would be stripped down to its Whitehall and Cabinet functions.

I was mindful of the divisions within the Welsh Labour Group and in retrospect I did not do half enough to overcome them. Whether I would have been successful is another matter. There was the division between North and South Wales and between the Welsh-speaking and non-Welsh speaking population. I tried to persuade myself that this was historical. There was hardly a time when Wales was governed by one authority within Wales. Our nation is made up of many tribes! How far this was relevant in the conditions in which I operated only historians can judge. I persuaded myself that the concept of Wales being governed from one internal point was quite novel. We had to get used to it – there had to be steep learning curve. Against this background it is almost miraculous that within a short time – between 1964 and 1998 – we have achieved what would be unim-aginable fifty years earlier when I started my political career – an elected Assembly sitting in Wales.

My first language was of great importance to me. It needed a lot of real encouragement, particularly officially, and, as always, resources. The question of how I could further provide practical support for the language without creating more divisions and feed the fears of my already divided colleagues was always in my mind. On one thing I was determined: any pos-itive steps I was able to take for the language should not be the excuse to open up further gaps in the Welsh Labour Party or undermine my attempts to establish some sort of cohesion and consensus in the Party for devolu-tion. Devolution had always to come first. If I was able to achieve any suc-cess for the language I would not publicise it, hence my long silent battle for nearly five years to provide the framework for the eventual setting up of S4C, the Welsh language television channel.

Those were my priorities; providing work for people in Wales and seeking the powers and setting up organisations under the Welsh Office to achieve it; repairing the democratic deficit in decision making in Wales through devolution, and doing what I could to improve conditions for the language to flourish. I believed that in setting up a Welsh Assembly, an elected national organ for government in Wales, which had eluded so many of my predecessor politicians, I could provide the machinery to achieve this – directly accountable to the people of Wales.

fifteen
WORKING OUT OUR DEVOLUTION PROPOSALS

THE PRIME MINISTER, HAROLD WILSON, had ennobled the eminent constitutional historian, Lord Crowther-Hunt, so that he could be a minister. He was one of the signatories of the minority report of Kilbrandon and I understood his role to be the eyes and ears of the Prime Minister as a constitutional adviser. He was expected to give a sort of 'good housekeeping' approval to any government proposal.

As a politician, conscious of both the lack of interest in the Parliamentary Labour Party (PLP) and the divergent views within the Welsh Labour Group, I had reached an early conclusion that an executive form of devolution was the furthest I could carry the Party. Attempt anything further and Scotland would have gone off on its own to legislative devolution and I would have been left with nothing, or at least very little. Anything less than our manifesto commitment to Wales would have been regarded by the supporters of devolution as a failure and would undermine the government's precarious position. I was reasonably confident that the PLP would wear this and it would satisfy the majority of the people of Wales. As it turned out, I was not a good assessor of either.

I have since noted a curious attitude among my fellow Welshmen. Many of those most vociferous and partisan in the matches in Cardiff Arms Park, particularly among 'the establishment' were then the most reluctant to support any political Welsh constitutional development. I believe that this has now changed to some degree.

The committee stage of any devolution bill or bills would have to be taken on the floor of the House. Such a committee stage, particularly when a government has a minuscule majority is a wonderful opportunity for MPs without much else to do to suddenly manifest an interest and take an opportunity to speak. The fact that it would be a government 'flagship bill' would not matter much to them. There would be no accusations of left or right disloyalty, as the overwhelming number of their constituents would not be interested at all. I did not relish the thought; so for political reasons I had decided that I would limit the dangers by going for the least provocative of proposals. I had outlined my views very early in office, though I was probably working towards this opinion before that. I believed I would never carry the day with the Welsh Labour Party for full legislative powers. It had to be something less and it would be easier to justify by comparing its powers with other bodies. Quite frankly, an executive form of devolution was the most that I thought I could get through Parliament. This was not ideal, but it was the maximum I thought I could achieve. I had no previous political baggage and neither had the government. As R. A. Butler MP, the Conservative statesman once said: 'Politics is the art of the possible.' This was my guiding perception.

We were elected as a minority government. Labour had 301 MPs, the Conservatives 297, the Liberals 14, the SNP 7, Plaid Cymru 2, and others 14. There obviously had to be another election in 1974. Our majority meant that the Prime Minister would have to try to seek a fresh mandate fairly soon, hopefully with a majority. This time the results were a little better. Labour had 319 MPs, Conservatives 277, Liberals thirteen, others twenty-six. We had a small majority.

I had a message from the Prime Minister between the two general elections to consult widely as to what the people of Wales wanted. We had after all promised in the Queen's Speech on 12 March 1974 that: 'We would initiate discussions in Scotland and Wales . . . and bring forward proposals for consideration.'

With the assistance of Lord Crowther-Hunt, I carried out extensive consultations in the summer of 1974 with every major organisation representing the people of Wales, including the political parties, employers and unions and local government. The White Paper (CMD 5732), which we published in September 1974, rejected separatism and federalism as solutions and concluded:

> It does not follow that Scotland and Wales must be treated exactly like each other . . . what is important is that the needs and aspirations of the Scottish and Welsh people are properly met.

It also emphasised the Kilbrandon Commission's unanimous conclusion that:

> Directly elected assemblies ought to be established for . . . Wales to meet the legitimate desire of . . . people for greater control of their affairs.

This was the catalyst I had prayed for in taking the risk of endorsing the idea of a Constitutional Commission.

Opinion among those consulted was divided. The majority was in favour of a directly elected assembly for Wales but there was no general agreement on what it should do. Opinion was also divided between those who favoured legislative devolution and those who were for executive devolution. Of the written representations from organisations about one-third were in favour of legislative and nearly half preferred executive devolution! We concluded that no consensus of opinion on the form of devolution for Wales had emerged.

There was considerable animosity towards the government's nominated bodies in Wales – the quangos. They were decision makers spending public money without sufficient democratic control, if any. There was a strong view, and I am sure I am right about this, that their powers could be taken over by an all-Wales, directly elected body which should also discharge some of the executive functions of government departments in Wales. It was one of the strongest arguments for furthering the devolution cause in Wales. The public view had been clear on this issue.

We therefore proposed setting up directly elected bodies for Scotland and Wales, which differed in the powers proposed for them. We also concluded that there were a great many matters of details which would require very careful and thorough study before the government was in a position to put forward fully worked-out proposals.

There were three schemes before the Cabinet: a draft White Paper prepared by the two secretaries of state for Scotland and Wales, under the chairmanship of secretary of state for consumer affairs, Shirley Williams; a paper concurrently prepared by the Home Policy Committee of the Party and a draft paper prepared at the Prime Minister's request.

Summing up, the Prime Minister said that a movement towards devolution had been started by setting up the Kilbrandon Commission, and the present government was committed to a White Paper. Given that commitment, the government should not seem to put forward its proposals in a grudging or reluctant spirit . . . the government proposals did not commit on the scope of powers and functions to be involved. The precise nature and timing of the devolution could then be given the light of more mature consideration. The best consideration for a White Paper was Annexe A.

Annexe A was the Prime Minister's draft White Paper.

A small drafting committee including the Chancellor and the two territorial secretaries of state was set up again under Shirley Williams's chairmanships to revise the documents for Cabinet consideration. The revised draft came before the Cabinet the following week (CC (74) 33rd Conclusion) and the White Paper was approved on 17 September 1974. Throughout, the government was developing a policy of a step-by-step approach, and seeking to carry with it departmental ministers who had reservations. I knew this would be a continuing battle.

Although I was happy to presume that there was an irresistible momentum for devolution, every step towards legislation had to be carefully examined, considered and set out cautiously. I had not anticipated the crossfire that so many senior members of the Cabinet would repeatedly bring to bear on our devolution proposals over the next few years. The fire came from different directions and from different people, depending on their mood. Some were, of course, indifferent or did not take part in the debate. Ted Short was a valiant defender of his proposals as chairman of the ministerial committee; but in retrospect steady support seems to have been confined to him and the authority of the PM.

It is difficult for anyone who has not been involved in preparing legislation to understand the care that is given by all Whitehall departments, both directly and marginally involved, to trying to get it right. The publication of the White Paper was a major step forward. I had managed to keep in tandem with Scotland; Wales was not going to be 'any other business'. A Labour government had many other priorities for the majority of the Cabinet's members. We had managed to push devolution to the top of the list of priorities – it would be the government's flagship bill and both countries would be legislated for at the same time. Putting the two countries in the same bill, although the proposals were different, meant a lot to me. It was a scenario beyond my expectations.

We were moving forward, but I was conscious that the main battles still lay ahead – firstly to try to keep the Welsh Labour Group reasonably united – a task that had met with little success in the past, secondly maintaining the interest and loyalty of the parliamentary party as a whole. Hopefully they would do the arithmetic of our numbers in the House and the importance of the strength of the minority parties. Despite the euphoria of success in getting the White Paper through, I did wonder from time to time just how far we could maintain a majority on the floor of the House.

Bernard Donoughue's two volumes of diaries as head of Harold Wilson and Jim Callaghan's Policy Unit touch quite frequently on the issue from the viewpoint of Downing Street's political advisers. As early as November 1974 he put in a memo suggesting an architectural competition for the Welsh Assembly. Donoughue relates in the first volume of his diaries that there were three full-day meetings of ministers at Chequers when most of the Cabinet were present.

At the first meeting, in January 1975, many ministers thought we were going too fast. Among them were Crosland, Elwyn Jones and Prentice. The blame was put on Ted Short, deputy leader of the Party, who now chaired the Devolution Unit. Prentice and Varley thought that we were on a slippery slope towards the break-up of the UK. Donoughue records my early intervention, 'We have promised devolution to Wales and we will have to deliver it.' Elwyn Jones spoke strongly for slowing down 'The most important decision in our lives'. Merlyn Rees was against speedy action as it would disturb his situation in Northern Ireland. Roy Jenkins wanted to go slow as he did not like the destination. Tony Wedgwood Benn and Peart supported him. Ted Short wanted his bill in 1975 while we still had a majority. With all the power of a Prime Minister, Wilson summed up on the lines advocated by Short, although we, the devolutionists, were clearly in the minority. Despite the extent and seniority of the opposition within Cabinet, Wilson was steamrolling it through. Only a Prime Minister with considerable strength can do this. Wilson was a powerful Prime Minister.

In June 1975 there was another all-day meeting at Chequers for the devolution committee. Donoughue relates that about this time there was a big move for a retreat, led by Jenkins, Crosland and Healey. In September we again met at Chequers. Healey, Callaghan, Shirley Williams, Peart and Jenkins are reported by Donoughue to be against. Willie Ross warned his colleagues that it was too late, despite having himself warned against devolution years earlier. Healey argued that Cabinet had never agreed to the policy.

I have no reason to differ from Donoughue's contemporaneous diaries, but there is one matter on which I do differ, and it is a matter of opinon: Donoughue believed that the Prime Minister had not really supported devolution. His position was that we were committed to it, that we had proposed it, we had put it in our manifesto and we had produced a White Paper, therefore we could not go back on it.

I doubt if Donoughue is wholly accurate in his assessment. Wilson never disclosed all his cards, although Donoughue was as close as could be to the PM. It was Wilson who, according to Crossman, in his massive and detailed diaries, had first noted the possible importance of devolution and the regions. He was genuinely interested in constitution making.

In support of this I refer to Crossman's diaries from as far back as May 1968:

It was eighteen months ago that I went to Harold and got agreement to have a committee to look at a proposal for some positive and constructive response to nationalism. H W had been swaying to

and fro. Eventually I got H W's agreement to all the recommendations for my paper. . .

Crossman, who had been appointed Lord President of the Council, had
been given some responsibility for devolution. He writes in May 1967 that
Harold Wilson had commented several times that the question of decentralisation and regional government might become the explosive issue at
the next election.

He adds that when there was some opposition to setting up the Royal
Commission in 1968, Wilson and Callaghan circumvented it by getting a
signed agreement from Willie Ross and George Thomas.

> These two have been bought out easily because they are anti-
> nationalist and this is a way of doing nothing.

And he records that on 24 October 1968 Peter Shore, Tony Greenwood and
Judith Hart had come to Cabinet 'breathing fire and slaughter' and were
told that there was really no choice as the Prime Minister and Jim were
convinced of this and had carried us along.

It is difficult to conclude that the Prime Minister did not have belief in
his actions over two decades. Wilson had manifest determination to drive
through each discussion and reach a result satisfactory to devolutionists.
He fully understood the momentum that he was encouraging. The sheer
numbers of the opponents could well have discouraged him from time to
time and he may have expressed his discomfort to his immediate policy
advisers. However, although he had many opportunities to abandon the
whole project, he allowed it to carry on.

Reflecting back I just cannot understand how I kept my head. Here
we were 'quarrelling like monkeys' accordingly to Donoughue, and yet the
momentum was carrying us forward to the preparation of a bill. It does
show how important a manifesto commitment is and how, although I and
Willie Ross were in a minority, we managed to keep it going. We owed a
lot to Ted Short, who had been given the job of driving the preparations
through, ably assisted by Gerry Fowler, his minister of state and to Michael
Foot, assisted by John Smith, who eventually took over his role.

Donoughue does not record Foot saying anything in these discussions
so far as I can see, although I may have missed it, and I have no recollection one way or another, but he certainly took on the cause with great
vigour when it was allocated to him. Michael did not do anything he
believed in without passion and conviction. He was certainly a devolutionist by conviction.

The whole weight of the Civil Service was eventually put to work on devolution, albeit not without some initial hesitation. I remember pausing at the head of a rather steep series of stairs to the secretary of state's room in the Commons and hearing a conversation two or three floors below between Hywel Evans and John Lloyd, my private secretary. Hywel, as a newly elevated permanent secretary now attended the regular gatherings of permanent secretaries at Sunningdale. He had just returned and revealed the mood of his fellow mandarins. As I was waiting for John Lloyd, I could not help hearing Hywel tell John, 'The secretary of state can have anything. . . ' meaning any increased powers he wants, and I was at the time busily campaigning for more and more transfer of functions orders, '. . . anything but devolution'. Hywel had not won his first battle.

It put me on my guard, but not long after there was a complete change of heart and Whitehall's finest were drafted in to prepare the bill. Michael Quinlan, a deputy secretary, who later rose to very great heights in the Civil Service, became head of the Devolution Unit in Cabinet Office. I have found that a good barometer of the seriousness of a government's intentions in any field is the quality of the civil servants put in to manage it. This gave some indication that finally every ounce of power was behind the wheel. The Devolution – Scotland and Wales – Bill really was to be a flagship of the government.

In the course of time our tiny parliamentary majority after 1974 was weakened by losses and we had to reach an arrangement with the Liberals, which worked remarkably well. But the Liberals gave notice on 25 May 1976 that they would end the agreement at the end of the 1976–7 session, which would at least ensure we could complete the devolution legislation. We were at the mercy of the minority parties throughout the life of that Parliament.

On many Sunday mornings I had long discussions with Lord Crowther-Hunt, from either of my homes in Wales or London. It was a fruitful period. He was the first hurdle that I had to clear in my advocacy of an executive form of devolution.

I well remember attending one of the Cabinet committees under the chairmanship of Harold Wilson. I said that my proposals were more modest than Scotland's. I hoped they reflected a substantial consensus in the Labour movement, although there were some dissidents. I proposed an executive form of devolution.

First, we have a fairly delicate presentational task, resulting from the fact that on one hand Wales is – for good and sufficient reasons – going to get something different from, and in certain key respects, less than what Scotland gets; and that on the other hand not all Welsh opinion will welcome or fully understand this. As a result, it will be politically important to maintain parity, both of substance and of presentation, to the maximum extent that the facts of the situation allow.

What we are committed to for Wales is something of a constitutional novelty. It involves the devolution of wide powers of executive and subordinate legislation, but the reservation of primary legislation to Westminster; this is a split new to British constitutional practice . . . we are therefore dealing with what is in some respects a more complex and more experimental structure than that envisaged for Scotland . . .

On future primary legislation for Wales, I myself see great attractions in the concept of moving progressively to a broader 'framework' type of statute, leaving the Assembly free to operate policies flexibly in the particular circumstances of Wales. I hope we shall aim at this, even though there is no way of ensuring or entrenching it.

The most difficult aspect of the system we propose is to find the right balance between genuinely wide Assembly participation in government and properly firm, efficient and cohesive operation of the very substantial practical responsibilities we shall be devolving. There is no neat solution, and much room for judgment, and we must be ready to make adjustments.

I commended the proposals, which had unavoidably some novel features and complexities, but would meet our commitment to Wales.

The more generally we legislated, the more opportunities we gave to the Assembly. Parliament generally dislikes what are called 'Henry VIII' Clauses – broad clauses giving powers to ministers to fill in the details – but I could point out that powers of sub-legislation were not being given to a minister but to a democratically elected body. When the Whitehall machine goes into action on new and pioneering legislation, every morsel is ground down to the finest particle.

Years later when new devolution proposals were brought forward in 1997–8, I recall, as Attorney General, sending for parliamentary counsel and pointing out to him the wide variations in the detail that primary legislation went into, some bills allowing great discretion to ministers in statutory instruments and others being pretty basic, detailed and therefore inflexible. So far as legislation affecting the Welsh Assembly was concerned, I sought to persuade him that we should aim to make it as general as possible.

I argued with my back-bench doubters that in offering secondary legislation I was doing no more than the National Parks could do, or British

Rail with their statutory powers. Local authorities, once they got a private bill, could introduce secondary legislation. This is what the Welsh Assembly was getting and I thought it was a reasonable parallel. Nevertheless, it was an uphill task. The major objection within the Welsh Labour Party was that power was being given to an all-Wales body. I have often thought that if I had divided Wales, like Caesar's Gaul, into three parts and given each of the individual parts secondary legislative powers I would have had far fewer problems. But the story of my life has been the creation of, or at least support for, all-Wales bodies.

There was no question of a referendum then. My task was persuading Cabinet and Welsh Labour MPs. I won on the first, but there was a vociferous minority against me amongst the second. They just did not want devolution. Their interests were the commanding heights of the British economy. It happened to be my interest too, but not the only one. Some of the opponents had inherited the emphasis their predecessors had placed on internationalism and devolution was a divergence from this. It was a form of nationalism to some of them. But a Labour government, with proper whipping, can usually get most of what it wants though it may have to trim at the edges.

I spoke on a debate on the Devolution White Paper. Minutes before I rose to speak I agreed to a suggestion that the word 'Senate' (*Senedd*) could be the name for the elected body. I had considerable distaste for the word *Cynulliad*. It may have been quite irrational on my part in retrospect.

The use of 'Senedd' now adopted so many years later by the National Assembly proved a disastrous decision and was interpreted by a minority of Welsh MPs to mean that what I really had in mind was a Parliament for Wales. That was my first mistake. The other was, for the first and last time, taking part with other parties in one joint campaigning meeting. I had over the years, after one misadventure, refused to do joint meetings with other candidates in my own constituency at election times. I always got the worst of it. My opponents could play to the gallery and promise the moon. I couldn't. I was going to be elected. I was persuaded by Michael Foot to take part in a joint-party meeting in Llandrindod Wells. My presence was ammunition for my opponents.

The Scotland and Wales Bill was unfortunately suspended following the defeat of the ggovernment's timetable motion. Separate bills for Scotland and Wales were presented to Parliament in November 1977.

The House of Commons gave a second reading to the Wales Bill on 15 November 1977 by 295 votes to 264. The bill set out the government's proposals for a referendum in Wales in response to views expressed in the House.

In the debate that day, I said that the bill would bring decision making closer to the people, not only in terms of geography but in the sense that more decisions would be taken in a democratically elected assembly as opposed to by a minister or nominated body . . . devolution was nothing to do with separatism, on the contrary it was essential for the underlying unity of the UK. There was nothing wrong with diversity and flexibility within a united country.

The Conservative Party has always opposed any significant transfer of political responsibility to Wales, from the campaign to set up a secretary of state to devolution. Through its spokesman, Mr Nicholas Edwards, MP (Lord Crickhowell) they maintained their traditional role, in the terms:

> The reality is that they (the government's proposals) were dealing not with administrative devolution but with national devolution that is offered for short-term political considerations on the basis of a claim to nationhood. . .

Six Labour MPs, including Leo Abse (Pontypool) and Fred Evans (Caerphilly) voted against the second reading. We suffered a number of important defeats at the committee stage when fifty Labour MPs, amongst others, voted against the government. The government lost an amendment which provided for the bill's repeal if less than forty per cent of those entitled to vote in the proposed referendum voted 'yes'. The bill was given a third reading on 9 May 1978 in the Commons by 292–264. The bill received Royal Assent on 3 July 1978 having been debated for 29 days over a period of 9 months.

When the Scotland and Wales Bill was lost, I contemplated momentarily the idea of resignation. It was a government defeat after all, not my mine alone. I decided to soldier on. If I remained I would be able to participate fully in salvaging the position. My resignation could be counter-productive to the cause into which I had put so much effort. To my surprise, others thought I might go. Dafydd Elis Thomas MP, on behalf of himself at least, came and saw me in Gwydir House and tried to persuade me not to resign. It was thoughtful of him, but it was never on the cards. My job was to go on and win the next battle. I was not going to give up now.

The opposition was led, in Wales, by some of my friends. Donald Coleman (Neath), my political neighbour with whom I worked very closely on most things; Ifor Davies (Gower), my friend for years; Don Anderson (Swansea), Fred Evans (Caerphilly) and, of course, Neil Kinnock (Bedwellty) and Leo Abse (Pontypool). They were, in varying degrees, burning with indignation.

George Cunningham, the MP for Islington and a Scotsman, was an opponent of all our devolution proposals and had proposed the referendum amendment requiring forty per cent of the registered voters to vote 'yes'. A referendum had been canvassed years earlier by the Caerphilly constituency and there may have been other attempts, but they had come to nothing. The carrying of the referendum clause in the form proposed made it impossible to carry or put our legislation into effect in either Scotland or Wales. It was to prove an insurmountable hurdle in both countries.

Michael Foot rang me up one night during the first bill and told me that to get the legislation through in reasonable time – we did not have the majority for a guillotine – we would have to concede a referendum. So we did, but it was a black day for our cause, and the Tories cackled their triumph. They were the beneficiaries of our caving in. Our general standing in Wales was shattered. In the subsequent general election, while we maintained our support in the valleys and industrial South Wales, we lost Ceredigion and Merioneth. Emlyn Hooson (Liberal/Montgomery) who had given us considerable support, lost his seat to a Conservative. However, we managed to win Carmarthen, just. The results of the May election recorded a spectacular increase in the Conservative vote in Wales.

The referendum campaign was fought from one end of Wales to the other. I spoke in a number of places, but should have done more even though I was pushing myself physically to the very limit. Some of the meetings were badly organised and mountains of literature remained undistributed in Labour's Cardiff office.

One meeting in the Brangwyn Hall in Swansea went particularly well. Jim Callaghan, who was the main speaker, followed me and the general secretary of the TUC, Len Murray, also spoke. I travelled to the meeting with Jim and I fondly remember him putting on his overcoat as he went into the car. I told him the weather was quite mild and he wouldn't need the coat. He replied: 'I have over many years taken this precaution when going to big meetings and rallies, just in case someone throws an egg at me. It has never happened but you never know. Should it happen you can take your overcoat off and have a clean suit for the meeting.' Wise words from an old campaigner.

I knew, of course, from all the intelligence I had, that we were marching to defeat. At a lunch given to me by some of the executives of HTV close to referendum polling day – it felt like the last supper – I made it quite plain that I would have one go, and one alone, in delivering a satisfactory devolution scheme for Wales. It would be for others to carry the baton thereafter. It would need new leadership and possibly a more flexible one.

The result, of course, was a defeat so crushing that no one had been able to forecast it. To lose by a four-to-one majority meant that our proposals were off the radar screen.

The referendum had come at the close of the 'winter of discontent'. It had been a complete shock when Jim Callaghan, having led us to believe that there would be a general election in the autumn of 1978, called it off. The shock all around the Cabinet table that morning was incredible.

The trade unions, I fear, had fought their own government on pay restraint right through that winter. The atmosphere could not have been more dismal. I had dead bodies awaiting burial in a chapel at Newport and rubbish piled up outside a Cardiff hospital which – through the good offices of George Wright, general secretary of the Wales TUC, after a telephone call from me, was removed. George was always a tower of strength, both from the political and trade-union viewpoint. I went on television one Sunday to say, with a heavy heart, that I had had to request the army to bring out their old 'green goddess' fire engines to provide cover. I suppose with hindsight, we might have deferred calling the referendum.

In the event, the government's low esteem and the campaigning of the opposition, joined by our dissidents, defeated us and undoubtedly paved the way for a Conservative win at the general election.

I had to go on television, I believe it was the Nine O'clock News, on the night we lost the referendum to make the most of a bad job. There was no ammunition to do what so many politicians try to do and justify a bad election result, and most of us do it so badly. There was no possibility of minimising our defeat, or the scale of it. I merely said, 'If you see an elephant on your doorstep, you know it's there.' The election was a horrendous defeat, a knock-out blow. It was the best I could do and it was my way of explaining the catastrophe on the main TV news, which I did from the few words I had hurriedly put together. I had put so much into the whole project that our defeat left me utterly dejected.

When I saw the detailed results of the referendum I could take a little comfort from the reasons. In South Wales the electorate had been persuaded that the Assembly would be run by bigoted Welsh speakers from the north and the west. This was the kind of propaganda that Leo Abse would have trilled. In the north, too many of the electorate had been persuaded that the Assembly would be run by the Glamorgan County Council 'Taffia' and the like. It was a no-win situation. It was undoubtedly the biggest disappointment of my life and I found it difficult, given the size of the defeat, to believe it could ever be turned around by any referendum in the future.

I could not help noting that whilst the electorate in Gwynedd was prepared to elect nationalist MPs to represent them at Westminster, they did not have sufficient confidence that a Welsh Assembly in Cardiff would look after their interests. I found this divided approach difficult to understand. To lose in industrial South Wales was easier to comprehend and the 'No' campaign was most active there. Jim Callaghan in *Time and Chance* noted:

> It was the adverse result of the referendum in Scotland and Wales that finally ended the government's life. Both were held on St David's Day, for John Morris, the secretary of state, had hoped that the compliment would strike a patriotic chord in Welsh hearts. But the valleys were dead to the sound of our music and rejected the blandishments by a huge majority of four to one.

Jim telephoned me on the night of the result. There were no recriminations and he conveyed the sympathies of others; one had kindly said 'I hope he was not too disappointed.' I fear I was. Michael Foot was also deeply disappointed as he had overcome every obstacle to get the bills through Parliament.

The Scottish nationalists put down their own vote of censure, indicating no confidence in the government, on 28 March 1979 and the Tories latched on to this. We had done our best to keep the Welsh nationalist MPs on board and this had included pressing ahead with a measure to provide compensation for Welsh slate quarrymen who suffered from respiratory diseases brought on by their work. The Labour Party had done a lot of significant work on this, including the Welsh Council of Labour, the TGWU in north Wales and Elwyn Jones, MP for Conwy and a solicitor with deep experience of the issue. Harold Walker MP, an old miner and junior minister at the Department of Employment, with strong encouragement from myself, had presented his proposals in the summer of 1978, and the bill was already promised in the Queen's Speech. All the nationalists had achieved was accelerating it by a couple of months, but they claimed all the credit. It was one of my earliest experiences of 'spin'; the spin in this case being against us.

On the day of the vote of censure the managers had to decide on the numbers they needed. There are usually some essential pairs, whereby one MP cancels the other on the opposite side. The arithmetic can become quite complicated as minority party members tend to go their own way, and discipline is probably laxer – they have their own priorities. Unfortunately over the years all the parties have failed to reform a system that can be quite cruel in demanding the physical presence of each member, if his or her vote is to count, in the precincts of Parliament, although the whips are content to check the presence of an MP in an ambulance.

Dr Broughton was a senior and esteemed Labour member. He had been very ill for some time, but nevertheless volunteered to come down from Yorkshire in an ambulance, aided by oxygen, to vote. He was at death's door, and Walter Harrison, the deputy chief whip to his eternal credit, spared him. He died a few days later but his vote would have spared us. Gerry Fitt, the Northern Ireland MP, voted against us, and another came from Belfast especially to abstain in person.

I was in North Wales on the day, having convened a meeting to address the employment problem in Gwynedd. I had the use of an aeroplane of the Queen's Flight and brought back with me Dafydd Wigley MP. He and Ellis Thomas loyally voted for us. We lost 311–310. It was an own goal for the Scottish nationalists, who had called for the vote, for we then faced eighteen years of Tory rule. As Jim Callaghan said in the course of the debate, 'the SNP would walk through the division lobby like turkeys voting for an early Christmas'. In the general election that followed on 3 May they lost nine Members out of their flock.

Not surprisingly, when I became Attorney General, I was made a member of the Cabinet committee dealing with our latest offering on devolution in the post-1997 government. I was not there as a policymaker, I was a legal and constitutional adviser and I confined myself to that role.

The second time round the drafters of the Devolution Bill in 1997 inherited the enormous amount of good work contained in our 1976 Bill. In reality, apart from the additional members, there is little difference in substance. There are other additions, but that does not detract from what I have said. The years of hard work in preparing the first bill, using all the resources that Whitehall placed at our disposal were not wasted. Our original legislation, with those qualifications, saw its way onto the statute book.

Through the efforts of Ron Davies – a convert and a welcome one to devolution – and a much wider segment of the Labour party and other parties, the referendum was just about won on the second time of asking in 1998. It was the slimmest possible endorsement. By this time it had become generally acceptable in the Labour Party to support devolution. The whole climate had changed during the Thatcher era. Some of the opponents of the past now supported it. For me it meant the culmination of nearly fifty years work.

It was generous of the Assembly to invite me to play a role as Attorney General at the opening of their first session on St David's Day 1999, by Her Majesty the Queen. It had been a long journey. When I got there that morning, the Lord Mayor of Cardiff quipped that the opening must be legal otherwise I would not be present as Attorney General. I was given a bound volume with a skeleton of the Act creating the Assembly. The document was in both Welsh and English.

My task was to proffer it to the Queen to initial. I presented both copies, the English version being on the left hand side and the Welsh on the right. I put my hand on the appointed place on the left for the Queen to sign. I doubt whether she had ever been asked to sign such a strange document. She had, of course, already signed the original bill, The Government of Wales Act (1998), as part of the normal legislative process. She was now being asked to ceremonially initial a dummy Act, which she did. I then pointed to the opposite page for the Welsh version to be initialled as well. She did exactly the same, although I confess my heart did accelerate a little just in case a hiccup occurred before she signed the second time. She graciously initialled the document on both pages.

It was up to the Assembly from now on to do its best for Wales.

sixteen
MORE POWERS FOR WALES

The Welsh Development Agency (WDA)

I HAVE BEEN CONVINCED since my earliest political activity of the immense value of statutory bodies, authorised by Parliament to tackle particular problems and to report to it on its spending of a specified budget. I had learnt from my experience in mid Wales that, despite valiant efforts by a variety of organisations there, they did not have appropriate powers to bring about real change. I set myself a challenge: I would try to get a slot in the legislative programme each year to create the necessary authorities. It was a formidable test.

When we were elected in 1974 I could see that if I could keep in step with Scotland, I would have a better chance of legislation. Willie Ross, my equivalent in Scotland, regarded the issue of oil around the coast of Scotland as the main reason for the success of the Scottish nationalists. 'Who's oil is it?' was the question. 'Scottish,' was the answer of the Scot Nats. In United Kingdom terms this was palpably a nonsense. The oil was in the North Sea surrounding England, Scotland and Norway. I would not dream of claiming any oil found in the Celtic Sea as Welsh oil (CMND 5696 Para 21). Willie thought that if he could get an organisation to recycle part of the national revenues, particularly oil revenues, back to Scotland for urgently needed development, it would be a trump card to beat the nationalists and there would be no need to bother with devolution. The ambiguous benefits of devolution would be nothing compared with what would flow to Scotland from real development, or so he thought.

Between the two elections in 1974 he put forward a proposal for a Scottish Development Agency. I argued for a Welsh Development Agency, but with no oil card to play I did not get very far. However, the principle of a Welsh Development Agency was accepted by colleagues and I got inserted into the 'United Kingdom Offshore Oil and Gas Policy' White Paper (CMND 5696), which we published in the summer, a promise of the setting up of a new agency in Wales 'as oil exploration develops in the Celtic Sea'. I was actually in a telephone box in South Wales at the time – the government machine wanted to get on with publishing the White Paper and I would not give my agreement without some recognition of Welsh needs. I got what seemed to be at the time, a crumb, however I sensed it could be an important crumb.

A few months later, on the eve of the second 1974 General Election, at a joint meeting of the Cabinet and National Executive to agree to the manifesto, I moved an amendment to the proposal to set up an SDA – to commit the Party to a WDA as well – without qualification. The argument became quite heated; Willie Ross maintained that to allow Wales to have a similar body would severely blunt his attack on the SNP. I could well understand that, but I argued that anyone cross-reading the manifesto in Wales would soon see how emptyhanded I was. It would make my task of leading the election campaign in Wales particularly difficult.

My colleagues realised my dilemma and sympathised with me. Welsh MPs representing the National Executive included Walter Padley MP (Ogmore), and Jim Callaghan was in the chair as Party Chairman as it happened. The meeting had much broader issues to settle if they were to agree the manifesto that morning and Willie Ross and I were an unnecessary diversion. Jim soon put an end to it by saying, 'If John wants it he can have it. Willie, there's more of us than you.' It was realpolitik. The meeting went on to agree the manifesto, including my amendment.

In due course I was able to move the second reading of the Welsh Development Agency Bill (No.2) on 26 June 1975. What I was seeking to do was to bring Wales's industrial development organisations under one roof – a 'one stop shop' for developers and industrialists. The clearance of the scars of the industrial revolution had been vigorously pursued by the Land Clearance Unit, set up by Cledwyn Hughes in the aftermath of the tragedy of Aberfan. They had worked in cooperation with local authorities, providing them with an eighty-five per cent grant. I increased this to 100 per cent so that there would be no excuse for delay in clearing valuable sites which would provide a more environmentally friendly area, and in some cases much needed land to develop factories. In many of our valleys, land was at a premium. North Wales, both in the north-west and the north-east, had its own problems too. It is later generations that have to pay the price for the activities of their predecessors. I hope that if today's rash of wind farms ever becomes redundant, there is built-in machinery for the developers to restore our landscape.

What is heartening is that when Welsh unemployment escalated from the 65,783 (five per cent) in 1979 to 166,683 (thirteen per cent) in 1986 some of these very powers which had been so fiercely fought over by the Conservatives were the ones they used to empower the WDA to do what it could to ameliorate Welsh unemployment. I was always conscious, and said so repeatedly, that the main factor influencing the level of Welsh unemployment was the state of the national economy. However, I firmly believed that with a budgetary provision of £100 million rising (at 1974 prices) to £150 million we could do a great deal ourselves by identifying the worst areas and bringing all the economic tools that we had into play. We had the advantage of being on the spot in Wales. The secretary of state could set limits to WDA action and the bigger investments had to have the secretary's approval.

I looked around for a chairman who would carry confidence in Wales and chose Sir Dai Davies, former general secretary of the Steelworkers' Union. There was a good choice of applicants for chief executive and I chose Ian Gray, former chief officer of the Board of Trade in Wales. I met them every month when the WDA's programme would be put before me. A few of the investments inevitably went wrong. The WDA was not there to take the safest course as a banker would. Their job in lending was to go the extra mile when necessary. What was important was that their general pattern of investment was sound, showing more enterprise and inevitably taking more risks than traditional investment sources would, otherwise there would be little point in giving them those powers.

I had authorised them to purchase land banks and to build large numbers of factories. Unhappily, through circumstances beyond our control, the further giant expansion for Hoover at Merthyr did not come about. It was a very big disappointment for Merthyr and myself.

The setting up of the WDA was the most significant of my activities in encouraging development. I was particularly proud of it, and saw it becoming, with one or two problems on the way, as a respected institution in Wales doing outstanding work. It established a brand of its own, known to industrialists and many others across the world. It developed its overseas contacts and through effective advertising Wales was known more and more as a good place to invest. Whenever I took the plane to America it was inevitable that I noticed a WDA advert, either on the way or when I got to my destination.

While I fully understand the desire of the Welsh Assembly to make a bonfire of the quangos and bring decision making under more effective democratic control – this, after all, was one of the main attractions for many who supported devolution, I regretted the loss of the name of the Welsh Development Agency. So much money had been spent on its projection. It had acquired a good brand image world wide. It had worked hard for many years in establishing a sound reputation and it had served Wales well. I do not know enough about the machinery of government in the Assembly to say whether it would have been possible to salvage something of value from the flames in the retention of the name within a more democratic framework.

An important duty of the opposition and members of the Welsh Assembly is to probe the worth of the machinery for encouraging industry. Are the staff sufficiently experienced and qualified in industrial matters? Do they draw on the wisdom of both sides of industry? How quickly do they react to the demand for help from industry or the need for new development? If a factory closes down, particularly one with its headquarters abroad, how soon do they make contact and at what level? In short, is it as good, better or worse than the Welsh Development Agency?

The Development Board for Rural Wales

I had indicated at second reading of the Welsh Development Agency bill that while it had an all-Wales remit, I was conscious that the main thrust of its activities would be in our industrial areas and we would be giving careful consideration to what else might be needed in rural Wales. I was signalling my future target.

Contrary to expectations in the Welsh Office, I won another place in the legislative programme to introduce a bill on a subject which was very dear to me – mid Wales. I learnt by accident that such was the lack of confidence by the permanent secretary that he had pulled off the civil servant, the late Mr Hall Williams, who was working on my bill, and directed him to some worthier task!

The department knew of the priority that I was giving to a steady annual flow of new Welsh legislation. Wales had never before had a series of legislative proposals put before Parliament. I was breaking new ground each year and the department was always surprised at my success in winning places in the legislative timetable. These places were not won without assiduous lobbying of parliamentary colleagues and success was the result of their friendship on many occasions. I had learnt these lessons from Barbara Castle who, when in the prime of her performance, never failed to canvass her colleagues before an important Cabinet committee. In the Westminster village, as it is currently known, members of the House of Commons lived together day and many nights for many years and this intimacy frequently paid off.

I was deeply disappointed with my department. It was the only time so far as I know that a strategic decision was taken in the department without my knowledge. I told the permanent secretary that I wanted Hall Williams back to work on the bill. In fairness his analysis of my chances was, on a historical view, nearer to the reality of the situation, but he had not reckoned with my determination to get this particular bill as it meant so much to me. The bill team was back at work soon afterwards and, under Hall Williams, good work was done.

I have referred to the deep impression that a report by the Advisory Council for Wales and Monmouthshire made on me as young man, and how I had used the report and a phrase from it as the keynote for my speech when I tried to become the Labour candidate for Cardiganshire in 1953. The phrase that impressed itself on me was the one that referred to 'depopulation as a form of economic adjustment' in mid Wales. It was cold and clinical. But true then.

On a recent visit to an area school in Llangybi, Ceredigion, that I had opened more than thirty years before, I learnt that ninety per cent of the children were from English-speaking homes, presumably a considerable number from families that had moved to the county. I was pleased, however, that they were being taught through the medium of Welsh under the guidance of enthusiastic teachers.

It was a different picture in 1974. I had made many speeches in political meetings in the county on the problems of the young having to migrate due to the lack of affordable homes and the lack of job opportunities. The majority of the children in my class at the grammar school had already left when I returned to Aberystwyth to work for the farmers in the mid 1950s.

I was determined to do something to try to remedy this through the setting up of a statutory body with particular powers to stem the tide, and with appropriate resources. It would build on the diverse bodies already operating in mid Wales. My mission was not to scrap them, but to take advantage of their knowledge and energy. Unfortunately, despite their good intentions, they had failed to halt depopulation, due to lack of resources.

The special problems of rural Wales, and particularly mid Wales had concerned my Labour predecessors. Jim Griffiths's idea was to build a new town in mid Wales, expanding on Newtown, Montgomeryshire. My recollection is that the concept was far too grand and eventually nothing came of it. Cledwyn Hughes grappled with the issue too, and proposed a board structure for mid Wales which covered all its industries and included agriculture. Unfortunately it was proposed that the board would have compulsory powers to acquire agricultural land in order to facilitate restructuring when an opportunity arose. This proposal resulted in uproar amongst the farming community. My peasant blood, with dozens of ancestors having farmed such land in mid Wales would have warned me of the dangers. A public inquiry was set up, and took evidence for a long period at sittings in Aberystwyth. The farming unions put their objections strongly. The result was that Cledwyn's proposals did not go ahead.

In retrospect, withdrawing the compulsory purchase powers would have been wise as, regrettably, so much money was lost to mid Wales. I was determined not to go along this path and my instructions to my staff were to avoid including agriculture in the remit any new board that I proposed might have. Since agriculture was such an important part of the mid Wales economy it was not entirely logical, but logic had to give way to political reality. Lessons had been learnt by all.

The variety of bodies I found operating there included the Mid Wales Development Corporation, the Mid Wales Industrial Development Association, the Development Commission – a British body set up by Lloyd George – and the Council for Small Industries in Rural Wales (COSIRA). Two were able to give grants to tourism – the Welsh Tourist Board and COSIRA. I hoped 'to bring these powers together, to better utilise the resources available and sharpen the attack'.

I eventually got the agreement of all my colleagues to a Development Board for Rural Wales.

When moving the second reading of the DBRW Bill in 1976, I said that we should build on successful institutions and cut down on the overall numbers of bodies operating there. The board proposed would provide facilities to supplement the primary industries of the area. It was a broad mission, but one with specific targets. 'It is the fine touch of the paintbrush that is required in mid Wales,' I said.

I believed the new board would make an impact from the outset. We had had enough of reports for mid Wales. I wanted to accelerate the development of that part of Wales which 'bridges North and South Wales'.

I got my bill through Parliament and I chose a board widely representative of many interests in mid Wales. The DBRW became a respectable and active body until its functions were absorbed by the WDA. I do not dissent from that decision, but at the time, given the issues facing the WDA, it was appropriate to found the DBRW as well. In due course the whole position could be looked at again, in particular in the light of the success of the WDA in its many tasks.

The Land Authority for Wales

On the initiative of Ted Rowlands and John Clement, who headed my industrial division from 1976, I succeeded in getting an important part of an England and Wales bill devoted to the particular needs of Wales.

Clement was an old Welsh Office housing civil servant who had joined the Civil Service straight from school. He had a wonderful story of being taken by his parents to Cathays Park to take up his post and being surprised at the presence of the Band of the Welsh Guards and the red carpet. He was soon put right; the band was not for him, but for King George, who happened to be opening the offices of the Welsh Board of Health. Clement now presided over the activities of the Land Reclamation Unit. Ted, as housing minister, was conscious of the need to adapt proposals for housing action areas that suited England but did not quite fit in with the Welsh need for 'the fine touch of the paint-brush', to paraphrase my own words. They persuaded me of the advantage of quite small areas, even single streets, receiving infusions of government money for improvements. We could do better in this way than the large action areas envisaged for England. It was frequently a problem of scale and the need for special measures. This was the strength of the decentralised Welsh Office: its civil servants had a deep knowledge of Wales's needs.

It was the same philosophy for our part of the Community Land Bill, introduced by Tony Crosland as the secretary for state for the environment in 1975. There was a desperate shortage of land for industrial development, particularly in our narrow valleys. I was persuaded that we needed an all-Wales body with powers to package various pieces of land capable of development, but owned by different owners. The current situation often resulted in no development at all. We wanted to dove-tail the powers a new authority for Wales would inherit from existing organisations, adding new powers, and some of the provisions of the Community Land Act.

I was persuaded that these new powers should not be given to local authorities. They had a vital planning role and it was important not to mix compulsory acquisition powers with that role. Hence I was persuaded to ask for a Land Authority. The fact that this was another all-Wales body made the task of my advisers that much easier. Unfortunately local authorities in Wales got wind of what we had in mind and feared they would lose some of their powers. As I was travelling to a Cabinet committee meeting dealing with the bill in Whitehall, Ted Rowlands jumped into the car and solemnly warned me not to give way to the local government bigwigs, otherwise my devolution campaign would in turn be doomed. They would envisage a similar loss of powers again. On the other hand I recognised the dangers of alienating local government to our devolution proposals, but this was a risk I was prepared to take in this instance. It's true we are a nation of tribes; it was yet again a turf war.

In my speech (Hansard, House of Commons 29 April, Cols 236–81), I set out what the Land Authority would do:

It will be a National Land Authority exercising powers flexibly, deploying scarce staff resources at national and local level.

In cooperation with local authorities it will be the means by which gratuitous profits, made at the expense of the community by land speculation, will accrue to the people of Wales. We envisage that £20 million a year will accrue to the Welsh people. It will mean that 2,000 acres of land per year, urgently needed for private housing, industrial and commercial development, will be available at the right time and in the right places.

The earlier criticism of the local authorities had evaporated. They now understood what we had in mind and they were particularly pleased by the agency proposals which had been put to them as the way the bill would be implemented in Wales. This was the compromise which we had devised.

I added that nothing in our proposals derogated from the traditional powers of local authorities. In retrospect, I wonder what all the fuss was about. I fear that councillors had been set up by their officials to oppose my proposals because of the fear of the loss of local government jobs and perhaps, more importantly, the fear of the diminution of the empire over which councillors reigned and in which they had not always distinguished themselves.

We got the bill. I wanted a particularly tough chairman for the authority and I did not have to go further than a former minister in the Welsh Office, Mrs Eirene White, now Baroness White. So tough was she that on one occasion, it was said, she refused to be retired as a junior minister by Harold Wilson and came back from North Wales to say so. Bearing in mind that she was a member of the National Executive, he gave way. I cannot be sure of the exact number of staff that she was offered to run the Land Authority. For the purposes of the argument, it could have been sixty-five. A week later, having studied the field, she came back and surprised the mandarins by saying she could do the job with, say, forty-five. She would have made an outstanding permanent secretary.

The Land Authority did an excellent job under Eirene's chairmanship and set about, with full local government support, acquiring parcels of industrial and similar land for redevelopment. They did a very good job in my constituency, again with the support of the local council. In accepting our proposals, Parliament was again providing the machinery for industrial development and jobs for our people.

seventeen
THE CATHAYS POWERHOUSE

I WAS STILL VERY CONSCIOUS of the Welsh Office's limited powers and I was determined to win more. I had some powers over industry, but I was determined to have greater responsibility in this field, but the attitude of ministers was common. They had no wish to be ministers for industry for England alone. This included Tony (Wedgie) Benn.

It was a period of considerable government action to provide incentives to industry. There was a whole system of encouragement that could be brought into play in such an interventionist era and attractive packages were available for both the creation and maintenance of jobs. But Whitehall feared that if the Scots and the Welsh offered more incentives than England it might distort industrial development. There were many parts of England that suffered the same problems as Wales. As a London Member, Peter Shore MP was prone to argue that London had its problems too, and there was considerable truth in this.

The challenge was to administer industrial development in Wales while maintaining the unity of the United Kingdom. I was confident that once the principle of devolved administration was accepted within the UK we could exploit whatever was devised to Wales's advantage, given the nature and gravity of our problems, and we did.

Eventually industry ministers gave way, though without much grace. The new powers required a Transfer of Functions Order in Parliament, which was obtained in July 1975. In Parliament I said:

> In a matter of days there will be transferred to the Welsh Office major industrial powers.
>
> These proposals add up to an unprecedented shift of power and effective machinery for decision making to Wales (Hansard Col 984).

Another obvious candidate was education. Education was the province in the main of local authorities and they jealously guarded their independence. I was a great admirer of what had been achieved in my adopted county of Glamorgan from the Depression onwards. There was no suggestion then of further accretion of powers by the Ministry of Education in Whitehall and I had no proposals to change the system. Given the bilingual issues that we faced there was no subject which had a stronger claim for administrative decentralisation than education. But I suspect the politicians and administrators of local authorities would have been happier to maintain their link with Whitehall than come within the influence of Cathays Park.

Unfortunately, Shirley Williams MP, then minister for education, was loath to diminish her empire. I wanted to extend the powers that I had, which were confined to schools only – primary and secondary education – a power transferred in 1970. I wanted higher and further education (including universities) as a necessary follow-on. I wanted to break, as far as I could, the umbilical cord between my education officials in Cardiff and Whitehall. The dual loyalty of my senior educational staff, who commuted to Whitehall as well as serving me in Cardiff, was a problem for me. Their views seemed to me to be coloured by what they heard in Whitehall.

When I suggested trebling the administrative grant to the Welsh medium nursery schools (Ysgolion Meithrin Cymru) which were run by volunteers, I faced considerable opposition from my departmental advisers. I think only about £30,000 was involved and I resented the energy I had to use in order to win the argument. I clinched it by increasing the grant to the English medium schools as well, which was equitable, although my poor adviser bewailed the knock-on effect in England. I think I remember that I got round it by using some health money for what was in substance education. They bordered each other. On a visit to Cardiff during the National Eisteddfod Dr David Owen MP, then a minister in the Department of Health, marvelled that we had managed to switch health money to an education cause, with which he had considerable sympathy.

The manoeuvring served an even greater purpose: it alerted me to the need to win powers from the Treasury to enable a Welsh Secretary to switch expenditure from one head to another generally. This was to be a battle for the future, a battle I won with the Treasury in 1978. I always tried to take the long view. On many occasions I kept my aims to myself. Timing was always important and I tried to limit my battlefields to one at a time.

The question of dual loyalty to Whitehall and Wales was nothing new. In the early days of my political career, one of the most distinguished Welsh education under-secretaries had been Sir Ben Bowen Thomas, and a very persuasive civil servant he was too. It was facetiously said of Sir Ben that so skilled he was that he never came out of a committee except on the winning side. This had more than one interpretation! Be that as it may it was said that he preferred to be based in London, where he thought he could be more influential, and he could not be persuaded to move to Cardiff. In fairness, in addition to his Welsh responsibilities he had acquired an important role in UNESCO as well.

I have fond memories of Sir Ben. When I was travelling back from a public inquiry as a barrister, where I was arguing successfully against the closure of the Barmouth railway line, I met him at Wolverhampton Station. At the other end of the platform was the Presbyterian divine, Dr Martin Lloyd-Jones. Sir Ben commented that the 'reverend gentleman' had been at the Presbyterian gathering, Y *sasiwn*, in Wrexham, causing 'difficulties'. 'There he is,' he said, 'wearing an overcoat and carrying a macintosh – no faith!'

At least in my time the education under-secretary was based in Cardiff, although I was not attracted by his stance on this and other matters, such as my proposal to give a grant to the Urdd children's magazine. In fact, I got fed up with having to spend valuable time arguing over fairly small issues and it increased my determination to extend my powers in this field. I got the transfer of this function.

The same problem of dual loyalty manifested itself in agriculture, though by this time the direct influence of political ministers was waning with our acceptance of the Common Agricultural Policy and more and more decisions being taken in Brussels. I got quite close to my agricultural under-secretaries based in Aberystwyth. We spoke the same language, the language of the farming community, and despite their dual loyalty they were effective in looking after Welsh agricultural interests and were regarded by the farming community as 'one of them'. With five of my brothers farming, I had my own links with what was happening. I shall avoid using the term 'grass roots'.

During his period in the Welsh Office Cledwyn had failed to get agricultural responsibility transferred to the Welsh Office. The Agriculture Minister, Fred Peart, had resisted the transfer at every stage. So I had inherited a strange system of political responsibility. In 1969, after Cledwyn had left the Welsh Office and became minister of agriculture, partial responsibility only was devolved to the Welsh Office. As a result Wales had two ministers of agriculture, the minister in Whitehall, who at the time happened to be a Welshman, and the Welsh Secretary of State. Why this particular arrangement, which was a constitutional anomaly, came about I could never be sure. The better view is that the Whitehall civil servants were loath to let go of Wales and persuaded Cledwyn of this.

It was ridiculous. No decision on Welsh agricultural matters could be taken without the agreement and signature of both ministers including statutory instruments. The civil servant in Aberystwyth had a duty to advise both. No one had worked out the possibility of a conflict of interest. There could be such occasions, or at least the need for a different emphasis in policy for Wales, which civil servants in London might fear would have a knock-on effect in England.

I was determined to end this. I did not rush to broach it with the minister, my friend, Fred Peart, who I knew would be against it, as he was against all devolutionary proposals. While training in Aberystwyth during his RAF service, he had met his future wife, who was of course Welsh. On this basis he claimed to know Wales and Welsh aspirations!

I waited until another friend, John Silkin MP, became the minister of agriculture. John was proud of his Welsh links. His father, Lewis Silkin MP, was a particularly distinguished Labour Cabinet minister in Attlee's government – the pioneer of new towns, national parks and basic planning legislation, who had put up his first brass plate as a solicitor in Neath and Port Talbot. One late night in the Commons, it so happened that there were four Welshmen sitting on the government front bench. John was the government chief whip. When this was pointed out to him he corrected his informant, '. . . No . . . four and a half!'

John agreed easily to the transfer of functions. It was the easiest and quickest victory I had.

There was one important matter which I deemed it right to do before the transfer became effective and that was to accede to the Farmers' Union of Wales's claim to government recognition as an organisation representing many farmers in Wales. It was a battle that I had played a part in many years before, and it was long overdue, but I thought politically the correct thing was to grant recognition while there were still two ministers of agriculture. I did not wish it to be seen as my decision and mine alone, but as the decision of the government, which was proper and better. We delayed the transfer of functions for a few weeks so that we could inform both unions, the FUW and the NFU, that recognition had been granted by the two ministers on behalf of the government.

On 1 March 1978 I took over formal ministerial powers for Welsh agriculture at a ceremony in the National Agricultural Service Headquarters at Trawscoed Mansion, Cardiganshire. I was due at Trawscoed at about 2 p.m. on a Friday, a comfortable time and day for everyone. Unfortunately my great uncle, J. M. Jenkins, the doyen of Welsh Black cattle breeders, had died at the venerable age of about 102. It was obvious that I should make every effort to attend the funeral, which was quite close by in Talybont.

The ceremony of transfer was put back a couple of hours on that Friday afternoon. I hope I was forgiven by the guests. It was a coincidence that it was the Earl of Lisburne of that period, owner of Trawscoed, who had ejected J. M. Jenkins's father and grandfather from their tenancy in 1875, and they were my ancestors too. My ministry had now acquired the ownership of Trawscoed. It was befitting it was on Uncle James's funeral day and that I should delay the transfer so that I could pay my respects.

There were other small additions to my responsibilities including The Manpower Services Commission's operations in Wales. Their planning role fitted well with my powers over industry. Another interesting transfer was the responsibility for ancient monuments, including the castles of Wales. This included the folly of Castell Coch near Cardiff built by the Marquis of Bute. I do not recollect ever officially visiting any of this part of my 'empire', although the use of Castell Coch for entertainment was once raised. I was, however, not in the entertainment business. I kept a tight ship on all expenses and I usually paid for entertainment myself, other than a dinner for the dignitaries of the National Eisteddfod. To the disappointment of my staff, I resisted all attempts to refurnish my offices in Cardiff and London when I heard the cost. I was a 'Cardi' with public money. I make no apologies.

I doubled the size of the Welsh Office during my stewardship – doubling both functions and staff. It was a far cry from the few responsibilities that Jim Griffiths was able to claim. The bigger picture for me was work for the Welsh Assembly to do when it came into existence. I was determined it would have all the responsibilities that had been won by my predecessors and myself as building blocks.

In doubling the responsibilities of the Welsh Office I also doubled the number of its staff who, in 1974, amounted to 1,270. By 1979 there were 2,600. This is a firm illustration of the sea-change in the office during my time. It was not matched by public expenditure so far as I can ascertain from the statistics. It may have increased in size but there was a considerable dip in money in 1977–8 due, I believe, to the cuts imposed at the time of the IMF crisis. It then recovered to an increase by 1979–80.

I had achieved a major shift in responsibilities from Whitehall to Cathays. In fact, apart from playing a role in national and budgetary matters, the fewer responsibilities that remained to the Welsh Office when the Assembly came into existence, the better from my point of view. My successful transfer of functions, coupled with setting up the WDA, the DBRW and the LAW gave me powerful weapons to tackle the economic and industrial problems of Wales.

eighteen
OTHER WELSH OFFICE WORK

CONTRARY TO APPEARANCES, devolution was not the issue that took most of my time at this point. An equal, if not a greater demand for my attention was the bread-and-butter issue of intervention in the industrial areas of Wales, hence my other legislative programme just described.

My daily concern, as part of an interventionist government, was, through the Welsh Office industry department, to encourage firms to invest and provide new job opportunities or help to preserve existing jobs. I had many meetings with liquidators of firms. Every effort was made to provide financial packages which would help both the lame ducks, and those who could waddle. It was time-consuming; every week seemed to have its problems. A minister would go to Ebbw Vale once a month to steer all the organisations that were active there in dealing with the area's problems.

I travelled to America and Japan, leading the Welsh Development Agency, seeking new investments and advertising the advantages of Wales. I went to about five cities leading a delegation on industrial development. At one of my meetings in America I was addressing the number one Rotary of the World in Chicago where Rotary was founded. The delegation entered a large hall with about fifty small tables set for lunch. Sir Dai Davies (Chairman of the WDA) noticed a small glass of red liquid on each place plate, and turned to Emrys Evans of the Midland Bank. 'This looks like communion wine to me,' he said. Back came Emrys, 'You've got a good memory, Dai.'

The rewards would come in the years ahead. I was determined to do what I could to try to correct the imbalance of public and private employment in Wales and take advantage of new industries and new techniques to make up for the inevitable shortfall in the old basic industries.

After a particularly concentrated four-day visit to Japan, leading a delegation from the whole of the UK, including Wales, and seeing banker after banker – the bankers were the key to individual firms' investment decisions – I returned to Hong Kong for a day or so to recuperate. The Japanese already had a firm footing in South Wales and appreciated the welcome they received from us. I took a list of Welsh golf courses with me to the Japanese as part of the bait – the cost of golfing in Japan was astronomical. The firms that settled in Wales with the practical encouragement of the Welsh office before, during and after my time have provided immensely valuable livelihoods to generations.

I still smile at recollections of the time I was introduced to the president of the Japanese Rugby Union at the British Embassy in Tokyo; he was an ex-kamikaze pilot. 'How can you be an ex-kamikaze pilot?' I asked. 'Oh,' he replied, 'I lost two engines on the way and was ordered to turn back. It needed some bravery to face my colleagues.'

Our greatest coup was attracting Ford to Bridgend. The competition from other parts of the UK was intense. Ford already had a plant near Swansea and after a chequered labour history in its early days, had settled down well with exemplary labour relations. Memories regrettably died hard and I was told that Henry Ford himself had come down to Swansea to check for himself. At any rate, someone from the very top management in Ford came down and took back a good report. Jim Callaghan, then Prime Minister, took an active interest in the American owners. He had his own connections too and knew which lever to pull.

Things were going reasonably well but one final haul was required, according to John Clement. Ford was demanding the freehold of the ground as apparently they did elsewhere. It was not the government's policy to sell a freehold. I was easily persuaded by Clement's arguments to agree the request – 'Sell them the freehold,' was my response. I was not prepared to lose. He cautioned me that the English departments might object, to which I responded, 'they'll be too late'. No one could really re-open the book once we had landed Ford safely. It was a clear example of industrial powers being used to the maximum extent in Wales through personal decisions. As it turned out there was not a murmur that I was aware of about our initiative.

I always kept in close touch with the unions about my intentions if I could. They played a particularly prominent part in all our Japanese plants. The Japanese insisted on having one union only per plant, whatever the skills. On each visit I made, the management fielded a full-time trade-union officer who was present during our discussions. Pay was not high, but labour relations were exemplary. Hardly anyone left voluntarily, and if there was a problem then management and the union would reach an agreement. It was a very paternalistic relationship and quite new to us in Wales.

I discussed the Ford project with George Wright, the South Wales secretary of the TGWU, who had a big interest in the motor industry. I suggested to George that because labour and labour problems could be such an important factor, that he might defuse future trouble by importing his own potential shop stewards from Swansea, a few miles down the road, to Bridgend with ready-made jobs. He knew his men. He, like me, wanted a successful plant such as we had by now in Swansea. Labour was probably as important as capital investment. It was his business what he did with my advice, I was not to know. All I can say is that both Swansea and Bridgend, whatever the early difficulties at Swansea, have had exemplary labour relations for very many years. George was a wise counsellor and got things done.

As part of my deep interest in maintaining and providing employment, road building was also important to me. I do not think there was any Party policy in Wales before 1974 on this or on many of the other things I did. I was incensed that the building of the remainder of the M4 had crunched to a halt when I took office. Not a spade was being used. No JCBs in sight. The department did not seem to have a policy on this, unlike my old Ministry of Transport. What they had done was to build a piece of motorway here and then move on some distance and build then another piece. They called it 'pepper potting'. Traffic speeded up on one piece, only to revert to a slow crawl for the next. The concerns expressed in my maiden speech in 1959 for the Port Talbot by-pass had been met, but to the east and west it was the same old misery.

I gave instructions that we would pretty much stop other road building and concentrate all resources on a good east-to-west motorway in South Wales. In the meantime, we should get on with planning a new A55 in North Wales. Some improvements could be made in the meantime in northeast Wales as they were urgently needed for industrial purposes.

I believed that two good east-to-west roads would provide the basis for making industry more attractive to the western parts of Wales as well as the east. In South Wales the old problem had been enticing industry west of Bridgend, and wherever I went in North Wales, conscious as I was of the need for advance factories, we built many – the further west you went the more difficult it was to attract tenants. Anglesey was always up against it. Wrexham had its own transport problems in connecting to markets and I went up to see for myself and discuss it with the local council. Access to the markets of England for our produce was paramount. I fear that despite the obvious need for better north-to-south communications, it was not on my programme at that stage.

We did get on with extending the M4 and opened section after section of it. I got Joel Barnett, the chief secretary, to open one part. The Treasury had, after all, provided the money and I suspect a grateful client had never asked a Treasury minister to do such a thing before. Despite having fixed the line I was unhappy that my successors did not get on with completing the Baglan to Lonlas section as urgently as I had envisaged. It retained its virgin state for too many years. The Treasury was not so helpful in agreeing to a third lane around Cardiff and in the interests of having a continuous road I had to be content with building a two-lane piece. My decision would have to be corrected one day – many years later.

I was already turning my attention to the A55 so that Denbigh, Caernarfon and Anglesey had their opportunity of attracting industry too and there was a requirement to have a public inquiry. Foolishly I thought this might be brisk. It was not to be. I heard that when the inquiry started counsel took leases for their personal accommodation for about a year and I exploded. To add to my sense of injury I heard the inquiry only sat some days of the week and sometimes only in the mornings. As always, I was in a hurry.

I wanted to send for my counsel, Michael Mann, QC (later Lord Justice Mann) to see if the Inquiry could be speeded up. I received strong legal advice that this might be an improper interference with the Inquiry, so it trundled on. I was an unhappy client and resented the restraint upon me, following legal advice. One interesting facet was the original proposal to build another road bridge over the River Conwy. Procedurally the proposals were in my name and I refused to agree to any such thing. Regrettably there was insufficient evidence that a tunnel under the river Conwy could be built, so I deferred my conclusions on that part of the road until the evidence could be obtained. This was successful after my time and the environment benefited from the later decision to build a tunnel, which pleased me. I think it was on the upper deck of a jumbo jet journey to Japan that I studied the conclusions of some of my planning inquiries. It was very much a 'hands on' role, no line was left unread or undigested. As a barrister involved in fraud cases, I knew the dangers of leaving one document unread.

I was desperate to improve communications to Ebbw Vale after the announcement of the closure of the steelworks. I argued with Joel Barnett, the chief secretary, whose mission it was to 'say no' to more public expenditure. I took the road access to Ebbw Vale to Cabinet – and, unusually, I won.

Closing steelmaking at Ebbw Vale was particularly painful for me, and I knew a little of how steel communities felt. I went up there to announce the closure, and Michael Foot, the local MP was with me. A huge and very angry crowd had gathered. There were more policemen present than I have ever seen together in Wales. Michael, deeply concerned, and unhappy too, wanted to make the announcement himself from the balcony in Ebbw Vale.

I refused his request as I was the secretary of state. Despite his Cabinet seniority, he was only the local MP. It was my job to announce the bad news. He would speak afterwards. I hope both of us did it with as much dignity as we could muster in those circumstances which were so painful to both of us.

I was driven back to London exhausted and emotionally drained. When I got the newspapers the following day, Saturday, the *Guardian* ran the story that I had refused to face the crowd. This was totally untrue. The journalist who wrote the story must have arrived late. I had insisted on making the announcement myself, and held a press conference afterwards to outline our plans for dealing with the aftermath and a promise of monthly ministerial visits to Ebbw Vale. I was extremely concerned, as the good work and care we had shown was being undone. Fortunately the editor of the *Guardian*, Alistair Hetherington, was known to me, and he lived in Blackheath a short distance away. I got the promise of a retraction in Monday's *Guardian*. To make doubly sure that there was no misrepresentation of my interest I decided to make an extra journey from London to Ebbw Vale the following day, Sunday, to meet the council and spell out what we intended to do. There was to be no doubt as to how the Welsh Office would tackle its responsibilities, but it was a return journey I could have done without.

Unfortunately on the way back on the second journey the driver, probably tired by now, crashed into the central reservation on the M4 and I crawled out of the overturned car only to be admitted to Swindon Hospital with shock. I could only smile when I received a telephone call as I lay on my hospital trolley, from Stanley Charles, the Welsh Office's 'fire brigade man in Whitehall' that he 'had a plan for all eventualities'. I suspected plan A was a state funeral in Llandaff Cathedral. I hope he was not too disappointed and I pulled his leg about this for many years.

An apocryphal story in connection with this accident was that that in addition to messages of goodwill from many councils all over Wales, one mayor insisted on coming to see me in my bed at home with the news that a message of good wishes had been passed the previous night by his council by a majority of one, the mayor adding that I was safe in his hands as he had the casting vote if necessary.

There has been a great deal of controversy recently on the unfairness of the Barnett Formula. My recollection of the time is that whenever there was a UK allocation of additional money for, say, health or education, both the press and my officers would be anxious to know how much our share in Wales was. I would go along to the chief secretary, Joel Barnett, and the back of an envelope calculation of extra money for Wales, based on population was five per cent and for Scotland, ten per cent of the additional money. I gladly accepted this rather than argue endlessly for something different.

It would not have produced any extra money; it was done on a 'take it or leave it' basis. There was no question of an assessment of need, and I had something to tell the Welsh press immediately that I had the money in my pocket, rather than face an endless argument. Getting a more equitable arrangement would have to wait for another day. It was never graced with the title 'formula' and Joel has been the first to agree that he never intended it to be a permanent arrangement.

Our needs, of course, were quite different. In my first period in office money for housing was open-ended. The need for more houses in Wales was great. So much of our housing was old and of poor quality. I sent Ted Rowlands to meet each of Wales's twenty-two authorities and told him 'to bust the bank'. To his credit he did and after this, not necessarily because of this, the rules were tightened. The stable door was shut but the horse had already bolted. I was, however, so concerned about the need for more housing that I put in a fresh bid. Unhappily this coincided with the IMF crisis, when we had about five or six Cabinet meetings in three days. Jim Callaghan, then Prime Minister, could not believe his ears that when everyone was being allocated a cut, I was arguing for more. I suspect he had difficulty keeping a straight face.

nineteen
THE FAMILY AND LATER YEARS IN THE WELSH OFFICE

ONE SHADOW DOMINATED OUR LIVES as a family in 1976. On the then current state of medical knowledge, doctors had been unable to diagnose a serious medical problem from which Margaret was suffering. At a small dinner to celebrate the knighthood of my old pupil master, Alun Talfan-Davies, Lady Emund-Davies suggested she try Garfield Davies at the Middlesex Hospital, a renowned ENT specialist. After a blip when the NHS mislaid her X-rays, she was eventually operated on for an acoustic neuroma. The particularly long operation, as it was in those days, was immensely successful; the loss of her hearing in one ear was permanent, but her life had been saved. It was a close-run thing. The prognosis could not have been worse. John Davies, my private secretary and friend, kept piling up the work during the day to keep my mind busy. On the night of the operation, John and I dined at the Commons. I don't think either of us tasted the meal. My girls must have been hogging the telephone as Garfield could not get through. It was a long evening for all of us.

This was at a time when I was battling on all fronts on devolution. My problems at home for the moment were much bigger than the ones in the office. Getting our three young girls, Nia, Non and Elinor, away to school in the morning was the day's first priority. We had no family to help us and managed it together. Friends helped to feed us. Ready-to-eat meals arrived from neighbours, for which I was grateful.

I shall never forget the period of the few days between the diagnosis and admission. The NHS then moved incredibly fast. Margaret and I went to a dinner of the Glamorgan Society where I was the speaker, Garfield Davies, the surgeon, was the president and Cliff Morgan, one of Wales's finest BBC commentators, entertained us as chairman. I tried never to break an engagement if I could and there were compensations for attending the dinner as I hoped it would while away some of the time. I still remember his stories. It gave me immense pleasure to see his name in the honours list a few years later for all his services to broadcasting, not forgetting rugby, of course. He lightened our evening immeasurably and I still express my gratitude to both.

During this period I used to have an annual, almost hour-long interview with the BBC – usually with my old friend and fellow soldier, Vincent Kane. I suspect I was not an easy nut to crack, so they put on two interviewers that year, Vincent and another distinguished journalist, Patrick Hannan. They were both good friends but very tough, though always fair, cross-examiners. I had to race back to pick up the girls from school, having just taken Margaret into the hospital for her operation. How different from the life of Cabinet ministers around the turn of the century with salaries that could pay for proper staff. At this time, with inflation more than twenty per cent, Cabinet ministers' salaries were frozen for some years. At the end of the day some time had to be found for the family, and from the sublime to the ridiculous, there is no one else to change the tyre on your wife's car or attend to a flat battery. Trivialities you may think? We were far away from family and had to get on with it. It had been the most anguishing period of my life.

One of the small burdens I carried in my 'gubernatorial' role was recommending suitable names to the Prime Minister for inclusion in the honours list. I think I got a good share for Wales. I do not think I ever failed to get one 'K' (a knighthood) in each list and many lesser honours. The honours system is an economic and efficient way of honouring those who had gone the extra mile in public service; holding a particular job at a substantial salary was not enough – medals did not just come up with the rations. I believe John Major developed and broadened the system – In my time just holding a particular job only did not get my nomination.

One matter that I am particularly proud of was making it possible to build St David's Concert Hall. Hywel Evans, my permanent secretary, came to me one day at about the turn of the year stating that he would like a concert hall built in Cardiff. He was the son of T. Hopkin Evans, the Welsh musician and conductor, and pedigree will out. I foolishly asked him why not an opera house? He explained that that was a totally different matter and would have to wait until another day. With my Cardi's mind on money I asked him, 'What will you build it with?'

'Well,' he explained, 'it's the turn of the year and we have a little money left over – a few millions.' Such were our accounting procedures that allocated money had to be spent within the financial year, or otherwise it would be reclaimed by the Treasury. He had also learnt that Cardiff City Council had money which had just become available because a proposed redevelopment could not take place. He proposed that I should persuade Cardiff to put the two sums together to build the concert hall. I readily agreed, and three of its party leaders were invited to see me at 8 a.m. the following day. What they expected or feared I do not know, but true to the finer character of good local government, they agreed on the spot to recommend the proposal to their council jointly. I did say, however, that since it would not be a wholly Cardiff venture it should be called 'The Wales Concert Hall'. They later decided to call it 'St David's' and I could not complain because that too underlined the all-Wales nature of some of the money behind the venture.

Looking back one of my deep regrets, apart from hardly ever seeing my daughters grow up over six years – I have since had the good fortune to correct this – was that I did not have enough time to give more attention to two important portfolios I had, namely health and education. Barry Jones managed the day-to-day matters of these tricky subjects for six years and I was most grateful to him. The fact that there were limits to our success was mirrored in England, and our successors are still battling for a better Health Service. In education my powers were limited to school capital building and disciplinary action against teachers who erred. There was not the centralisation of today. I was disappointed that Mid Glamorgan refused to allow its Director of Education to circulate a speech I had made in Rhyl advocating more languages and scientific teaching, 'it was none of my business'. The jury is still out as to whether matters have improved with the concentration of powers in central government since my time. I have my doubts.

By the time the election came, I suspected I was showing signs of the wear and tear of six years as secretary of state which, by current standards, is a long time in a department. Despite the tragedy of the devolution referendum, I had been able to build a formidable office of state in the government from rather modest beginnings. Little did I think that eighteen years would go by before someone else returned to the issue of devolution. Despite my despondency, I had a feeling in my bones that one day we might persuade the people of Wales that closer government is better government. That would be for others, but otherwise much of my political life would have been in vain. However at the time there was not much evidence of a change in the future.

At that stage, all I wanted was a long rest, and for the next three years I needed to stand aside from the main political battle.

Looking back, I had never been so absolutely exhausted physically and mentally. I knew I would get over this, as I have always done, but at that time I had no more to offer Wales. In my judgment others might succeed where I had not and justify and carry out the plans I had worked on so hard to bring devolution to the fore at Westminster.

twenty
THE WELSH LANGUAGE

THERE WAS NO DOUBT IN MY MIND that when I took office as secretary of state I had a clear duty to do what I could to take part in efforts to try to preserve and regenerate Welsh as a living language.

It was my first language, the language of the hearth, the language in which my wife and I spoke to each other. It was an accident of geography that we conversed in this way. We were both born in the same county, where the majority of citizens still spoke and understood Welsh. The majority of industrial South Wales no longer spoke Welsh – in my constituency only eight or nine per cent did. My wife and I did not have to make a positive effort to speak Welsh. Geography, where we were born and lived, made it easy.

What could be done? What should be done? I was clear in my belief in the need for government to face up to its responsibilities to one of the oldest living languages of Europe and, if anything was unique as part of the national heritage of Britain, it was the Welsh language. The calculated damage to the language had been exemplified by the Act of Union and continued later in government attitudes, particularly in education, in the nineteenth century.

The language was under pressure and had been for a long time. The dominant English language, spoken by all but a very few, was constantly encroaching. The development of radio and television and the lack of Welsh language papers with a wide circulation meant cumulatively that the language was under constant siege. I fear I am stating the obvious. It might be said that it was a depressing picture. Between the censuses of 1961 and 1971 there had been a fall of twenty per cent in the numbers who spoke Welsh. Despite the reality of the figures I did not share the pessimism of some of my friends. I suppose there was an element of wishful thinking in this soon to be corrected. Nevertheless I believed that certain steps in the field of education could do something to stem the tide and ultimately, since the media wielded such enormous influence, I came to believe that positive action through broadcasting could reap substantial benefits and that I should concentrate on this. I was soon to learn also that financial provision could be the key to a better future for the language. Money was as important as status. That was, I sensed, the real politique.

Politically I had a problem. My number one aim was to bring devolution for Wales and nothing that I did was to detract from its achievement. My Party was divided in general, but not wholly so. I was immensely grateful to my colleague from Port Talbot, Alderman Llew Heycock (later Lord), for his far-sightedness in setting up Welsh-language schools in Glamorgan. Glamorgan was not the only county but it had pioneered educational provision for the language in a difficult area. Rearranging schools could cause considerable social upheaval, for example by displacing non-Welsh speaking children whose parents did not desire Welsh education for them, to make room for the ever-increasing demands for schools with Welsh teaching.

Elected representatives were quite brave on many occasions in rearranging schools. I believed that increasing the number of those being taught in Welsh in the industrial areas, and the non-Welsh-speaking areas of Wales would be a significant factor in re-establishing the language. At the same time I took note of the invasion of non-Welsh-speaking children into Welsh areas and applauded the successes of teachers and education authorities in those areas who actively encouraged the teaching of subjects in Welsh to so many of their pupils. I am still concerned about the quality of Welsh spoken by some on the media and elsewhere. There is still more to be done in ensuring Welsh is spoken naturally and without an anglicised tone. My anxieties, despite recent enquiries, fall on deaf ears. We really do need a proper inquiry into the 'success' of our teaching, particularly how much Welsh is spoken after leaving school.

I only gradually became aware of the attractions of cheap housing in Wales compared with high prices in England. This, together with substantial council-house building makes Wales a magnet. My political problem was how to take part in the battle to save the language without frightening those of my colleagues who were not always its natural supporters. Politically, if devolution was to survive then I should forego any credit for whatever I was able to do for the language. I had to bear in mind the big picture all the time.

Responsibility for the language had been one of the first subjects transferred to the Welsh Office in 1964 and Cledwyn Hughes had succeeded in piloting the Welsh Language Act 1967 through Parliament. Apart from the importance of the bill that he presented, it was the first major exercise for any bill team in the Welsh Office to learn the process of legislation, and how to win friends in other government departments. It must have been a steep learning curve, and I cannot underestimate its importance.

I believe the Act helped to create a more understanding atmosphere in other government departments in Whitehall. When I was a junior minister in transport in 1966–8, I faced substantial opposition to Welsh forms for road tax applications and driving licences. The practical difficulties paraded by officials to any change were frequently overwhelming. In the future all that was to change and gradually the new understanding that grew made it easier to accommodate Welsh aspirations, frequently document by document, in any government department.

I was not very well served by my education and language advisers in the Welsh Office. Their dual obligation to both Whitehall and to Cardiff meant that Whitehall came first. For a time the civil servant responsible for the administration of my responsibilities for the language did not even speak Welsh, or at least I never heard him do so.

My predecessor Peter Thomas had appointed a body of distinguished Welshmen and women to advise him on the language. They had produced a valuable report proposing substantial expenditure, and part of that was to be on a fourth television channel in Welsh. Regrettably no action involving expenditure could be taken as we were in the throes of the IMF crisis. The report could not have landed in the Welsh Office at a worse time. I fear, if I recollect correctly, that because of financial limitations I was powerless to act. In any event, prominence to the needs of the language at that time just did not fit in with my strategy of giving priority to devolution. However it reinforced my awareness of the situation and made me more determined to pursue progress in the field that I thought would yield the greatest dividends, and that was broadcasting.

From my earliest days in office I had to take ad hoc decisions on measures to support the language. I did so in my practical support for the Urdd magazine, Welsh nursery schools, the Eisteddfod and Welsh publishing. These, however, were personal decisions taken on the basis of my limited knowledge and in the absence of official advice. I had no idea which of such initiatives would be most beneficial. I had learnt in my transport days of cost-benefit analysis – how pound for pound some activities would yield a greater benefit than others. It was not exactly the same result that I was looking for, but I needed some machinery to advise me on any initiatives I took in order to get the most worthwhile result in a period of scarce resources. I was not getting this kind of advice from the Welsh Office, and during my period there I was working, at least in my own mind, towards setting up a body with a remit not unlike, but obviously in a different way, the Historical Monuments Advisory Committee. My Welsh Language Advisory Council was not the kind of body I needed, what I needed would be small and more sharply focused.

Unhappily the chairman of the existing body, Mr Ben Jones, signed a published letter with other very eminent Welshmen demanding government action for a new Welsh television channel. I was deeply disappointed. I felt he was perfectly entitled to say what he believed in, but he could not be one of my principal advisers and able to enjoy the luxury of publicly demanding government action in this field, particularly when I was one of the government ministers principally involved.

I sent for Mr Jones, who was a man I liked very much. As always in a difficult interview, I thought it would be easier if I saw him alone – I had to spell out as best as I could the incompatibility of his actions and his role as chairman of my advisory body. The problem was that I just could not tell him what I was doing with parliamentary colleagues in my campaign for resources for a fourth channel. It was a major difficulty for me, but I kept my role in this campaign a close secret. From long experience to tell one person was to run the risk of all knowing and it was not my way of conducting ministerial business to tell the world of my discussions with colleagues.

Mr Jones had no defence or reply to my criticisms, but I noted he did not offer his resignation and I was not minded to ask him for it as I did not want to fan the flames. He was a good man who had given vent to his beliefs in an inappropriate way.

In the absence of advice I decided to do things my own way. The grant for Welsh book publishing was still small, but it had grown since I first raised it in Parliament as a young MP in the 1960s. I increased it, but more importantly changed radically how it would be operated. I decided it should be done by the Welsh Books Council, having been advised by its then director. In 1979, following a recommendation from the Welsh Language Advisory Council, I announced a totally new grant of £55,000 to assist in children and young people's publications and invited the Welsh Books Council to distribute this and to fill gaps in the market. Following this, as a result of my decision, for the year 1981–2, the Welsh Books Council took over the role of Welsh University Press in the allocation and distribution of grants for adult books.

All this extended considerably the strategic role of the Welsh Books Council. Even allowing for inflation, the total grant distributed for 1981–2 was £285,000. Since then its role has been expanded further and it is now funded by the Welsh Assembly. It is a sea-change from my cry in the wilderness for more money in my adjournment debate speech in the 1960s. I had been privileged to have had my opportunity of following that speech with positive action when I became secretary of state, and am grateful to my successors for doing so too.

I had been brought up, reading *Cymru'r Plant*, the Urdd Gobaith Cymru journal for children. The official advice was dubious, if not negative, about supporting the journal financially. The Urdd is a successful national youth organisation providing a whole raft of activities, from culture to sport. It was effective in part of my constituency. Later, when Jim Callaghan made his first official tour of Wales as Prime Minister, I built in a visit to the Llangrannog Urdd camp as part of his fact-finding mission. It helped to mark the government's endorsement of its activities, and I gave practical help to its publication in the face of official advice.

I fully supported the setting up of Welsh-medium secondary schools, but sometimes I would need strong evidence of need to have separate provision in a mainly Welsh-speaking area, and it was important that it would fit in to the education pattern of the area. My officials were enjoined to prepare their plans carefully and the school had to have a sufficiently wide catchment area to make up what I thought to be necessary numbers for a comprehensive school. I was a minister who was particularly interested.

My biggest disappointment in this field was the failure by governments to recognise the extra cost to education authorities of providing teaching and teaching materials in two languages. To my way of thinking, two books in different languages cost more than one. On taking office I immediately thought that I should examine the situation on the ground. I travelled to Gwynedd the first Easter after appointment and in addition to many industrial visits was invited to address Gwynedd County Council. The full meeting took the form of a short speech and a question and answer session. I said I would take questions in either language and answer accordingly. I had seen Prime Minister Trudeau do it in Ottowa in the Canadian Parliament, speaking and answering in either English or French, depending on the language of the questioner. It is a task not without its difficulties because of the speed of the exchanges, and I was pleased that it was accomplished. Involvement of people, particularly elected representatives, was important to me. They had to get to know me.

During the visit I had talked to the excellent chairman of the education committee. It was embarrassing to both of us that nobody had, it seemed, officially at any rate, queried the extra cost of bilingual education. The stock official answer was that it was covered by the Rate Support Grant. When I delved into this it was obviously a nonsense. Population density was one factor, the number of elderly another, but not the extra cost of the language.

I determined to remedy this. The RSG was not the right instrument, even the 'sparsity' of population worked out to sparsely populated Powys's disadvantage, so I had to invent 'super-sparsity' to help them out. Behind my back I suspect my leg was again pulled about the Cardi's obsession with money.

It was a long-drawn-out battle over four years to try to win the agreement of the Treasury but I was able to announce success for the extra cost of the language in my presidential speech in the Cardiff National Eisteddfod and to promise the necessary legislation. Wherever I spoke protesters were never far away, and considerable damage was done to the deserved publicity for intended government action by about twenty or thirty young people who walked out during my speech. Their actions were, of course, premeditated and they were not to know the content of my announcement. The language needed all the friends it could get, and approval of actions has a cumulative effect. This was an 'own goal' for the protesters. My successors took over my proposed legistlation when they succeeded me.

I inherited an unfortunate situation as regards bilingual road signs. An inquiry conducted by Roderic Bowen QC, the former MP (Cardigan) into the need for bilingual road signs found that both languages should be exhibited. I welcomed this, but then had to face the thorny problem of the order of the languages. I attempted to look at the problem logically rather than emotionally.

I was an old transport minister and a former chairman of the National Road Safety Committee. The roads of Wales were used by Welsh and English speakers, including English and foreign tourists – and unless you are Chinese you read the words of a language beginning at the top, and not at the bottom. I could not for the life of me see how 'Danger' – understood by everyone – could not but be at the top. In terms of peace and quiet I had years to regret my decision as at every public activity I conducted I was accompanied by protesters. One thing I would not agree to was local option. If we were one nation then the same policy should prevail from one end of Wales to the other. My successors took a different view.

About this time British Rail asked for my advice as to how they should exhibit their station signs, announcements and timetables, I was quite frank with them, and told them I would have put Welsh first on my road signs, but for my belief of the importance of safety considerations. I would be more than happy if they put Welsh first everywhere. This still prevails, although I have noted recently some unhappiness from some of my newer and younger colleagues who have limited knowledge of what an earlier Labour government had advised. I am glad of the advice I tendered as it is in accord with my belief that both languages should be the norm, and that this aim should prevail throughout Wales.

The National Eisteddfod was close to my heart. My family, in a small way, had been involved in it for a long time and I attended many in my youth. I had indeed met my wife at the Llangefni Eisteddfod, more important to me than winning the chair or the crown! I was concerned by the accounts in the press of its financial difficulties. As it happened, Harold Wilson had circulated a paper entitled 'Little things go a long way' to his Cabinet ministers between the two elections of 1974. What he enjoined all of us to do was to put up proposals which would both be popular and not cost a lot of money. An election was not far off.

Harold came to Wales to speak at a Party meeting in Bangor and the following day he and I were to speak at a rally in Aberystwyth. He decided to travel from Bangor to Ceredigion that night for no other reason except that many, many years before, when cycling in Wales, he had slept particularly well in Devil's Bridge. Many from the police force in North Wales had to escort him half the night to Machynlleth where Dyfed Police picked him up and escorted him to Devil's Bridge.

The following morning I came up to escort him and Mary round the Devil's Bridge Falls. We talked of the numerous rumours about his health and he boasted about his ability to 'keep up with me'. He said, 'Every Cabinet minister should be tested by his ability to walk round the Devil's Bridge Falls as fast as the Prime Minister.' Harold, Mary and I chatted, accompanied only by one plain-clothes man and I thought it an ideal opportunity to mention what I had in mind about 'little things'. I had no departmental advice. I explained the National Eisteddfod's financial problems, owing to its peripatetic nature. 'I know all about it, I've been to Llangollen,' he said. I then explained that the National Eisteddfod was rather a different thing. After a few more words, he said, 'Yes, a good idea – it certainly falls within what I had in mind. How much do you want?' I said it's the first grant ever, they may be loath to take it but I think I can persuade them. He found not accepting money a difficult concept. I said, 'What I had in mind was £50,000 to £75,000.' He said, 'Don't put it too high, you know what the Treasury are like – they don't like to open a new page in the book on expenditure and the more you ask, the higher it will go and the greater the difficulty.' I took all this on board. 'What about £50,000?' I asked. 'Done!' was the Prime Ministerial reply as we brought this most expensive tour of the Devil's Bridge Falls for the government to an end. My varied ministerial experience meant I was far from innocent in knowing which buttons to press, and when – perhaps equally important.

I was due to preside at the Carmarthen Eisteddfod at the opening concert on the following Sunday night. I got a message to Norah Isaac, the local committee chairman, whom I knew from childhood and admired greatly as the headmistress of the first Welsh school in Aberystwyth, that I wanted to have a word with her and the Eisteddfod treasurer half an hour before the concert started. This would minimise the risk of a leak, and hopefully time to consider a refusal.

We met in her office at the Eisteddfod where I explained what I was minded to offer with the Prime Minister's approval. I genuinely had no idea what the reaction would be. My admiration for her soared when she immediately said yes; supported by the treasurer. As realists they really had no option, but in Wales you cannot always be sure that reality will prevail. It was the beginning of many years of financial support from governments and I was able to announce the breakthrough in my speech.

That week, as a new secretary of state, I moved my office to the Eisteddfod field and all who wanted to speak to me could do so for the whole week as I dealt with all my governmental business there. My wife and I hardly missed an Eisteddfod, but this year the children and Margaret were accompanied by Special Branch men, who doubled at other times as drugs investigators and were dressed accordingly in jeans, to the approval of my teenage daughters. But after a week of being too much in the public eye, one of them did eventually ask, 'When can we get back to normal?' That was the only time in six years they had to share a public presence with me, and we were only there as a family because Eisteddfod presence was natural to both my wife and me. I was quite upset sometime later when after taking my eldest daughter, Nia, to Jesus College, Oxford, the alma mater of so many Welshmen and women, I noticed a chalked note on a notice board, 'what about the 4th channel, John?' in Welsh as I left the college. She was entitled to her privacy, despite being a politician's daughter. I did not tell her what I had seen. I hoped and prayed that her university days would not be affected. No such problem arose when I took my second daughter, Non, to my old college in Cambridge with an exhibition, and by the time Elinor, my youngest, went to the Royal Welsh College of Music and Drama there was no problem. I was by then one of 'yesterday's men' in Wales.

When I took office, my advisers were split down the middle as to the desirability of an all-Welsh television channel. In general the more Welsh-speaking their roots, the more they were against it. I was very troubled. Quite a few, albeit a minority, of eminent Welshmen and women were against it, including the articulate Professor Jack L. Williams and the redoubtable Jennie Eirian Davies. I did not come to an immediate decision for a separate channel. What I was sure of was that the existing provision for the Welsh language was completely inadequate. I also knew that only a small minority of my constituents were Welsh speaking, and there was the factor that when people did tune in to an English broadcast, they did not immediately switch off if it was followed by a Welsh one. I knew because if I was on they commented on my appearance and many had the gist of what I had said. As a follower of rugby programmes I was conscious of the value of Welsh sports programmes and the growing excellence and professionalism of commentators.

It was only by a rigorous intellectual appraisal that I came down in favour of a separate channel. Since 1973 protests in favour of some kind of special provision had grown. By that time there was a majority in favour of a separate channel, and the Tory government had set up the Crawford Inquiry to investigate broadcasting in Scotland, Northern Ireland, Wales and rural England. Crawford wrote to Sir John Eden MP, the responsible minister, that the case for defending the language was 'compelling' and the fourth channel in Wales should be allocated to give priority to the Welsh language.

It proposed that the government should pay for such a channel and it should be run jointly by the BBC and the IBA. However this should not be done before paying for colour television technology; many parts of Wales were severely disadvantaged in this respect. My predecessor, Peter Thomas, agreed that colour television should have priority, and proposed that the Welsh Language Council should consider the Crawford Report. The Home Office shared this view.

Shortly after I took office I started writing to Roy Jenkins, whose Home Office now had responsibility for broadcasting, telling him the issue was especially sensitive in Wales and I was looking for Welsh representation on the proposed Annan Committee. Jenkins was sympathetic. I corresponded with him again in May, July and August 1974 and proposed that the government should set up a Welsh channel when the previously appointed Crawford Committee reported. I then had a face-to-face meeting with Jenkins in August and demanded a fourth Welsh television channel. I continued to bombard him, 'In the light of the overriding view in Wales on the one hand of the crisis of the Welsh language, and on the other, the increasing agitation of non-Welsh speakers on having Welsh programmes on existing channels'. By now Jenkins was unhelpful, stating how difficult it would be to justify a situation, 'in which two or three years from now there were four channels in Wales, but three for the rest of the United Kingdom'. In any case there was no question of taking a decision before the Crawford Committee's Report.

About the same time, on 27 August 1974, Robin Butler, the Prime Minister's private secretary, was writing on behalf of the PM to his counterpart in the Home Office to ask, 'Whether there is a case for considering some interim arrangement for Welsh language broadcasts, perhaps on the joint responsibility of the BBC and Independent Television, on the clear understanding that these should not prejudice any arrangements made in the light of Annan.' Butler received a cold reply. I had also raised this matter a few weeks earlier with Wilson during our journey around the Devil's Bridge Falls and it had borne fruit. The lesson from my previous ministerial experience is that if you have personal time with your boss, you must use it most advantageously and try to cover your mental agenda. Small talk is no compensation for big business.

In August and September John Harris, the broadcasting minister at the Home Office, Gregor MacKenzie, with the agreement of Tony 'Wedgie' Benn, his boss at industry and John Gilbert at the Treasury all weighed in against me. The DTI view was that it would be a huge waste of resources. With an election approaching I wrote to Wilson seeking clarification and asking whether we could say in the campaign, that if the Crawford Committee's report supports a fourth channel for programmes in Welsh, together with programmes in English of Welsh interest, we would be prepared to act upon their recommendations.

But Denis Healey, as Chancellor of the Exchequer, expressed his doubts about giving priority to the channel. In the face of both Home Office and Treasury objection, Butler wrote to me that Wilson agreed the government 'cannot at this stage commit itself to accepting whatever the Crawford Committee may recommend'.

In November 1974 Crawford reported supporting the Welsh channel, but making it clear that the priority was completing the technical provision. It was then proposed by the Home Office that the costs of the Welsh channel should be looked at in more detail as well as how the BBC and IBA could work together. Hence the Siberry Report. Unfortunately the January 1975 White Paper on Public Expenditure made it clear that additional monies would be needed to provide a fourth channel for Wales.

During 1975 the costs had escalated, both capital and running costs, and the BBC thought it could not be met out of the licence fee. Jenkins wrote to the Treasury that the Home Office could not meet costs out of their resources but that a decision not to proceed on the channel would obviously give some rise to objections, some of which 'may take violent form'. On my behalf my private secretary wrote agreeing 'that there may well be serious political consequences if the government does not allow the project to go ahead or if they delay their decision'.

At this stage, Willie Ross, the Scottish Secretary, always unhelpful to Wales, wrote that to allocate money to Welsh television would pinch money from the process needed to provide colour television in Scotland. Roy Jenkins and the Treasury agreed.

I met Roy Jenkins again in February 1976 to discuss the proposed announcement that there was no financial provision for the channel. I was not prepared to find the money and sacrifice my objectives of revitalising the Welsh economy as my resources were limited. It was like demanding a widow's ha'penny. A promise of reconsideration when public resources allowed was all I could get. I wrote to him six weeks later. As we were a small department I argued:

> I am very concerned about reports I am getting about the vitality of the Welsh language. Despite considerable expenditure on bilingual education and manful efforts by voluntary bodies such as *Urdd Gobaith Cymru*, the signs are that the language is inexorably continuing to lose ground to English, even in the Welsh-speaking areas. A decision to delay the fourth service indefinitely would I am sure be seen as a tacit acceptance on our part of the continuation of the process which can only end in the extinction of the language.

I pressed the Home Office to seek additional money from the Treasury, and a firm timetable by the end of the year, otherwise objections might take violent form, and used as a pretext for disorderly behaviour during the royal visit to Wales in 1977 during the Silver Jubilee. At the meeting with Roy Jenkins in February 1976 I had argued that if we could not implement the Siberry Report there should be a clear understanding to consider the channel in a year's time. I was trying at least to keep the door open. I felt like Atlas holding the world up!

At this stage I was beginning to reconsider my refusal to meet the Welsh Language Society. I agreed that my officials could meet their representatives and this occurred on 28 July 1976.

In correspondence in July 1976 the Home Office concluded that the Welsh Office would have to pay for the channel from its own budget and additionally it would be better to await Annan's recommendations. Another meeting took place with officials of the Welsh Language Society on 3 September 1976 where they threatened action if a decision was not taken by their AGM, and some activity of the kind threatened took place.

I had a further meeting with Jenkins in December 1976 when I forecast that law breaking and disorder would worsen, hence I had authorised the meeting with the society. Jenkins insisted we had to wait for the Annan Report, which was due to be published in February/March 1977. Things were obviously extremely difficult for me. The BBC, trying to be helpful, asked if they could make a start in particular parts of Wales to save money. I refused, as it would be contrary to Siberry, and in any case

I wanted an all-Wales solution which was my philosophic line for all Welsh developments.

In 1977 Roy Jenkins was replaced by my close friend, Merlyn Rees, but there was no change in the Home Office attitude, however he did agree on 22 February 1977 that the government was bound by its commitment to the channel. Shortly afterwards there was particularly bad news from the Treasury that no expenditure could take place for four years unless the Home Office or Welsh Office could find savings to provide for it.

Annan reported on 24 March 1977 and called for setting up the fourth channel in Wales, ahead of the rest of the United Kingdom, to be run at first jointly by the BBC and IBA. It was unclear how the channel would be financed in Wales. In May I asked the Welsh broadcasters to extend the number of hours of Welsh language television. I frequently referred to Jim Griffiths's favourite maxim – *Deuparth gwaith yw ei ddechrau* – half the work is to begin.

The economic situation had become extremely bleak. We were heading for confrontation with the IMF and the view of some of my officials was that it would be counter-productive to keep on bothering Merlyn Rees. I fear I could not agree and wrote to Merlyn on 12 July 1977 asking him to request a small sum of two to three million pounds to commence the work and to make it additional to his usual bid for resources. Merlyn's reply was disappointing. However, in private conversations he made sure I shared the internal thoughts of the Home Office. My officials had previously found it difficult to find out anything that was going on there. His private views were that he was anxious to help but was constrained by the whole problem of finance. The Home Office had its own priorities for the kind of resources it won from the Treasury.

I wrote again to him in October that I had received 'the most disturbing report prepared by the HM Inspector of Schools on Welsh in the primary schools of Gwynedd, Powys and Dyfed. The deterioration in areas which we have always regarded as bastions of the language is really quite frightening.' Again, I pressed for two to three million to be set aside to do the preparatory work for the channel. I continued the correspondence with him in November and December 1977. In retrospect I am rather sorry for him. I knew where his heart was, but my persistence was bordering on fantasy. I had come across the problem of 'persistent litigants' in the courts. No minister could have faced such a bombardment of letters, particularly when the recipient did not have the wherewithal to accommodate the petitioner. Looking back I find it difficult to understand how I had the gall to continue at the same level of persistence.

All this was carried on behind closed doors. In modern times there would have been regular briefings to the press from the importuning minister. There were none and I had to be reminded recently of the details and length of my campaign, through invaluable research done for a programme to celebrate the setting up of S4C. My private campaigning is a major illustration of my keeping a very low profile on my efforts for the language. Nothing in this context was to jeopardise my efforts, inadequate as they were, for a consensus on devolution. At least on the fourth channel there was apparent agreement – most Welsh speakers by now wanted special provision and non-Welsh speakers wanted Welsh removed from the main BBC (Wales) channel to another channel.

By June 1978 I was pressing for money for more programmes for children following the recommendation of the Siberry working party.

In July 1978 my persistence finally paid off. The government published its White Paper on Broadcasting in Wales and promised to start the fourth channel in Wales by October 1982. In October 1978 the Home Office, however, protested about my statement that we had agreed to 'finance the channel'. The promise was only to 'institute a channel' and if there were any problems I would have to explain myself to the Treasury.

From the correspondence there is an impression that I was beginning to weary in my somewhat repetitive campaign. I wrote again on in October 1978 to Merlyn Rees saying, 'For us to go into an election campaign with no progress being made even on the limited front of children's programmes was asking for trouble.'

I had a small victory by 28 November 1978 with a promise from HTV and BBC that they would improve the provision for children from August 1979.

By December 1978 we began to believe there was a 'jinx' on the channel when the Home Office discovered that the IBA did not have the legal authority to erect the necessary transmitters. This would need legislation and there was little parliamentary time before the impending election. Michael Foot, as Leader of the House, and the chief whip were made aware of the situation and were supportive. The two nationalist MPs were also helpful.

I pointed out the political embarrassment to Michael Foot and that I was 'deeply disturbed with the state of affairs'. It was getting very close to the line and to my huge pleasure the government announced before Christmas 1978 that it would introduce the necessary legislation so that the channel could begin to broadcast by October 1982. The government was as good as its word and in the dying days of the administration the Leader of the House, Michael Foot, and Michael Colks, the chief whip, announced it would find time for the bill.

On 6 March 1979 it fell to Merlyn Rees to move the second reading of the Independent Broadcasting Bill. It had a general purpose of permitting equipment to transmit for the whole country, but of course, a special one for Wales to permit broadcasting by the autumn of 1982.

When the Bill was passed I felt an immense sense of relief. All the meetings and correspondence since my earliest weeks in office had paid off. I had worried Home Secretaries year in, year out, like a Cardiganshire corgi.

We were now out of office, having done the necessary spade-work in the face of considerable odds. The next Conservative government went through some U-turns before eventually (after considerable agitation and, among other things, threats of irreversible and tragic action by Gwynfor Evans) taking the right decision to set up S4C. Lord Crickhowell recently commented in the presence of Lord Roberts of Conwy, his junior minister at the time in the House of Lords (26 January 2011, Col. 993) that the crucial moment in that particular consideration was not 'the actions of Mr Gwynfor Evans but a visit paid to Lord Whitelaw and himself by Lord Cledwyn of Penrhos, the then Archbishop of Wales and Sir Goronwy Daniel'.

As a sad postscript, in the autumn of 2007 S4C presented three flagship programmes to celebrate ten years of the Welsh Assembly. I was looking forward to seeing them. The second programme made me sit up in my chair as it had as its 'thesis' the suggestion that the government's legislative proposals in the devolution bills of the 1974–9 government were based on George Thomas's letter to Harold Wilson in August 1969. Until that time, I had not known of the letter and since I was steering my proposals through the government machinery, I knew that George Thomas's proposals, which I have set out and which were so different from ours, received no consideration by the new government.

The programme concluded:

If Margaret Thatcher is the mother of devolution, then constitutionally George Thomas is the father. Devolution is a bastard child and neither parent gave a damn for it.

I wrote to the chief executive of S4C, Mrs Iona Jones, to complain about the programme. It appeared that nine people with some involvement in devolution had been interviewed in the preparation for the programme, but .this particular 'thesis' was not put to any one of us. Had it been put to me I would have strongly refuted it. I found the failure to put this 'thesis' to any of those who had some knowledge incomprehensible. While contributors have every right to put forward their views, commissioning editors had a duty under Ofcom rules to ensure there is a balance.

I was rather innocent of the complaints procedure, never having complained about programmes on the media in fifty years of politics. The correspondence with the chief executive batted to and fro for six months. She rejected my complaint time after time and took no step either to acquaint me of the complaints procedure or herself refer my complaint to it. My requests to have the matter considered by the board were ignored. Eventually six months later, in March 2008, having just become acquainted then with the S4C procedure, I lodged my complaint with the S4C Board secretary. After nine reminders he made his adjudication in November 2008. The secretary upheld my complaints that there had been breaches of two of the rules of Ofcom's Broadcasting Code, which specified that alternative views to those put forward by the broadcasters should be adequately represented. Since I was responsible for the policies in Cabinet and introducing the bill to Parliament, 'I should have been given the opportunity to answer the criticisms' made about the origins of the Act and the form of executive devolution contained in it.

I had only been asked by the interviewer about matters regarding different views within the Labour Party. In summary, the secretary adjudicated that I had not been given an appropriate and timely opportunity to reply to the 'thesis' relating to the origin of the devolution settlement.

After further prodding, S4C agreed to, and did, broadcast on 12 May 2009 an on-screen apology to me for breaches of fairness in accordance with the Ofcom Broadcasting Code. In addition S4C agreed not to repeat the programme on any of its TV services in future.

The long saga from October 2007 had at last come to an end. I must say I was disappointed with the body that I am proud to have played a small part in setting up. I surmise that for a minor complaint the existing complaints machinery of S4C is probably adequate. In my case, I had a major complaint that took an extraordinarily long time to deal with, and I was pleased that the thrust of my complaints were eventually upheld, and with the agreement that the offending programme would not be shown again. Fortunately, I had the patience, resources and the skills of my former special adviser in the Welsh Office, by now Lord Prys-Davies, to continue my battle. After another long gap the then chairman at S4C, John Walter Jones, eventually wrote to say that 'all concerned are committed to ensuring that all complaints are dealt with thoroughly and effectively, and our procedures are formulated to ensure consistency in this respect'.

Many years before, I had come to the conclusion that radical changes were needed to make the programmes of S4C more attractive. I had met the former chairman and former chief executive to express my concerns about the quality of programmes on a typical evening, and I questioned whether there was over-reliance on too few people (although as individual actors, presenters and entertainers many were very good performers). S4C did some things particularly well, but other programmes might be less appealing. Perhaps the fault was mine, but I had made my views quite clear. Above all, I found the overwhelming dominance of sport (despite being an ardent rugby fan) on some evenings disturbing – my late mother would not have enjoyed such evenings without *some* non-sporting relief, and I suspect her interest in soccer matches in distant parts of Europe would be limited. Tragically, the latest viewing figures, if they are accurate, reflect the fears I expressed many years ago. It has to be recognized that a new factor in the totality of Welsh speakers is that many live in towns, and Wales in any event is no longer an agricultural country. If viewing figures are to recover, programmes must reflect current tastes.

At the time of writing, the Coalition Government has proposed new funding arrangements, quite contrary to the provisions of the existing statute, for S4C, which involve a considerable diminution in finance over the years. I deeply regret that our political leaders in Cardiff have not taken the initiative to obtain the transfer of responsibility for broadcasting in Welsh, with appropriate compensation, to the Welsh Assembly, as I proposed in my 2002 lecture at my initiation as Chancellor of Glamorgan University. There was total silence in Wales to my proposal.

In my two meetings with Whitehall ministers of the Coalition government, I have expressed my anxieties about the future of Welsh television on the fourth channel in the context of modern broadcasting. In my view, it should be made clear that clear guidelines are required about the role of the BBC and S4C in the new arrangements. The government say they wish to maintain the independence of S4C and, if this is so, I believe they should spell out how this can be achieved. The licence money does not come from the BBC, but from those who pay for their television licences. The government should therefore pay whatever money is appropriate directly to S4C and not via the BBC. In view of the required timescale to review the BBC Charter, work should now commence on clearly setting out the role of S4C in charter form or equivalent.

I would be more confident then of the future of Welsh language television, and to justify the continued effectiveness of whatever small part I may have played in its creation.

twenty-one
PREPARING TO BE
A LAW OFFICER

T HE ROLE OF ATTORNEY GENERAL is unique in government and has been written about extensively, though not always understood. The Attorney General is at the same time a government minister and collectively responsible for government policies, its chief legal adviser and yet independent as a prosecutor, either directly or by supervising prosecuting authorities. The office holder is the guardian of the public interest to Parliament.

Contrary to the statement by Gordon Brown when he was Prime Minister, the Attorney General does not actually take a decision to prosecute unless bound by statute to do so, where there is a duty to do so the AG will authorise prosecutions – but only then. This duty covers everything from authorising war crimes prosecutions to prosecuting purveyors of cancer treatment under an Act passed in the heady days of 1939.

It was a bit of a mess and towards the end of my period as Attorney General I was preparing to clear it up. It needed legislation. The best time to get a slot was at the beginning of a Parliament when other departments are not ready with bills. I took advantage of this lacuna on another occasion and introduced a bill in 1997 and carried it through in all its Commons stages in about nine minutes, allowing the Solicitor General to do whatever the Attorney could. Their functions then became wholly interchangeable.

It had been my ambition to be a law officer since I entered Parliament, and possibly before. I remember being asked about my future hopes by the mayor of Port Talbot in the course of the 1964 election campaign. She was mildly surprised by the answer that I wanted to be a Law Officer.

Later, in 1974 I had asked Harold Wilson for the post of Solicitor General, should we form a government. I had already been a senior minister of state at defence and although some might have thought the Solicitor General's post a downgrade, or at least a sideways promotion, I would have been delighted.

It was not to be; to my astonishment I found myself in cabinet. It would be another twenty-three years before I fulfilled my ambition. I have said, and it is sometimes repeated to me, as I told a Sunday newspaper soon after being elected in 1959, that I was a barrister first and a politician second. I only wish I had had more time to hone my skills as a barrister. A circus artist would probably tell you that riding two horses is not without its difficulties.

The loss of meaningful experience, quite apart from the financial loss during those gap years from the bar while being a minister, is immeasurable. Your contemporaries will have made immense strides, your solicitors will have forgotten you, and your craft will have changed considerably. The years can never be fully made up. That is why, based on experience, I would counsel against such trick riding.

The electorate sacked us in 1970 and I returned to the bar, having been away doing three ministerial jobs in turn. My chambers were busy, and my clerk, Stanley, although he did not really like politicians as they were not totally under his command, gave me plenty of work. After one or two initial hestiations, I was kept busy. Stanley worked me hard throughout the whole of July and then, complete novice that I was, I hired a caravan for a month to travel to France, Italy, Austria and Belgium with my family. If restarting as a junior was not without problems, how much worse was it in 1979 and now in silk, with every judge and colleague watching my every step, or so I thought?

As I have said, I took silk in 1973 but with hindsight it was a mistake given the political events that followed. Once again, I had been a young man in a hurry. I was forty-two. It had not crossed my mind that within a little over a year we would win another election and I would be away again for six years.

Coming back in 1979 was sheer hell. Having no practice, few skills and experience only in the distant past, mainly of junior work, did little to counteract the daily fear of making major errors, or even small ones, as a silk. The learning curve was steep. Each day had new terrors and the going was slow.

I had been warned by two old friends in chambers that there was a dearth of work. The amount of work available can be cyclical; this was a low point, and we had excellent and more experienced silks in chambers.

After my return in 1979, there were periods when I was uncharacteristically despondent at the slow build-up of my practice. I well remember a walk in the woods with Margaret when we contemplated alternatives.

My biggest dread was death by a thousand cuts, passing the years on the circuit bench. I already was doing more sitting as a part-time judge than was required as an assistant recorder and then a recorder. A fortnight's sitting was as much as I could stand. The expected month's sitting at one go was never attempted; fortunately there was a monthly cheque from the Commons.

It took about three to four years to build up substantial regular work. Somehow or other work did come in from my own chambers, where I had a few contacts, and totally unexpectedly from another chambers in 3 Hare Court. The steady growth of work from Hare Court forced me to consider my position when I was involved in a long multi-handed case involving silver bullion in Lewes, in which some members of those chambers were counsel for the co-defendants. Approaches had been made to me earlier, but I had more or less declined, or at least showed a lack of enthusiasm. In those days, one did not readily move chambers. At least I was not a mover in search of greener grass elsewhere.

Hare Court was a fairly recently formed chambers that had attracted one silk, a fellow Welshman, Michael Lewis, QC, to head it. Work from Hare Court was increasing as well as from my own chambers. I dealt with thefts of large quantities of tea in East Anglia and then lorry loads of bananas – silver bullion from lead processing was a welcome change in commodities at least. I have fond recollections of defending one of the oldest of armed robbers to appear at the Old Bailey, one of the last to serve hard labour, when he suddenly said in cross-examination, 'OK gov'ner, I done it.' Consternation all round. The sentencing judge dealt with him saying, 'You and I have spent our life in crime, on opposite corners of the ring.' He left the court saying, 'If you can't do time, don't do crime'.

When the offer of moving chambers was re-put, it was done over lunch on the terrace at Garthwen, our home, on the only fine day in August that summer. The weather was a good omen. I decided I would move after Christmas, having spent twenty-three years at 5 Kings Bench Walk. It was the beginning of a long and happy relationship.

I had earlier taken an important decision as to my political role. To the surprise of Jim Callaghan, I decided not to continue dealing with Welsh affairs as shadow secretary of state in 1979. I had done six years in the Welsh Office and I had no more to offer at that stage. I had come up against a solid wall. I could see continual involvement in Welsh affairs with a never-ending series of delegations as well as leading the opposition politically in Wales unattractive. It would be a rehashing of what I had been doing for six years. It would also divert me from my aim of being a law officer. It would however, after six years in Cabinet, be a major, almost unheard-of departure from what might have been expected of a career politician. With so little to offer Wales at that moment, I took the view that my desperate need for physical and mental rest must come first.

A political shadow office would not make it easy to build up a practice. To abandon a 'political ministerial career' was to be one of the most important decisions of my life. Never again, particularly if we were a long time in opposition, which I envisaged, would I be considered for a senior political portfolio. My wife and family had hardly seen me for six years. My girls had grown up almost in my absence. I hope they will remember how August was always a sacred month to renew our acquaintanceship, a time when I tried to make up for the rest of the year.

I asked Jim Callaghan for, and got, the job of shadow Attorney General, a post I was to hold with only a small break for eighteen long years – I suspect this is unequalled, because of our failure to win elections. I wanted to get back into the law so that when we took office I could fulfil my ambition, although I reckoned this might take many years.

It was Michael Foot who interrupted my tenure of the shadow job between about 1981–3. I had understood that there was no tradition of the shadow Attorney General standing for election to the shadow Cabinet. I did once, and did not do well. My colleagues did not take kindly to a part-time MP as a shadow Cabinet minister. I agreed with them. Neither would I.

Peter Archer, who had been Solicitor General and was my deputy, won a place on the shadow Cabinet. Shadow posts were shared out, it seemed, on the basis of how well one had done in the 'beauty contest' of shadow Cabinet elections. Reg Prentice, later to desert to the Tories, came top of the poll about this time. To my surprise, perhaps it shouldn't have been, my post was given to Peter. I had earlier committed the apparently unforgivable sin of telling a parliamentary party meeting in about 1981 that neither Michael Foot, our leader, nor Denis Healey, my former boss, could win a general election, such as was the fragmented state of the party. I was interviewed regarding my speech for the main six o'clock BBC news that night, and since the only leader was Michael, I must have been asked point-blank whether it was true that I had said in the party meeting that morning that Michael could not win an election. I must have confirmed this, which was unwise. The fact that I had also included Denis Healey in my speech at the meeting did not count.

Probably Michael's friends and family were highly aggrieved by my unacceptable frankness. That was my strong suspicion. So it was not surprising that at the earliest convenient opportunity I was dropped from a great height. Michael telephoned me and I believe indicated in a roundabout way that something else might be found for me later.

There I was, having been a cabinet minister for six years, with my political prospects dashed, and my resumed practice at the same time still struggling. It would have been easier to take if I had really got going again at the bar, but the years of ministerial absence could not be overcome as speedily as I had hoped; two years later it would not have mattered so much.

Worse was to come. The following year I did not stand for the shadow cabinet. Peter Archer was re-elected and on the basis of a better vote, given the job of shadow Northern Ireland secretary. I had hoped that my sins would have been forgiven, and that I would resume my duties as shadow Attorney General.

Instead, to my great surprise, the job of shadow Attorney was given to another of my friends and a member of my legal team, Arthur Davidson, QC. I wrote to Michael reminding him of what I had understood to be a promise, or at least a clear indication that I would be considered for a post. He wrote back a most contrite letter saying that he had forgotten my availability. It was a curious letter but I reminded myself, 'Put not your faith in princes'. I felt sad because Michael and I had worked so closely on devolution and on the closure and part-closure of Ebbw Vale. I really had done a lot to save his bacon because it was said, scandalously, in Ebbw Vale that the works would not have been closed if Nye had been there. This was, of course, nonsense, but it was the talk on the street. In later years, Ebbw Vale, one of the strongest of our strongholds has proved its volatility.

I've already said how, as Welsh Secretary, I and my ministers put an enormous effort into to minimising the damage in Ebbw Vale, and one of us tried to be there once a month – I did a lot of travelling there myself and took the planning decision for a substantial new industrial area on the Rassau Estate, in the teeth of an adverse inspector's report. I was much criticised by the Conservatives – they staged an almost-without-precedent debate on it in the early hours of the morning – but I felt confident that I was right to reject the inspector's report which advocated piece-meal development. The area was crying out for substantial industrial expansion on a significantly large site.

It was no comfort for me that the next election under Michael was one of our biggest disasters both nationally and for me personally in Aberavon. Nearly 15,000 people voted Conservative or Liberal and my majority came down to 15,539. For quite a hard-working MP – at least in my own estimation – this was a blow. It was my only bad result.

The years in opposition were hopeless for Wales. I saw the ravages of Thatcherism, with neo-colonial governors from England running Welsh affairs. At least Nicholas Edwards had good Welsh roots and was committed to doing what he could within his remit. He understood some of our problems and was ably assisted by Wyn Roberts, who was always the bridesmaid at re-shuffles, never given the top job. So far as the Welsh language was concerned, he did a great deal, and deserved all praise for it.

The arrival of Keith Joseph in charge of industry and eventually, the final insult of John Redwood as Welsh Secretary, paved the way for recognition in Wales of the need for a change in the political system of government. It was said of Redwood, I hope not unfairly, that he sent unspent money back to the Treasury. Wales at that time, with coal and steel closures, was on its knees. The timing of his arrival and his actions was most unfortunate. He was an extremely bad choice as secretary of state; fighting for Wales and Welsh interests was not his forte. Yet when I went to him with a problem arising in West Glamorgan, he listened and indeed, for whatever reason, acted correctly, to my satisfaction.

The job of shadow Attorney General was not heavy. There were Parliamentary Questions once a month and any late night adjournment debate was handled by my deputy. If a bill came along, like the Contempt Bill, I returned all work for the duration. Of course, returning a good brief which would have run for some six weeks was a blow, but my clerk took it on the chin. However, this is what I was in politics for; this was the priority for me and there were many other opportunities later for reasonably heavy work to make up for it.

Over a total of eighteen years I was able, with the help since 1986 of the best clerk in the Temple for criminal work, John Grimmer, to build up a substantial practice in all aspects of crime. Professionally, they were the best years of my life. I was of good standing and now I was a criminal law specialist, increasingly prepared for high legal office in Parliament. It was, however, at an immense physical cost. My day started at 6 a.m. preparing for that day's witnesses at 10 a.m. The day in court was followed by my duties in the House – particularly in the lobby and occasionally advising colleagues with problems concerning bills and sometimes the constituency problems of MPs. I was always on call and always made myself available. When I wasn't doing such work I could work in my room preparing for the next day in court. I was usually home before 11 p.m. Looking back I am astounded that I kept going.

Malcolm, my agent, would ring up with any constituency problem before 9 a.m. and Margaret held the fort with the media, but it needed a lot of extra effort on my return after a hard day in court to agree to give a Welsh broadcast around 5–6 p.m. Huw Edwards, then a young BBC reporter, would stop me in the corridor and ask so charmingly for yet another broadcast in English or Welsh, as the case might be; usually both, one following the other, that is was hard to refuse. We were, in my younger days, desperately short of Welsh-speaking MPs and, tired as I was, I felt duty-bound to do much more than my expected stint for the language. I never refused.

At the Bar one has quickly to become an expert in a particular field for each case, and usually that expertise is rarely needed again. Stolen bananas, tea bags or lead – all these cases took many weeks, sometimes months to resolve. Murders, rapes and long VAT and mortgage fraud trials were also common. They all demanded detailed knowledge, and long weekends studying dozens of lever-arch files were commonplace.

The Broadwater Farm case and an important paedophile case at the Old Bailey were significant cases. I was fortunate that I was only involved in two paedophile cases in all my time at the Bar; they were not pleasant. I remember telling the new Archbishop of Canterbury, Dr Rowan Williams, when he came to give a lecture at the University of Glamorgan many years later, that the cases prosecuted were only the tip of the iceberg and that the problem was much more widespread than what appeared in the public eye. I was very troubled by this and remain so.

The great advantage of the criminal Bar, coupled with my constituency surgery, was that you had a never-ending fount of knowledge about what was happening at grass-roots level, albeit on either the murkier or the most vulnerable level of society. I had a real job, although only part-time, and my mind was constantly replenished by knowledge of people's problems. I became deeply aware of the growth and activities and deprivation of an underclass during a murder case I did at Stafford and cases at the Old Bailey increased, regrettably, my knowledge of problems which were all too often below the radar screen of most people. I knew them better than many.

When Neil Kinnock reappointed me to the front bench, for which I was very grateful, the shadow Cabinet frequently threw any unresolved matters which arose at their weekly meetings to the shadow Attorney General to advise on by the following Wednesday. It could become a hectic weekend for me and my slim support legal team. One instance I thought I could not deal with in this way was a proposal put to the shadow Cabinet to cancel the Channel Tunnel. The tunnel was already being built and the shadow Cabinet wanted to know what might be the measure of our compensation to the French. I had quite vivid memories of an earlier proposal in Cabinet to cancel Concorde, of the advice of Elwyn Jones, then Attorney General, and Tony Wedgwood Benn's vehement defence of the project – he was a Bristol MP where part of Concorde was being built. I went up to Cambridge to seek advice from Sir David Williams (a contemporary and then Master of Wolfson College), who directed me to another eminent don, an international lawyer, Christopher Greenwood (now a judge at the International Court in the Hague), who wrote a valuable opinion. I showed this to the shadow Cabinet and that was the end of the topic. It was a cul-de-sac that had caused me to make a substantial effort.

The other issue which sticks out in my mind was advice given on the constitutional duty of the Queen if the Prime Minister sought a dissolution of Parliament after winning an election but with an unsatisfactory majority. They wanted to know whether the Prime Minister could demand a second dissolution. After again consulting widely in Cambridge, I advised this would not be correct. I judged that the proper course in the event of a hung Parliament after an election would be for the Prime Minister not to ask for a second dissolution and, if he did ask, it would be proper for it to be refused. Sir William Wade, the eminent constitutional lawyer and former Master of my college, wrote that unless there was a genuine chance of the Prime Minister putting together a coalition 'he had no business to ask for a dissolution'. The Leader of the Opposition, commanding the support of a substantial number of Members of the House of Commons, should be given the opportunity of forming a government. Where a Prime Minister had been in office for some months since the previous election and had been defeated on an issue of confidence, he or she would have the choice between resigning or seeking a dissolution.

Neil Kinnock was obviously deeply concerned in the run-up to the 1992 election, but even so I was a little surprised when Charles Clarke, his political adviser, rang me up on the afternoon of election day to go through my written advice.

Another interesting request from Neil was for myself and Paul Boateng MP to visit South Africa, at a time when Mandela had only been partially released. We saw many of the leaders of the African movement, but although progress was being made it was difficult to form a view as to at what speed it would finally succeed, and when. It was a worthwhile experience and I wrote a report on it for Neil.

Elections came and went and my assumption that we were in for a long haul in opposition turned out to be too true. Nineteen ninety-two was the year of great disappointment. Losing, undeservedly in my view, to John Major was a bad result. I had had some hopes in 1987. I had just joined Hare Court and was leading a particularly busy junior in my new chambers, Bill Clegg, in a case in Winchester – it was a charge of persuading gullible old ladies to part with large sums of money for replacing a few tiles: they were quite tragic cases. The 1987 election was approaching and I was doubtful about taking the case, although it was only for a few weeks. I had a firm assurance from my clerk that Bill would not leave me during the case. With this cast-iron assurance, and my clerk's anxiety to please this particular solicitor, I took it on. Within a day or so, I had a message in Waterloo Station that Bill would not be with me; he had gone down with acute appendicitis. I was reminded of Robbie Burns's lines about the 'plans of mice and men often gang astray'. Then an election was called! I carried on, and Bill returned far too early from his hospital bed. I wrote my election address during the judge's summing up, and it was all the better for that.

Come about 1995, the Labour Party seemed to be becoming electable, but with a series of national election disasters behind us I was far from sure of the future. What if we lost in 1997? I would be sixty-five plus and my hopes of re-entering Cabinet in the event of victory would be nil. There were plenty of new young giants striding across Labour's political stage. I and one or two others were part of the 'lost generation' whose last ministerial experience was in 1979. I told my agent that I would probably retire at the election, but not to tell anyone until the final decision had been reached.

After a few months I asked to see Tony Blair. He was surprised at my frame of mind and assured me that the job of Attorney General was mine. He made it clear to me that he wanted me to do the job for 'about a couple of years'. I said I would like to do it; it had always been my ambition and it would help if he gave an indication that, short of me committing rape or murder, the job would be mine. He laughed and referred to a story in the same vein concerning Mark Twain, who had said that the only thing that could stand in his way was being found in bed with two small boys. I thanked him and told him that I would put the machinery of my proposed retirement into reverse. That was our only contact at the time and probably, with one exception, the only conversation I had had with him. Hence I remember it well.

The other conversation had been when he was appointed shadow Home Secretary a few years earlier. Unlike the Tories, Labour's shadow home secretaries used to hog all the quasi-legal work to themselves. My relations with Gerald Kaufman and Roy Hattersley as shadow Home Secretaries were 'proper' but distant. They regarded the shadow Attorney General as the fifth wheel of the coach. With the promotion of Tony Blair to the job, I hoped for better things, so I went to see him.

It was an interesting conversation. He did not show much interest in the law and in what I did. I told him, as I had told John Smith previously, of the desperate need for competent and experienced lawyers in the House, who could serve as the Solicitor General when the time came. He confessed he had never addressed an English jury in his life; he was a commercial lawyer. He agreed to do better and work with me, and presumably to consult from time to time. It never happened. Some of the blame for this is, of course, at my door, as anything other than a modest increase in my parliamentary duties would have interfered with my rapidly growing practice at the Bar, so I did not complain.

Against this background I had one of the biggest shocks of my life when, after dealing with Attorney General's questions one day, I was walking from the chamber rather pleased with myself, and Nick Brown, our Chief Whip, signalled that he wished to see me. He said he had been given a list of about six members who would be offered peerages if we won the election and I think that I was top of the list. I explained to him that quite a few months previously I had discussed the possibility with Tony Blair of my being Attorney General in the next Labour government and that Blair had agreed enthusiastically I should do the job.

Nick was a good friend of mine; he had been given his first job on the opposition front bench as my deputy. Now he was nonplussed. He had, I understood, been given the list by Sally Morgan, one of the Prime Minister's political advisers. He was rather thrown by his encounter with me, the first of his candidates for ermine. 'This is too big for me to handle,' he said. 'You'll have to see the boss.'

I immediately rang Blair's office for an urgent appointment. I went home to dig out a copy of the letter I had sent to Tony immediately after our earlier discussion about the Attorney General post, and I returned to the House. I told him the sequence of events that day, my recollection of our earlier conversation and how I had put off my retirement. Blair showed little, if any, knowledge of the background to the day's events and expressed himself completely surprised that I had been approached. To my immense relief, he also expressed his strong wish that I should be his Attorney General and that I should put any thought of retiring out of my mind.

I soldiered on until the election drew near and, as it approached, I refused all but short cases. I hardly ever left a case I had started and had no wish to be in that position. In the immediate run-up I successfully defended three fairly short alleged rape cases of about two to three weeks each. The difficulty of getting a conviction in a rape case where the defence is consent has, over the years, left a strong mark on me. These cases are usually just one word against another and any fragment of supporting evidence to undermine consent is invaluable. They are so very different to an allegation of rape by a stranger. When I eventually became Attorney General I challenged the CPS as to why my junior, as defence counsel, was paid more than their prosecutor. I advised that they pay prosecutors better in cases where it was difficult to get a conviction and so attract more senior and experienced prosecutors in the hope of getting a higher number of convictions.

The general election was eventually called in 1997. What a night! Not only was Labour electable, but as the results came tumbling out, like pennies from a slot machine in a never-ending cascade, we were overwhelmingly elected. I watched the results in a corner room as my ballot papers were being counted. The count at Aberavon is a seemly affair. My agents always took the view that if there was any dispute about a parliamentary vote we would give way. Given my majorities, it was not really a great act of generosity but common sense.

The usual experience, as I watched every ballot box being counted with eagle eyes, was for my supporters to come to me with snippets of news of some disaster or triumph. The futures of friends and opponents were whispered to me. This time a small room had been acquired for us, so sweet triumphs were enjoyed in abundance. My result was declared: a majority of 21,571, a swing to me of 2.7 per cent and 71.32 per cent of the vote. Despite our triumph I was a little sad that this eleventh contest was to be my last. I thanked the returning officer and all who had taken part. There was never a note of triumphalism or dismay in those eleven speeches I had made over the years; I always put on a good suit, a white shirt and a sombre tie. I was yet again the Member of Parliament for Aberavon, aged sixty-five and ready for office as Attorney General.

twenty-two
APPOINTED ATTORNEY GENERAL

WHEN MY WIFE AND I came back to London the day after the election in 1997, Tony Blair was summoned to the Palace, invited by the Queen to form a government and kissed hands as her Prime Minister. What a relief! It felt like the end of the long march in China, after all we had been in the wilderness for eighteen years.

I was full of expectations, but nothing happened. No call from Number 10. How different from 1964, when Elwyn Jones was one of the first called, to be appointed Attorney General. It may be because Harold Wilson had urgent Rhodesian problems and needed the Attorney's advice. I had to know my place; the Attorney General was low down in the government's political batting order, though of Cabinet rank and paid marginally more than a cabinet minister!

Saturday no news. Sunday the same. Monday no news; I was getting more than a bit concerned. Had the Prime Minister gone back on his promise? When I contacted an old friend whom I thought must know, I was told I was marked down as the Attorney General and I was slightly re-assured. If you touch the right button, there is always somebody who will be able to tell you things in politics.

Eventually Blair rang me. No explanation, no apologies. How different from my former Prime Ministers. Despite the age gap, I seemed so much closer to them, and so it turned out. I suppose there was a reverse age gap here but I could always talk to both Harold and Jim. They were generous with their time and understood whatever concerns I had, and there were not many. I had grown up politically with them and for that reason they wanted to know my judgments.

During the whole period I was in Tony Blair's government my only meeting with him outside Cabinet committees was when I was summoned to Number 10 together with Jack Straw as Home Secretary to discuss crime.

It was one of those 'sofa' meetings, where the three of us sat on a sofa or easy chairs. I have forgotten the precise point that was being discussed, but it was crime generally and prosecution.

I raised the question of reoffending. As a criminal practitioner and particularly as a sentencing recorder since the early 1970s, I was all too familiar with the problem of recidivists. I have always felt over my years at the criminal bar how inadequate was the training, education and frequency of psychological and medical help for prisoners. They were too often let out of prison or institutions with hardly any support. Unless they were fortunate to have maintained contact with their families, the temptation to reoffend was strong. I am not an expert on prisoner care, but from my side of the fence I knew, and still know, that something is very wrong. A little more money for, and better organisation of, the probation service, as well as facilities such as educational and medical services in prison, would be a good investment. As a judge I relied heavily on pre-sentence reports and the effort the probation service and colleagues put into them.

I touched on these matters with Tony. I knew it was a major problem. Tony was obviously not properly briefed on reoffending, if at all. I would not damn him by saying he was not interested – nobody had told him. It was not a problem he had put his mind to and I fear he looked through me when I raised the point. I am sure, giving him the benefit of the doubt, he was not bored, but he gave a very good impression of it. I felt like a visiting Martian.

But to go back to my long weekend. Apparently Charlie Falconer, who was unknown to me and had been Blair's flatmate, was to be my Solicitor General. However, he had gone away with his family for the weekend and had either left no telephone number or given the wrong one, hence the delay in the legal appointments. Why I had to wait, anxiously, continues to baffle me, although when I mentioned Blair's promise, to him, Charlie had a bemused look on his face. Had there been more than one promise? 'Put not your faith in princes!'

When I was finally appointed I immediately went over to 9 Buckingham Gate, the Attorney General's chambers, where I was met by David Seymour, the legal secretary, and head of the department. He had come in from the country every day over the May Bank holiday and had waited and waited, spending a long and lonely weekend in an empty building. At least I had had my family with me. I am sure the civil service was as unimpressed as I was.

As I walked up the stairs to my magnificent room, albeit oddly furnished with off-white leather sofas, I was, despite the trauma of the weekend, quite elated. Photographs and prints of my predecessors lined the stairs, among them one of Margaret's collateral ancestors of the Christmas Evans family – the Baptist divine, Sir Samuel Evans, who had been Solicitor General during the First World War. I recalled seeing a plaque to him in one of the workingmen's halls he had opened in my constituency, part of which straddled his.

David Seymour and I had a long and detailed discussion of the problems that would face me, and I told him what I was minded to do. He was ever-willing and enthusiastic. It seemed as if I had known him for years. Over the next day or so I met most of the staff. I had done this kind of interviewing, entering a new department and seeing senior staff over a couple of days, four times before on taking up a new office and I regret to say, despite the best endeavours of the staff, not all the briefing always sunk in immediately. I think I was given a hefty 'bible' of notes to take home. I was only dimly aware of the totality of my new responsibilities.

In addition to being HM Attorney General for England and Wales I discovered I had another job – quite separate – as Attorney General for Northern Ireland, with the cessation, temporarily I hoped, of a devolved administration there.

One lawyer had been at Buckingham Gate much longer than the others I met, Stephen Wooler, the second-in-command. He had originated from the CPS, but so wide were his duties he seemed almost irreplaceable. His throughput could only be explained by my suspicion that there was just a touch of the workaholic about him. I hardly ever drove to Wales at the weekend without a call from him on my mobile with some urgent business that could not wait. I had to explain this on one occasion to the police when I had pulled off the motorway. I was delighted when we carried a bill towards the end of my service which eventually, among other things, created for him the post of Her Majesty's Chief Inspector of the CPS, a post which has since been expanded. Undoubtedly horses for courses.

The senior lawyers were very hard worked, hence after a period it was necessary for them to move on. One never knew when the Attorney would be called to advise, frequently at short notice. I was to enjoy an extremely happy relationship with David, Stephen and all of them.

At my pre-election meeting with future senior advisers I had met Dame Barbara Mills, the Director of the Public Prosecutions. I knew her from her days in practice at the criminal bar, and I had appeared in some criminal trials with her, particularly the Broadwater Farm case, where she had appeared for one of the defendants, Silcott, and I for another, a Turkish man named Engin Raghip. When she came to see me, I believe she was armed with some figures and statistics about the CPS success story. I listened. It hardly tallied with the general impression the public, the profession and

I had of a service struggling to keep its head above water and subjected to a daily barrage of criticism from the press.

She was rather astounded and a look of horror crossed her face when I explained that I intended to have a full inquiry under a senior judge into the organisation and workings of the CPS. She nearly fell off her chair. She had not kept her ears close to the political ground. The interview did not go on for long after this. Obviously, from what I said it was the worst-case scenario for her and her organisation. We parted pleasantly, but I could see that she was deeply disturbed.

In my first discussion with David Seymour I explained my intention of setting up an inquiry into the CPS. This was to dominate my time as Attorney General. If I did nothing else, I put into place the machinery to identify the case for major changes within the CPS and, within the time given to me, got on with it.

There was considerable public concern about the workings of the CPS. The *Daily Mail*, among many other newspapers, was repeatedly putting the spotlight, not always fairly, on its errors and its workings, and all too often, both before and after the election they concentrated on its head, Dame Barbara Mills. There was the constant rumble of their guns, but they were not the only ones. I knew from my own experience that things were not right and most days in court would be reminded of this by colleagues at the Bar and in the judiciary, when I sat as a recorder.

The CPS had been set up by the Conservatives to take over most pros-ecutions from the existing Director of Public Prosecutions – previously quite a small office dealing only with the most important cases – some high street solicitors and police forces' prosecuting departments. The quality of these organisations had varied wildly and there was no con-sistent approach. When the original DPP department had been involved, the work was of very high quality. To receive a brief from the DPP was a pleasure. Everything was beautifully prepared and no stone was left unturned. Regrettably, little of this template had been carried through to the CPS run by the DPP. It was a very large and underfunded organisation. Basically, the Conservatives had nationalised most prosecutions and had failed to learn from the experience of other nationalised industries with their patchy record. They had failed to provide it with enough money, as both I and Nick Brown, who was my deputy on the front bench, warned at the time in debates in the House.

'Something must be done,' as the young king, Edward VIII, said famously on his visit to the depressed areas of South Wales in 1937.

The Labour manifesto had promised to reform the CPS to get more con-victions, adding:

> There is strong evidence that the CPS is over-centralised, bureau-cratic and inefficient, with cases too often dropped, delayed or downgraded to lesser offences. Labour will decentralise the CPS, with local crown prosecutors cooperating more effectively with local police forces.

I had some difficulty with my colleagues in getting agreement to what I thought needed to be done. Derry Irving, the Lord Chancellor, was not too concerned and was helpful. Paul Boateng, who was sometimes involved as a shadow junior Home Office spokesman, was more concerned with the accountability of the police, and Jack Straw, hummed and hawed. Jack seemed to be subject to persuasion by his advisers. His knowledge of practice was from a very long time ago, he had left the Bar after a short time to work for ministers, which was the Bar's loss. His experience was from a period before the creation of the CPS so he only had hearsay knowledge of the state it was in, but this was helpful in so far as it supported my own views.

I thought, after many meetings, we had got agreement to a document to be published and the basis of words to be put in the manifesto, and I went away on a delegation to Taiwan. I was absolutely flabbergasted to be faxed a document that had only a limited resemblance to what had been agreed upon. Many of the agreed points had been overturned. I faxed back about forty amendments, almost all, if not all of which were eventually agreed upon. The process of getting agreement did not augur well for work-ing together after the election. It is of the utmost importance when you battle with your own department and with colleagues, and particularly the Treasury, to have a manifesto commitment. Once elected, I moved quickly to set up an inquiry to fulfil the manifesto commitment and did so in June 1997, although Jack Straw jumped the gun by announcing it at a police superintendents' conference a few days sooner. Not a very joined-up gov-ernment approach. It was rather naughty.

We appointed ex-Lord Justice The Rt Hon Sir Ian Glidewell, whom I knew a little of as Treasurer of Gray's Inn, to be the chairman, along with recently retired Chief Constable Sir Geoffrey Dear, and Robert McFarland, a former chief executive in industry. It was a formidable team and they were asked to examine the structure, organisation and policies of the CPS including the role of its headquarters. The inquiry was also asked to look at whether the CPS had contributed to the falling conviction rate; the downgrading of charges and at its relationship with the police.

The report, which ran to 216 pages took nearly a year, much longer than expected and was delivered to me on 1 May 1998. It concluded that:

It was necessary to define more clearly the proper relationship between the three main agencies in the criminal system – the police, the CPS and the courts.

It also recommended forty-two 'areas' for the CPS, roughly in line with police areas at the time. It said:

> First, the CPS needs to give greater priority to the more serious cases. Secondly, it must have a new organisation, structure and style of management. Thirdly, it needs to establish firmly its proper role in the criminal justice process.
>
> If our recommendations are adopted, the staff of the CPS at all levels must accept the desirability of and understand the aims of these changes. New working practices and a new culture will be necessary if the CPS is to thrive and finds its rightful role in the criminal justice system.

The report was both clear and damning. It found establishing the facts on discontinuance and downgrading of offences daunting. They found it necessary to define more clearly the proper relationship and responsibilities of the main agencies of the criminal justice system. The aims and concerns of my colleagues and I in drafting our part of the manifesto were thoroughly vindicated. I duly presented the report to Parliament where it was well received.

The inquiry tried but failed to find an explanation for the disparity between the statistics supplied by the CPS and the judicial statistics for the number of convictions for recorded crime. The report recommended that the court service and the CPS should achieve agreement on counting statistics as soon as possible.

It was obvious to me as the evidence unfolded that there had to be, in addition to the organisational changes, a fresh start at the top and a new DPP at a convenient time. Drawing on previous experience replacing the Wales Tourist Board Chairman, and mindful of the considerable adverse publicity that Michael Howard had in dealing with his head of the Prison Service, I was determined to ensure the necessary changes were made as smoothly as possible.

In the meantime the courts had criticised the CPS severely in judicial reviews, for their decisions not to prosecute in three cases that had arisen from the deaths of prisoners in custody. Barbara Mills was not too happy with the idea of another inquiry, but accepted it was inevitable. The report of ex-Judge Butler was extremely critical. The three cases in question belonged to the central casework unit of the CPS. Butler found that the system employed by central casework to arrive at a decision as to whether or not to prosecute was 'inefficient and fundamentally unsound'. He found that the judicial review proceedings in the case of two of the deaths were 'dealt with in an unsatisfactory manner by the CPS'.

The central casework unit was one of the most important parts of the DPP's responsibilities and was found to be wanting. One of the basic problems in one case was who had taken the decision not to prosecute. The publication of this report immediately would have undermined the DPP considerably. It was important to me that, whatever my intentions, I should not undermine her while in post. I told her at some social occasion in the AG's chambers that I would not be publishing for the moment. I wanted the Glidewell Inquiry to proceed to its full conclusion and hopefully, she would see that a new start was necessary. There were bigger fish to fry and the Butler Inquiry was an untimely but necessary interruption.

She subsequently tendered her resignation to take place in a few months' time and I attended her farewell party in the Middle Temple. I believe I was rather gracious in my thanks to her and bought her a coffee-table book of paintings by one of my favourite Welsh artists, Sir Kyffin Williams.

The truth of the matter was that the CPS was a difficult horse for anyone to ride and not all the problems which beset the CPS were of its own making. The proper boundaries between the CPS and the courts had not been appropriately delineated and, as the report said, 'Other agencies had not made the space for it to assume its full role.' Any lawyer without adequate administrative experience would have had a grim battle; Barbara was a distinguished criminal practitioner. When the time came to appoint a successor I put in as well a senior administrator from the Civil Service who, with the DPP, would report to me.

Open advertisements were placed and a head hunter engaged, as is now customary. I was receiving messages from the direction of Number 10, and the Cabinet secretary, Sir Richard Wilson, rang me up to inquire whether I would be happy to work with whoever was eventually favoured. It was my appointment by statute, but obviously I needed to take fully into account whatever views emanated from the centre and apparently Sir Richard came to see me.

Eventually, after these discussions, I was delighted to appoint David Calvert-Smith, now Mr Justice Calvert-Smith. I knew that I was in good hands with him. I had crossed swords with him many times at the Old Bailey when he, as Senior Treasury Counsel, had prosecuted some of my clients. He was fair, industrious and extremely well thought of by the Bar.

He, too, lacked much administrative experience, but I had met that problem by the appointment of an up-and-coming civil servant as an administrator.

In successfully completing the Glidewell Inquiry and appointing a new DPP a great weight was lifted from my shoulders. There would obviously be a need for more good work in future, but the new foundations had been laid. It had taken the lion's share of my time, but I knew that it was only the beginning.

One of the tricky issues which occurred early on in my tenure was the arrest of the Home Secretary's son for allegedly selling cannabis to a journalist. Jack Straw was an old friend and rang me up one evening in the recess feeling a bit helpless like any concerned parent. He inquired about legal advice and whether there had to be publicity about the matter. I suggested that Bindmans would be the firm to handle it. Geoffrey, now Sir Geoffrey Bindman, had wide experience of public affairs and would be very wise. I said I had not been in a juvenile court since my early days at the Bar, but my wife was a juvenile magistrate of many years' experience and my clear recollection was that the proceedings would not be in public. I said that from my considerable experience in dealing with adults I had many, many times seen a press prohibition order posted on the door of the court for proper reasons. There were clear rules on this. That was the end of the conversation, apart from expressing my sympathies. I had a clear impression there would be no publicity and presumably told him so. Juvenile courts sat in private. I sensed relief on his part.

There was, in fairness to Jack and myself, no other conversation between us on the matter. I had put him on his way to getting legal advice and he rightly assumed I had no further appropriate role. As a father and grandfather, my sympathies were very real.

A little later, it being Christmas, I was driving to the Hackney Empire to take some of my grandchildren to the pantomime on a Saturday afternoon when I had a call from Stephen Wooler. The impression is frequently conveyed that Her Majesty's Attorney General takes his important decisions at leisure, surrounded by a cohort of advisers, in oak-panelled rooms or the like. However, I was driving my car and Wooler wanted an urgent, immediate decision. To my surprise he mentioned Jack Straw's son. The press had got hold of the story and wanted to run it the following day. Would I agree to apply for an injunction to stop publication at this late hour before the presses started running? He explained that I would only be doing what I might do for any juvenile if it were to come to my notice.

The application would be based on the Contempt of Court Act (1981). It would be founded on the argument that there would be prejudice to any proceedings brought as prior publication of the name would set at nought the statutory anonymity to which the juvenile would have been entitled under the Children & Young Persons Act 1933, as amended, for a juvenile who had been charged or summonsed (although in this case no decision had been taken).

My advisers and I would focus on the wider point which was of general application. It would not have been right for any juvenile (William Straw or not) to be named prior to charge so that the statute was effectively overridden.

Even as I drove to the theatre, Wooler was grappling with the issue, having been telephoned by Jack Straw's private secretary on Boxing Day. He had been liaising with the solicitors throughout the following day and was receiving updates about what was running in Fleet Street.

I had no direct experience of taking such action. All I had was a firm recollection of the notices I had seen outside courts on innumerable occasions. I relied on Stephen's advice and undoubted experience. It had nothing to do with the juvenile in question, save that there would have been little or no press interest had it been Johnny Jones's son at No 27 Blankshire Street. I agreed to the application being made. I drove on and the injunction was granted by the duty judge. I can't say I enjoyed the pantomime; I kept hearkening back to my interrupted journey. In the event, nothing was printed in the newspapers.

The situation unfortunately developed in an unexpected way in the next few days. The news of the arrest, I believe, appeared in the French newspapers. I would never learn who leaked the story but the French newspapers were being sold in the streets of London. The news was broadcast on continental radio. It may have been on the internet. There was no means of stopping that. The law had not anticipated this development. We had not applied to have an injunction in the Scottish courts against Scottish newspapers, as Scotland has a separate jurisdiction and it has always been the case that restrictions there were of no effect south of the border. They were on sale in England, carrying the story. The situation was becoming very difficult as the dam was bursting all over the place and there was the inevitable further application before the duty judge to lift the injunction.

My officials had sought urgent advice – what a Christmas! Philip Havers, son of Michael Havers, my old chambers contemporary, usually did contempt cases for the AG's office and I had continued the practice. As Havers was away, we initially took advice from another of the AG's panel and made the application on his advice. Collectively we took the view that the status quo had to be maintained until the court ordered otherwise, as well they might in a fast-developing situation. Charlie Falconer was on holiday in the Caribbean and I had his agreement on the phone. Two minds were better than one. But

I did miss having a conversation in depth with him, when all the nuances could have been explored. The clock was ticking. We agreed that young Straw would be treated like any other juvenile. 'Stand by the status quo until ordered otherwise,' were the instructions to Havers, who was racing up from his home in Canterbury to appear on my behalf late that afternoon.

What we did not know was the attitude of the defendant himself (he was about seventeen years old) or even of his father. Sitting in my chambers on that weekend while the court was being convened I did not, rightly or wrongly, feel it appropriate to contact him and he did not contact me. It was some relief to know that Bindmans, who appeared for young Straw, also opposed in court the lifting of the injunction. I could only guess as to what instructions they had, or was Geoffrey Bindman, or his associates, acting, like we were, on his own instinct and professional feeling?

When the matter came for hearing a second time, the injunction was lifted, which in all the circumstances was right at that stage. With hindsight, and more time we should have considered in greater depth the lifting of our objection.

On New Year's Eve, while driving with my wife to see friends on the south coast, I was extremely surprised to hear on the news that the family had always wanted the ban lifted. This was news to me, since I had not spoken to anyone after my initial conversation after the arrest. Whether anyone had been in touch with Bindmans, who had been engaged to act for the boy, I did not know. Certainly the attitude of Bindmans in court, I was told, was clear and unequivocal. I have never had an explanation of the family's position. It was a strange episode and an illustration of how, despite your best endeavours, a situation can blow up in your face. I suppose the AG is always a useful fall guy.

I was almost equally surprised at the press reports of my intervention on the Land Mines Convention issue. HRH Princess Diana had campaigned and raised international concern at the use of landmines and the appalling human tragedies that could follow. There was an expectation, or at least a considerable feeling, that the convention banning their use, which had been agreed in Ottawa, should be ratified by the Government by September 1998, the anniversary of the Princess's death. The ban would then have full legal effect.

The Foreign and Commonwealth Office were getting quite a lot of stick in the press for the many months of delay. They defended themselves by saying the law officers had to be consulted and made it clear apparently, in their press briefings that the law officers were to blame. Newspapers followed the FCO briefing and blamed the AG.

There was indeed a tricky and novel legal problem to be solved. Fortunately my legal advisers came up with a solution overnight. It broke new ground, which I found attractive, and agreed to, despite its legal novelty: it met the needs of the situation. We had turned the whole problem round and given our helpful decision within about thirty-six hours. Blaming the law officers was quite uncalled for. Had they asked for advice earlier and not sat on the problem I suspect they would have avoided the criticism which had been levied at them. When I spoke afterwards to a leading political correspondent who had printed the story, and told him that the delay had been in fact the FCO's and that we had turned it round in thirty-six hours, he commented that he would never trust Foreign Office briefings again.

Under the Prime Ministerial code any minister who wants to take personal legal action, particularly for libel, has to consult the law officers. There are good reasons for this; political, personal and ministerial interests are frequently intertwined, but I did not expect when I entered the AG's chambers that I would shortly have a long queue of ministers, some seven to nine, who in the flush of the excitement of winning the election wanted to sue someone. My advice to all of them was to think carefully, and remember that they might have to consider their ministerial positions if they sued, as it could turn out to be too time-consuming to launch a libel action and devote time to their ministerial duties. Not surprisingly in the event none of them resorted to the courts.

Stephen Richards was my treasury common law counsel but was promoted to High Court Bench. Charlie Falconer had wide experience of the civil courts and its practitioners which I did not have. I relied on him as he would know most of them. I asked him to find a replacement for Stephen. The name he recommended was of a young man named Philip Sales. Not unexpectedly, given that my experience was solely at the criminal Bar, I had never heard of him. I believe Charlie had consulted Derry Irving who thought very highly of him (he was from Derry's chambers, and so knew him well). I accepted the advice and sent for Sales. When I saw him I made it clear that though I had received advice, it was my decision and I was pleased to offer him the appointment, which he accepted. He is now a High Court Judge.

Unfortunately two lady barristers decided to sue me for unlawful discrimination on gender grounds. In fact, neither had been on my radar screen. I was looking for somebody with a particular and wide experience in public law, and despite his youth, from what I was told, I had every expectation that Sales would deliver.

The hearing was fixed for Croydon in midsummer and I was the defendant. This was a real pain as about three to four weeks had to be set aside for me to be available to take part in the proceedings, although my expectation was that my evidence in chief would of necessity be quite short. What would happen thereafter was not in my hands. Given the enormous amount of work that we had in the law officers' department, it was a burden I could do without.

No man should be his own lawyer, and I sought the best advice. Three QCs were consulted on various aspects of the case. The view taken was that we were in unusual and relatively uncharted territory and it was not possible to predict with certainty what might happen during a three-week trial at the Croydon employment tribunal. Despite my firm belief that one was not comparing like with like in Sales and the disappointed barristers, I was becoming less and less enthusiastic at the prospect of wasting my time on what to me was a peripheral issue. It had not crossed my mind to exercise any prejudice.

Doubts began to emerge at the breadth of the work Charlie had done in preparing his recommendation. He had chosen a good candidate, but did he have the evidence to justify his choice? What did other practitioners and judges think? His witness statement set out the consultations he had undertaken. I believe the Lord Chancellor had a somewhat similar action against him at the time.

In the run up to the hearing, I examined in more detail the soundings Charlie had done and my doubts of success at the hearing increased. I finally consulted counsel again and the advice I received made me more wary. I instructed my staff to see if I could settle the case on appropriate terms, as it was becoming a real nuisance, and I just could not see how I could afford the time for the distraction. The throughput of work in the AG's office was formidable, making it virtually impossible to be away from my desk for any length of time. The plaintiffs proved amenable and the terms of the settlement were agreed on 11 June 1999.

In fact, since July 1998 all appointments to act as counsel to the Attorney, including the first junior counsel to the treasury, which was the post in dispute, had been by transparent and open competition. In the terms of the settlement, I stated that I did not accept the applicant – the lady barrister who sued me – or any other prospective appointee had in fact been subjected to discrimination. Nevertheless I readily accepted that it was unsatisfactory system until I had changed it in 1998. Although several women barristers had been appointed to the supplementary panels as standing counsel to other departments, only one had been appointed to the main chancery and common law panels of treasury counsel. Informal consultation may have a tendency to result in the recommendation of people known personally to the consultees and the purpose of the new system that I had set up was to end such consultation. I recognised that the system of appointments which was previously in place may have contributed to the under-representation of women on the main panels. In recognition of this, I agreed to make a donation of £5,000 to the Fawcett Society.

The applicants withdrew both their claims, in each case with no order as to costs.

When Derry Irving heard of our intention to settle, I believe he was incandescent, or so my staff informed me. The deadline for agreeing was fast approaching, on a Friday afternoon. I was content to dispose of the case. I told my staff I was just not available for further representations from anyone. I had done the equivalent of 'gone fishing'. I heard no more.

It illustrates that the Attorney General, however able he may be, cannot be a master of all the 'trades' demanded of his office. He was to rely on the advice of others, so wide are his responsibilities, and then reach his own judgment. Long before the settlement I had set up a review, under my new Solicitor General, Ross Cranston, into the appointment of counsel to do government work. The Solicitor General, the treasury solicitor and David Seymour, my legal secretary, worked out a scheme for those wishing to be on the list of counsel for government work, and they had to apply to be on it. There would be open advertisements as has now become customary for public appointments and, where necessary, an interview procedure. It was hoped to end any suggestion of cronyism, the wink and the nod, and the alleged favouritism for some chambers. There was some whining on the way, but I was anxious to pursue a policy of transparency in this field. After all, they would be highly prized and lucrative appointments, and there would hopefully be no more litigation.

My real regret was that I was not able to go on more occasions such as the War Crimes case into court as Attorney. I found that the combination of the Glidewell report and Kosovo just left me without the time and energy to do more. I suppose I had grown up in a field where for the duration of a case my mind was fairly exclusively on that. The daily issues of the Attorney's life as the government's chief legal adviser took too much time for me to be able to spend a lot more in the courts. The lesson of Michael Havers, when Attorney General, going to the Old Bailey to prosecute and intending to accept a plea of 'diminished responsibility' from the Yorkshire Ripper, only to have it turned down by the trial judge, whereupon Michael was stuck with a full-blown trial of many weeks, was always in my mind.

I did lead in a difficult four-or-five-day human rights case in the House of Lords, but after opening the case and replying to the Law Lords' questions, the rest of the work was done by my counsel, David Pannick, QC, (later Lord Pannick), although I would return to court whenever I had a little time to follow the argument.

Cases in Strasbourg were quite easy as they only took a day. An expert junior would prepare the argument for me, after initially consulting with me in my chambers on the line to take. I believe I was limited to about half an hour's speech. There was no questioning by the huge bench. There was no interchange between bench and counsel and I found it very unsatisfactory, although I enjoyed the limited challenge. It was not the kind of advocacy I was used to.

I knew, in accordance with the indication given to me well before the election by Tony Blair that my time in office was not unlimited. I was thinking my departure would come sometime in 1999 and my promise of the office was on the basis of a 'couple of years'. By July I had served about two and a quarter years. In July 1999 I was suddenly sent for. There was to be a ministerial re-shuffle and I was called from home to come and see the Prime Minister. He was very kind, as I would expect, and told me that he 'had nothing against me', but he had to make room for younger people coming up. Of course I did not argue and I immediately suggested that I would send a letter of resignation indicating my retirement as soon as I got home, which I did. A warm reply followed.

Gareth Williams, then in a junior post in the Home Office, was appointed to the job and I wished him well. The circumstances of his interest in the job I don't know, but he had left the Bar some years before and was without either chambers or clerk – an essential for an attorney. John Grimmer, my clerk, generously agreed to continue to act in the meantime.

I did not want to be bothered by the press, so my wife and I left on the ferry for a short, much-needed holiday in Brittany. Curiously, my private secretary and his wife were on the same boat.

After a couple of days my daughter, Elinor, who was then my secretary, rang to ask me to ring Downing Street to speak to Jonathan Powell, the Prime Minister's chief of staff. I rang and he said that the Prime Minister was minded to recommend a knighthood for me. I was delighted to accept.

Letters of good wishes came from all sorts of people; the one I valued the most, putting me on a very high plane as Attorney General was from the treasury solicitor, Sir Anthony Hammond. All I had tried to do was to do the job without fear or favour. We had worked well together and I valued his judgement and advice. I hope I had maintained the tradition of the independence of the Attorney General's role, particularly on Kosovo, which I surmise had not endeared me to the centre!

When the House returned it took some weeks for the knighthood to be gazetted and one of my young colleagues, Gareth Thomas, MP for West Clwyd, asked me what kind of knighthood I had, whereupon I replied it was the usual kind for Attorney Generals and high court judges – a knight bachelor. His slightly cynical comment amused me greatly, 'Oh, a bog-standard knighthood'.

Above: TAKING
CONSTITUENTS
AROUND HOUSE
OF COMMONS,
*c.*1970

Right: TAKING SILK
IN 1973

Above: CABINET OF THE WILSON GOVERNMENT, *c.*1974

Top right: DECLARATION OF ELECTION RESULT FOR ABERAVON, 1974

Bottom right: ALL FIVE SECRETARIES OF STATE FOR WALES TOGETHER IN 1974–5

Top left: PRINCE CHARLES VISITING ST JOHN'S PIT, BRIDGEND, 1976

Bottom left: WITH PRIME MINISTER JAMES CALLAGHAN AT CYNHEIDRE COLLIERY, 1976

Below: WITH PRIME MINISTER JAMES CALLAGHAN AT THE WELSH OFFICE, EASTER 1976

Above: AT PORT TALBOT STEEL WORKS WITH SIR BRIAN MOFFATT, MD, c.1990

Right: WITH GRANDSON HARRY ON THE WAY TO BE SWORN IN AS ATTORNEY GENERAL, 1997, WITH SOLICITOR GENERAL LORD FALCONER

Above: WITH HM THE
QUEEN AND LORD
ELIS-THOMAS AT THE
WELSH ASSEMBLY, 1999

Right: GARTER CEREMONY,
2003, WITH MARGARET

twenty-three
KOSOVO

THE TEN-WEEK WAR IN KOSOVO dominated that period of my time as Attorney. It is important to spell out what my role was. It was not unlike that of my predecessors who had had to make similar assessments regarding our earliest involvement in Iraq and I followed their decisions, as to what actions we could take in the absence of Security Council resolutions, closely. It is important to spell out the decisions that were taken and the limitations imposed on the government's activities. I would be loath to do so ordinarily, but so much has been said and written, that the history of events should be set out in the public interest.

Over the years there have been a number of occasions when the Law Officers' advice to Government has been revealed. Edwards, on 'The Attorney General, Politics & The Public Interest', quotes some instances: 'These comparatively recent precedents certainly fall within the flexible role governing the confidentiality of the Law Officers' opinions. Talk of an absolute prohibition against such disclosure is totally unsupportable.' He comments in this context that 'the readiness to disclose . . . must enhance those independent qualities of their offices'.

Nevertheless, I approached the question of referring to my role in Kosovo very carefully. Why should I deal in this book with my part in history nearly 12 years later?

First of all, as I will shortly set out, the impression has been created either by ministerial statements or briefing apparently from Number 10 that I, as Law Officer, had agreed all the bombing targets. This was not true, as events unfolded. Whenever I am asked about my role as Attorney in the bombing, I explain that every target passed my desk and my advice was sought on the requests of the military. To that extent the statements are true. However, I did not agree with them all and, eventually, towards the end of the war I refused my consent – and it is right that this is known. I believe it to be in the public interest and in accordance with Edwards's precept.

Secondly, the Cabinet secretary Sir Gus O'Donnell, on the issue of the Attorney General Lord Goldsmith's advice to the government, has stated, 'I have considered the matter carefully and believe that, given the very exceptional nature of the Iraq Inquiry, this particular material can be disclosed without prejudice . . . to the convention in relation to the Law Officers' advice'.

One of the unintended consequences of this decision was that repeatedly in the evidence my role in Kosovo was referred to, as was also my apparent role in the drafting of earlier United Nations Resolutions 1154 and 1205. I suspect there are other instances in the evidence of references to me. The basis of the long standing 'convention' regarding the standard of 'an arguable case' has been referred to and I have been quoted as precedents in this and other respects such as the revival argument.

I developed the distinct doctrine for the legal basis without a Security Council Resolution for action to avert an overwhelming humanitarian catastrophe. The late Lord Bingham of Cornhill, in his book *The Rule of Law* states 'that the doctrine of overwhelming humanitarian catastrophe is controversial' and that the revival argument, although it had been consistently supported by British Law Officers and had been endorsed by the Secretary-General of the United Nations in 1993 and by the Legal Adviser to the United Nations, had been questioned by such eminent lawyers as the late Lord Alexander, QC of Weedon, and by Professors Sands, QC and Professor Lowe, both experts in international law. I refer to Professor Christine Gray, who dealt exhaustively with the subject in her book, *International Law and the Use of Force*.

Towards the end of this chapter, since the doctrine is likely to remain controversial, it is in the public interest for me to explain how I arrived at that decision in the same way as Lord Goldsmith has been permitted to explain his decisions.

In order to try to meet reservations expressed on behalf of the Cabinet Office, I have done my utmost over a long period to limit my observations to the bare minimum. Hence I have now drafted this chapter for the purposes of the present book in a narrative form, setting out the story but deleting specific documents in which my actual advice was tendered. I have further shorn this chapter of a considerable amount of detail to come some way to meet the concerns of the present Attorney General.

For most of my time as Attorney, I was fortunate not to have my name in the newspapers. I was advised early on by my officials that if I made news as Attorney General it was probably a bad thing. If I was out of the news, I was probably doing well. I sought to respect this advice. It was sound.

It was therefore of some surprise to me to read a report of a speech that George Robertson, the Secretary of State for Defence, had made during the Kosovo Campaign in Bonn, Germany, justifying our actions in Kosovo. My recollection is that he said all the UK's activities had to pass the scrutiny of the Attorney General, and therefore all that was being done was legal on the advice of the Attorney General and complied with the Geneva Conventions. The surprise to me was that he had made this speech in public. I fully understood why the badge of the law officer's approval was most useful. The public use of it was rather new to me, and was contrary to standard practice regarding the publication of a law officer's advice. However the position has now been transformed by the publication of Lord Goldsmith's view on Iraq and by his evidence and that of my former legal adviser before the Chilcot Inquiry.

About the time of George Robertson's speech, I read a report in London's *Evening Standard* as a result, apparently, of a briefing from Number 10 to the same effect, that all our actions had the approval of the Attorney General and that he, the Attorney, had satisfied himself of their legality.

As history unfolded, it was not the whole story as it eventually transpired. It was not quite as simple as that, and therefore it is useful and right that I should explain what happened and how decisions were actually taken, and the limits on the government's action. The limitations are important, as are the restraints imposed, otherwise those who might be interested could form an inaccurate picture.

The Labour government from 1997, apart from during the two world wars, was probably one of the most warlike of modern world governments and it did not take much for troops to be sent to any part of the globe. There have been five major interventions by the UK since the Labour government was formed in May 1997. In 1998 bombing in Iraq; 1999 Kosovo; 2000 Sierra Leone; 2001 Afghanistan and the Iraq invasion of 2003.

We had a Prime Minister in Tony Blair who was ready to commit British troops with a frequency unparalleled in modern times. He seemed to revel in interventionism – hardly an apprenticeship to be a world peacemaker, despite his enormous success in Northern Ireland, particularly the Good Friday Agreement in 1998. He and Sir John Major before him had invested an enormous amount of prime ministerial time to Northern Ireland's problems. Apart from Robin Cook in the Iraq War, no significant member of the Cabinet demurred consistently at that time. I suspect that this had something to do with the fact that none of my colleagues then, or since, had any military experience whatsoever.

Mine was only briefly as a National Serviceman, but I had lived in the officers' mess in the Welch Regiment after their return from the Far East and had long and earnest conversations with battle-scarred senior NCOs who had recently served in Korea, including a senior subaltern with a Military Cross and another soldier with a Military Medal. I had missed Korea by a hair's breadth as I had completed my university education before doing my National Service. But I had smelt a little of the fear and atmosphere of war and I was instinctively against jeopardising lives. It was reflected in my immense caution in decision making in this field. My earlier experience as a defence minister during the conflict in Nigeria still weighed on me.

As ministers we are obliged under domestic law and the ministerial code to obey international law; likewise servicemen and civil servants. Hence ministers are always anxious to get legal cover. This is where the law officers' views were of vital importance. They try to give an objective and accurate view of our legal duties and obligations.

The Geneva Conventions and their protocols were our guidelines and they, many years after their ratification, were still sound. Consideration should however be given to whether they could do with some updating to meet modern conditions of waging war.

I never attended Cabinet as Attorney General. I frequently attended many Cabinet committees, particularly on the issue of Kosovo, where I or my Solicitor General would turn up, frequently at short notice, if a meeting was called in Number 10.

During the whole of my involvement with Kosovo I never had a personal meeting with Tony Blair. The contact was solely at the above committees or by correspondence. It was an 'arm's length' relationship between the Prime Minister and his principal legal adviser. This to me, as the months went on, was an astonishing state of affairs. The same aura exudes from Lord Goldsmith's evidence to the Chilcot Inquiry. I found this odd.

On one occasion in Cabinet committee, Tony Blair almost questioned my presence and role. I was a little taken aback, and at the next meeting I took care to spell out exactly what my and our obligations were. After all, I had been summoned by the Cabinet Office secretariat to attend – I had not just turned up. He never seemed eager to invite me to speak, but that did not inhibit me when I felt it necessary.

I had, in addition to attending these 'war cabinet' meetings, a close personal relationship with the Ministry of Defence on a day-to-day basis. It was of some help in understanding their needs that I had been a middle-ranking defence minister in the 1960s. It was the Ministry of Defence particularly who wanted the security of my legal advice. They had their own in-house lawyers, and they worked with Foreign Office lawyers too but more often than not they wanted my personal advice. Perhaps I spoilt them with my ready availability. There was legal advice in the interpretation of the rules of engagement available in the field to all commanders, and if any difficulty arose it would undoubtedly have been referred to me.

In every significant instance the rules of engagement for both big operations and also for smaller deployments had to be approved. On one occasion I was summoned back from a legal conference in Sweden to advise the trade department. No part of the earth was too far to get at me. They wanted me back in the Attorney General's chambers.

The Kosovo campaign, involving air strikes, aged me a little I believe. I was never actually conscious when my hair turned white, but I am sure it was greyer at the end of the sixty-eight-day Kosovo campaign than it was at the beginning. I was either in London or at the end of the telephone for every one of those days, save for just a few hours when I attended a college function in Aberystwyth.

The problem arose from the need to authorise all targets of any significance in a war carried out from the air. The targeting had to be in accord with our Geneva Convention obligations. There had to be minimal civilian damage or loss of life, and the least disturbance to ancient monuments and the like. Our actions had to be proportionate. Each case had to be decided on its merits and, of course, other countries were involved as it was a NATO operation. This applied to the use of British forces or British bases used by allies.

There was undoubtedly a degree of subjectivity in decision making, but all it needed was a lot of common sense, adherence to principles and proportionality as a key issue. It was not too demanding intellectually; right and wrong, with some effort and study, could be distinguished. While it was a nuisance to the military that lawyers had to be consulted, the wiser heads preferred, nevertheless, to have firm legal advice behind them. Illegality could be punished by the courts and in the future by the International Criminal Court, for which I and our government had pushed so hard – we were entering a new field.

Over that period the military, usually headed by an air force officer of the rank of group captain and then air commodore, I believe, accompanied by his lawyer, came along with a folder of targets, photographs and maps. They quite soon came to know my ways and each case was meticulously prepared, for they knew that there would be a detailed investigation by lawyers. All the material put before my lawyers and I would be examined with great care, and if it was deficient more would be demanded

If a more senior rank was fielded, like an Air Marshall, then we instinctively knew that they must think they were on weaker ground. Life at the criminal Bar was of some help in scrutinising motives; if you are briefed as a silk in the magistrates' court, they are usually doubly wary. I was immune to bluster; I wanted the facts from whatever source they could provide. They soon learnt to tailor their requests to meet our wishes.

The military frequently came in the late afternoon, or evening, for a decision to bomb that very night. I surmised that we could not trust some of our allies from leaking had a decision been taken earlier in the day to bomb a particular area. I guessed some countries were the weaker sisters in our enterprise.

Sunday night at my home was a favourite time for them to arrive. I could not be more fortunate than to have my own lawyer, Iain MacLeod, a Foreign Office secondment, at my shoulder at all times. He would hurry over from his home in south-west London. He worked extremely hard in giving me detailed and invaluable advice on each and every application.

On the rare occasions when I was not in the Attorney General's chambers or in my London home, we had to consult by phone. To maintain some degree of security (encrypted mobile phones were not available at that time), he and I had agreed on cards numbered A, B, C and 1, 2, 3 etc. representing the essential factors. Relying on his assessment of the grade the target was in, I could quickly understand what was being proposed on the telephone and give my decision. There were not many occasions when I was unable to have a face-to-face meeting with the MOD, Iain and others. In fact they were very rare. The card machinery was devised for the exceptional occasions when I was home in Wales or in my constituency.

The legal basis for armed intervention in the air strikes in Kosovo was not without its complications. Article 2 (4) of the UN Charter prohibits the intentional use of force except for self-defence, or with the authority of the Security Council. During my time circumstances prevailed when it was impossible to get a necessary resolution from the Security Council to allow the use of force in a particular circumstance.

The United Nations Charter forbids the use of force unless there is a decision of the Security Council or in self-defence. Self-defence, of course, is subject to many interpretations. Broadly it is not too difficult to identify actions in self-defence, though one can enter into difficult waters when steps are taken in anticipation of action by another country by way of self-defence. There was no decision of the Security Council expressly authorising the use of force in relation to the situation in Kosovo.

My Conservative predecessors had to consider whether force could be used by the United Kingdom on humanitarian grounds in 'Iraq One'. I believed, like them, that circumstances had become much more demanding than the founding fathers of the UN could have anticipated. The only clear basis for armed intervention, apart from self-defence, was a resolution of the UN Security Council. The principal resolution relevant to Kosovo was

Resolution 1199 (1998). This did not authorise the use of force, indeed paragraph sixteen stated that the Security Council would consider 'further action and additional measures to maintain or restore peace and stability in the region'. It seemed to all of us that it would not be possible to get a clear and unambiguous resolution from the Security Council in the future on this issue because of the attitude of the Russians and their bond with the Serbs.

Like Lord Goldsmith much later, I had reviewed the advice given by my predecessors in 1991 and 1996 on Iraq. They had concluded on the particular facts before them that there was a respectable argument to justify the use of force on the grounds of an overwhelming necessity to avoid a humanitarian disaster.

'No-fly' zones for Saddam Hussein's aircraft had been set up to prevent Saddam from murdering the Kurdish population in the north, and the Marsh Arabs in the south. The same principles were applied in Kosovo to prevent Milosevic from murdering and forcibly evicting thousands of Kosovars in his ethnic-cleansing campaign.

The principles we adopted in Kosovo were the same as those relied upon earlier in Iraq by my predecessors.

There was ample objective and independent evidence of that need in Kosovo, from the reports of the UN Commission on Human Rights and from statements and resolutions of the Security Council, in particular Resolution 1199 (1998), and statements of the President of the Security Council on the issue in late 1998 and early 1999. The first condition which I have set out had been clearly met, in my firm view.

Whether the second condition – that there was no practicable alternative to the use of force – was satisfied, was largely a diplomatic and military judgment. My colleagues were convinced of this, and although I was not a policymaker I saw no reason to dissent from this in view of the evidence known to me. The UK was not alone in forming this view. One problem was that we were breaking new ground in one respect, compared to what we had done in Iraq. We were going further. Our actions in Iraq could be described as 'passive'. In Kosovo what was being proposed was undoubtedly 'pro-active'.

It was particularly important to emphasise the third condition for action, that the proposed use of force was the minimum necessary to achieve our objectives.

My colleagues in the foreign and defence secretariats were approaching the whole situation with great care. There had been a good deal of coming and going between my lawyer, the Foreign office lawyers and lawyers at the Ministry of Defence. In furthering the emerging consensus it was clear at all times that any targets proposed would have to be considered carefully.

It seemed to me that pleasing the Americans, or at least keeping in step with them, was far too often uppermost in the mind of the Prime Minister and his small circle of advisers in Number 10 headed by a Foreign Office diplomat. I suspect the reception that my lawyer, Iain MacLeod, sometimes got there could only be described as frosty. Whether he was always invited to all these meetings at Number 10 I shall never know. The curious thing was that the actual presence of other Foreign Office lawyers in my chambers was infrequent. It seemed to me that their top lawyer, Sir Franklin Berman, QC, was frequently away in foreign parts. I did send for him from time to time and when I did he was very helpful. What was important was to get it right and if the issue was looked at later, we had to be confident that we had adopted the right legal position and that we could defend it with confidence.

What is surprising, given the accidents and catastrophes that occur in war, was that we could not be blamed for them. I believe our 'hands on' policy paid immense dividends in that we were not blamed for any catastrophes.

Frequently the nub of our problem was that some of our targets in Kosovo had a dual use, such as roads or rail used to carry troops and also civilians. We had to estimate the extent of civilian traffic and reach a decision as best we could as to whether it was within the letter and spirit of Geneva, so as to minimise civilian casualties. I was fortunate that I had no knowledge of the American decision to bomb what turned out to be the Chinese Embassy. This was a huge blunder occasioned by faulty and out-of-date maps, which did not show accurately where the embassy was. The result was that the bombing was followed by highly vocal Chinese protests; they had a major grievance. It was about this time the bombing of a hotel which was used in part by the Yugoslavian secret police was authorised by me. In retrospect it was too close for comfort.

Many years later, after I had ceased to be in the Commons, I was visiting NATO headquarters in Brussels to listen to a briefing by the NATO Supreme Commander. He mentioned the UK's part in the Kosovo war. He was a deputy commander of NATO at the time and said, not knowing of my presence, how the Americans appreciated the legal advice given to British forces, and added that if the 'Brits' thought it right, it must be right. It was something firm upon which they could rely.

I was glad he did not know me. I was rather embarrassed and pleased, as I knew the practice of American administrations was 'if you don't like your lawyers, change them'. This perhaps explained why I could never make contact in this field with my American legal equivalent.

There were many awkward decisions which had to be taken in the course of the Kosovo campaign. Although it had been proposed by the secretaries of state for defence and foreign affairs that all actions must be cleared by the law officers, the machinery did not always work as smoothly as it should.

There was a strong temptation by the government to cut corners. The government wanted to keep in line with the Americans. On the great march to victory it would be pretty bad form for us to find it difficult to keep up with the others (that is, with the Americans). Law officers were seen as a brake, or the fifth wheel of the coach. I had the clear impression that advice from government lawyers was not always welcomed. Because we were initially not given a formal role it was often unclear that we had been consulted on a particular relevant issue. One of the well-publicised events was the bombing of the Belgrade TV Station. As I understood it, it was not one of our actions. It was extremely doubtful whether it was an appropriate target.

One of the constraints was that so many nations were involved in the NATO enterprise and decisions had to be unanimous. The consulting protocols did not always work smoothly in the time available. I could understand the impatience of the military who wanted to get on with the job. Hence I ensured I was always available and ready to discuss. In the same way my involvement in the war cabinet, the defence and overseas policy cabinet committee was rather haphazard initially, but it soon became more formalised and either I or the Solicitor General would be present.

The Yugoslavian attack on the Albanians of Kosovo was horrendous and brutal. It was rightly termed 'ethnic cleansing'. Thousands and thousands of people were treated in a barbarous fashion. The world could not, and should not stand idly by while all this was going on.

How could we be confident that our actions were on a sound legal basis? Downing Street knew that if we used force we would be breaking new ground if we acted on a significant scale.

My approach, like many other conclusions when adapting the law to the facts, was rather a simplistic one. If a burglar, having entered your house, was intent on setting it on fire, and the local constable seemed reluctant to act, you could not just wait and complain to the chief constable, let alone to the police committee – you had to act. Some of the lessons of the Holocaust, which haunts so many of us, should have been learnt. International inactivity has unacceptable memories.

Sometimes the best one could do was to say I believed we had 'a respectable argument' or 'an arguable case'. This is Foreign Office speak and, indeed, law officers' speak. It implies that we cannot be one hundred per cent sure. Even in common law we frequently cannot be one hundred per cent sure, but we do have fairly firm indicators to help us to steer our case to safety. There is an element of constructiveness about interpreting international law. Things are more fluid than in domestic law, and new situations demand the means to deal with them.

I was reacting to an international nightmare where thousands of lives were being lost; Kosovars were being killed and maimed by the Serbs. It became NATO's task to prevent more of these human tragedies and restore refugees to their homes.

I attended many of the meetings of the 'war cabinet' (the Defence and Overseas Policy Committee, or DOP). On 15 April 1999 it was reported to us that the UN Commission of Human Rights had carried a resolution condemning Yugoslavian actions in Kosovo by a majority of 44–1 and six abstentions. The Prime Minister rightly believed that Milosevic had started the war, and that the campaign would continue until he was defeated.

From my earliest days as Attorney, I realised that I would be deeply involved in the consideration of various aspects of international law. But I had never anticipated the degree of my involvement. By the time the campaign in Kosovo reached its peak it was a daily event to be briefed on current developments. The diary had to be constantly regeared to meet ever-increasing demands. I devoted an enormous, perhaps a disproportionate, amount of time to meetings with defence officials and the military. In retrospect, how I found time to carry on with the Attorney General's unremitting flow of work on a whole host of other issues concerning government and prosecution I do not know.

The rule of law is of fundamental importance to me. The need to obey both domestic and international law is enshrined in the ministerial code. Civil servants and the military are equally bound. Hence officials, particularly the military are anxious for legal cover. To some of the more excitable ones, the involvement of government lawyers is a nuisance. I suspected that some of the officials in Number 10 took this view. The wiser ones, particularly in the military, valued the security that legal advice gave to their actions.

My first political campaign, when I was eyeing the possibility of becoming a Labour candidate in Carmarthen in 1956, at the height of the Suez invasion, was based on Labour's slogan underlying its adherence to United Nations resolutions. It was 'law not war' – hardly remembered by the younger generation today, but still of paramount importance.

To revert to the legality of our actions – to justify extending the permitted use of force by nations, strict criteria had to be met. The circumstances must be exceptional. There must be some kind of human catastrophe. It would be helpful – hardly the right word – if the catastrophe is easily recognisable by its scale. One would not wish to argue one's case on the parallel of the Holocaust, but this clearly meant the circumstances for action would have to catastrophic. The use of force must be a last resort: everything else must have been tried. Thirdly, it must meet the test of proportionality, and lastly, there must be a high probability that the use of force would achieve a positive humanitarian objective.

For the reasonable, the need for something to be done was inescapable.

Milosevic was clearly putting the lives of thousands of Albanians in jeopardy and even after the Rambouillet Accords, following the Rambouillet Conference during January to March 1999, no progress was being made, indeed the opposite was happening. I noted the advice of my predecessors in 1991 and 1996 regarding Iraq. In that instance Saddam Hussein had backed down and had agreed unfettered access to the UN weapons inspectors. If there was obstruction, action would be taken against him. It was concluded that a respectable argument for the use of force in Kosovo could be justified on the grounds of overwhelming humanitarian necessity.

This doctrine, still in the course of development, is not without its problems. I was building on the view taken on our intervention in Iraq. However, the circumstances were rather different. Our action with our allies in Iraq was to protect the Kurds and the Shias. It was a strictly limited encroachment onto Iraqi sovereignty consisting of protective actions – the establishment of safe havens and no-fly areas. But as in Iraq, our actions would take place against the background of previous Security Council resolutions and I supported their objectives in Kosovo. The actions in Kosovo would, however, be positive; they would be proactive, and the scale would be substantially different. The common element would be establishing the probability of a humanitarian disaster and the need to avert it. To that extent it was extremely innovative and not yet wholly accepted. Should similar situations arise it is my earnest hope that this policy will be followed, and that in due course it will receive universal acceptance, or at least an acceptance that such humanitarian situations demand and justify some response by other nations. I believe that there was a respectable argument for action in Kosovo, accepted by the government lawyers. This was developed in the following way:

- There had to be convincing evidence, generally accepted by the international community as a whole, of extreme humanitarian distress on a large scale, requiring immediate action and urgent relief.

- There was, in all the circumstances, no practical alternative to the use of force, if lives were to be saved.

- The proposed use of force was necessary and proportionate to the aim being pursued (the relief of humanitarian need) and was strictly limited in time and scope to this aim, ie, it was the minimum necessary to achieve this aim.

In the absence of a Security Council resolution, our actions would be weighed against these criteria. My colleagues accepted from the beginning that particular targets would have to be assessed against these criteria.

It hardly needed emphasising that there had to be convincing evidence of a humanitarian catastrophe, and Security Council Resolution 1199 (1998) explicitly recognised that such a situation existed. It also had to be clear that the humanitarian catastrophe could not be averted unless Milosevic was dissuaded from further repressive acts, and that only the use of force would achieve this objective. My ministerial colleagues in defence and the FCO were of the clear view that these were the facts and I agreed with them.

There was no convincing evidence, indeed no evidence at all, of Milosevic's compliance with the Security Council resolution. In fact his continuing conduct was a 'material breach' of Resolution 1199 (1998) and no doubt also exacerbated the humanitarian problems. But the fact of material breach did not of itself authorise the use of force in this case: in this case the legal argument was that the use of force was justified to prevent a humanitarian catastrophe. The material breach argument (ie material breach of UNSCRs establishing a ceasefire) was of course the legal argument relied on to justify the use of force against Iraq in 1998 and 2003 (and earlier). There was agreement among colleagues on the use of force, provided it was deemed necessary, that it was proportionate, and strictly limited to this objective.

Tony Blair was adamant that Milosevic had started the war, and that he was a continuing threat to the Albanian population, and that the campaign would continue until he was defeated. The broad-brush approach of some of these sentiments would have to be carefully considered when the time came on any proposed action. Regime-change had no legal foundation.

At all times the need for proportionality was clear, ie that the proposed use of force was the minimum necessary to achieve the objective, and that this would need to be discussed in more detail when a list of proposed targets was prepared. Anything beyond the strict legality of our approach was not in order. Perhaps with hindsight there was at least the colour of St George slaying the dragon about Tony's words.

I had observed the words in Security Council Resolution 1199 (1998), paragraph sixteen, that

Should concrete measures in this resolution not be taken . . .

the Security Council would:

consider further actions and additional measures to maintain or restore peace and stability in the area.

It was made clear that it was important such consideration took place before military action was taken.

I was clear in my own mind that we must be able to show we had respected the pre-eminent role of the Security Council in international peace and security and given it every chance to deal with the deteriorating situation.

This sentiment seems to have been forgotten in the justification of the second Iraq War. Whatever the arguments on both sides on the legality of that war, the situation was crying out for exhaustive efforts to devise an internationally agreed political solution from the Security Council. The equivocation of the French before the Iraq War is not an argument for failing to try for a further sustained effort, or was the die already cast? The Chilcot Inquiry may tell us. Regrettably there were no useful developments from the Security Council as regards Kosovo in early 1999.

The role of the government lawyers was to approve the legality of airstrikes flown from the UK. Colleagues had agreed our role very early on. It was emphasised that the law officers were to be consulted as soon as possible on this. We had been told that the details might not be communicated until a brief time before the air strikes were to take place; nevertheless it had been agreed that the Prime Minister and colleagues were to be advised on the legal basis for attacking such targets to ensure they were satisfactory and that principles such as proportionality were observed. The same principles applied to Kosovo as to the operation of aircraft bombing in Iraq.

A very important event occurred on 30 March 1999, when I was told there was a strong political will to move to what was termed 'Phase Three' of the action, involving attacks on Serbia itself, in addition to the attacks on mobile targets in Kosovo.

I was told that the military planners were confident that, on the basis of the high degree of accuracy of their weaponry and bombs, civilian casualties could be kept to the minimum. The casualties would be lower if the attacks were at night. I urged the military planners to bear in mind the advantages of night attacks.

I believed the aim had to be the immediate relief of a humanitarian disaster. It could not have some more general or ulterior motive, such as reprisal or punishment, nor could it be designed simply to degrade Yugoslavian military capability. The aim had to be confined strictly to this one objective.

At the same time there had to be constant care to limit civilian damage. Excessive damage was prohibited by the Geneva Convention. There had to be a definite military advantage (Article 57 of the Additional Protocol 1) and where there was a choice of military targets, the object selected should cause the least damage to civilians and civilian objects.

Previously I had had another briefing, on 19 March, about a range of targets which might be attacked by cruise missiles. The bombs in question would be high velocity and I accepted the MOD's view that it was reasonable to base the collateral damage on their view that it would be low.

Around this time I had particular concern about the location of targets in downtown Belgrade. It was suggested that the location of these targets meant that attacks on them could pose more risks to surrounding civilian property than might be the case for attacks on military facilities in the open country. I was particularly concerned about two targets, which were in proximity to buildings that had a civilian/humanitarian function. I accepted that no one could plan for damage caused by missiles which misfired or went astray and I noted their proven accuracy during Operation Desert Fox in Iraq (a factor which I regarded as important). Nevertheless, the risks inherent in such locations would have to be balanced against the military advantage to be gained from attacking these targets.

We were anxious that the attention of the Defence Secretary and the Prime Minister should be drawn to the proposal, and that it should be made clear to them that the attack on such locations risked significant casualties to civilians as well as military personnel. This was in accord with my scrutiny and advice – before an action was taken civilian casualties had to be assessed as 'low'. The risk here was indeed higher than we were normally were prepared to agree.

Subject to these comments we believed that, on the basis of information supplied to us, the attacks were proportionate, ie ministers would have to be satisfied that the attacks were necessary to alleviate overwhelming human need. In law, the attacks were necessary and proportionate. The legitimacy of the use of force had been assessed in the light of circumstances at the time.

Would a decision to bomb be politically wise? One has heard too much since in other operations of casualties through friendly fire and accidental damage. It boiled down to the advice, 'go ahead if you must. It is legally open for you to do so, but is it politically wise?' As no one could guard against all eventualities, the political damage from accidental and unanticipated damage to the inhabitants of nearby buildings would be calamitous. Fortunately, authorising an attack would be for the policy makers.

So far as I know the attacks on these locations took place on the authority of the Prime Minister and the Defence Secretary with no unintended casualties. Were we too careful – who knows? I, at least, slept that night.

It was agreed that if targets were to be expanded then further consideration would have to be given in the event of a specific proposal from SACEUR (Supreme Allied Commander Europe). This was in fact a rejection of a proposal by the Defence Secretary who wished to have delegated authority to attack a wider range of infrastructure targets, but no specific targets. He had to concede that the present SACEUR had made no proposal to include infrastructure targets which were not directly related to the Serbian military effort. He had to be content that there might be circumstances as the campaign developed in which it would be necessary to look at this again.

This was a clear example of the MOD trying to limit the direct involvement of the lawyers on a case-by-case basis. The Foreign Secretary seemed to agree with the principle of intensifying, but agreed that targeting should be confined to those targets with a clear military objective.

I sensed a reluctance on the Prime Minister's part to call me to speak, so whenever necessary I called myself. I had been a Cabinet minister twenty years earlier. On one occasion, it may be this one, the Defence Secretary mentioned the need for my advice on the legal position. The Prime Minister scribbled a note to George and pushed it over to him. What it contained I do not know, but George did not mention the need for legal views again. However, I had spoken earlier on the general position.

The possibility of intensifying the air campaign was raised by the chief of the defence staff. It was being resisted by our allies Portugal, Canada, Greece and Czechoslovakia due to the fear of civilian casualties. Later on the MOD claimed that if the campaign were to be effective it needed to be intensified, and that the air attacks were affecting the morale of the Yugoslavians.

Whilst I knew where George Robertson stood, I was not always sure of what Robin Cook really wanted. He seemed uncomfortable. I eventually went to see him to express my concern that we should both be on our guard against the chipping away of legal safeguards. The meeting, at my request, was quite good and I believe we agreed we should keep in touch. It was clearly agreed with colleagues that there should be no change in the criteria for targeting, namely that targets should be confined to those with a clear military value.

Looking back on events, the power to widen air attacks was never asked for. I knew at the time that it was a try-on, a brave try-on. Constant vigilance paid off. However I was, before this, becoming increasingly concerned that the legal position which had been agreed might not hold and that the state of play should be summarised. It must have been very tedious to the Prime Minister and, where they were informed, to colleagues.

We were reaching an important juncture. So far so good, but it was time for me to collect my thoughts and summarise them.

There were several important considerations that the Prime Minister and colleagues had to be aware of, the importance of which I could not underestimate. It was important they were reminded of the legal justification for what we were doing in Yugoslavia and the legal constraints which necessarily applied. The Prime Minister and colleagues were fully aware that what had been done was to put together a respectable argument of human necessity as the basis for the acting outside the ambit of a Security Council resolution.

I made it clear that our actions could not be designed *solely* to degrade Yugoslavia's military capability or punish Milosevic. The aim of the action could only be the immediate relief of an overwhelming humanitarian disaster.

Also I was unhappy about some of the targets of the NATO campaign. No matter how Milosevic behaved, the alliance must not cause indiscriminate or unnecessary harm or damage and must focus only on military objectives. I recognised that problems could arise where infrastructure had a mixed use, for example, bridges used by both the military and civilians.

The relative proportions had to be borne in mind. I became concerned about reports of attacking regime targets, such as Milosevic's residences, the headquarters of political parties and TV stations, and some commentators believed that we might have as our objectives the crushing or humiliating of Milosevic rather than relieving human suffering.

I believed that if there were a risk of civilian casualties or damage, such targets could only be attacked if the civilian consequences were not excessive in relation to the concrete and direct military advantage anticipated. I had found some recent events troubling. I did not know how the headquarters of political parties, radio and television stations etc, could have qualified as 'military objectives'.

I was also concerned as to whether the alliance of which we were part had evidence that these facilities were contributing *directly* to the military action in Kosovo. If so, a case could be made for attacking them. Similar concerns had been expressed by others regarding attacks on hydro-electric and other industries. I wondered what assessment had been made of the impact of such attacks on civilian life. I assumed (because I was not asked to approve these attacks) that the UK had not been directly involved. But even if we were not, attacks carried out by the alliance in our name, and if press reports are accurate, with our full endorsement, could cause real difficulties.

I also wondered whether we had been able to examine the lawfulness of these attacks which had taken place. In short, did we have effective control over the NATO military strikes? From my recent meeting I said to colleagues that Robin Cook was worried about the extent that we and the rest of NATO were kept in the dark about some of the actions of the US.

My concerns were not theoretical or academic. I believed we could expect close scrutiny after the event. This scrutiny need not stop in Parliament. The UK courts had jurisdiction under the Geneva Conventions. Prosecutions could be brought against anyone, whether in the UK or not, who committed or aided, abetted or procured the commission by any other person of grave breaches of the Conventions. The International Criminal Tribunal for the former Yugoslavia had power to prosecute persons 'violating the laws and customs of war'. Unjustified attacks on civilian property and unjustified casualties to civilians were very much within the scope of that court. We could expect any NATO actions which came close to the edge of lawfulness to be brought to the attention of the (independent) prosecutor. Our actions would come within the ambit of the International Court of Justice, the European Court of Justice, or the European Court of Human Rights. Litigation in any of these would quickly bring under judicial scrutiny the legal justification for our actions against Yugoslavia. The outcome of that scrutiny could not be guaranteed.

All this reinforced my belief in the continued need for the most scrupulous adherence to legal requirements. As the campaign intensified we had to be careful that we kept in the forefront of our minds the legal constraints which govern the use of force by our servicemen and women and those who authorised them. I believed that the limits of the legal basis for our actions in Yugoslavia and the constraints which apply to the use of force should be constantly and carefully kept in view as the campaign developed.

Although colleagues from the Prime Minister down were aware of my concerns, other than my earlier meeting at my request with Robin Cook there was no reaction and no other meeting. I expected to be summoned to Number 10 to explain myself immediately. There was no such summons. There was no attempt to challenge my fears, or indeed to acknowledge that they existed. There was no doubt in my mind that the Prime Minister, the Foreign Secretary and the Defence Secretary were made fully aware of the consequences of illegality.

Little did I anticipate that within weeks, we would, as a country, be summoned before one of these courts as a defendant with our other NATO allies.

One of the most important events in my constituency was the 'mayor making' in the council chamber in Port Talbot on 21 May. My wife and I tried to be there, and normally we succeeded. It was a joy to meet old friends and it was a recognition of the importance of the event that the MP was there. I would sit on the platform with the councillors and my wife while the new mayor and his entourage were duly sworn in.

While sitting there on 21 May 1999 I had an urgent message. My senior advisers wanted to see me. They had collared an aircraft and were to arrive shortly at St Athan's airfield close by. During the proceedings a further message came that they had arrived and at a convenient moment I left the platform for a room that had been assigned to me, and met, I believe, senior RAF officers, David Seymour, Iain Macleod and other Foreign Office lawyers, I believe, including Michael Wood, their deputy chief lawyer. It was a formidable delegation in retrospect, which underlined its importance. In the event, I missed the mayor's tea!

An urgent decision was needed for a raid that evening, hence the nearly 200-mile air dash. It was to be a substantial bombing attack. I had a very short time to consider their pleas and an instant decision was required.

The scale of the proposed attack would be considerably larger than what I had understood as regards previous raid. The crucial issue was whether the harm and damage to civilian life would be excessive in relation to the concrete and direct military advantage. On the basis of what I was told, the consequences to civilian life would not be severe. The proposal was unobjectionable and not unlike similar ones in the past. I believed the attacks which risked disruption to civilian life on the scale anticipated were at the very limit of what could be justified in law, assuming accurate delivery.

I understood that all NATO countries endorsed the intensification of the attacks, having in mind the time of the year. The underlying problem was the belief that NATO could rely on air attacks to achieve their aim without committing ground troops. The attacks so far had not reaped the desired dividend.

I drove back the 245 miles from my home to London on Sunday – I always drove myself as I had been on constituency business and was coming from my home in Wales, and therefore whatever the pressure I was under, was never offered an official car. From reports of more recent ministerial activities, it seems that past principles have got somewhat blurred on this issue, but a car would have helped when I was under considerable pressure. Tiredness from long-distance driving is not a proper background to good decision making.

On the way I decided it was important that my concern about the intensification of bombing should be understood generally.

Article 57 of the First Additional Protocol of the Geneva Convention refers to "direct and concrete military advantage". This was of paramount concern to me.

I knew that the lawfulness of what NATO was doing in Yugoslavia was already under review before the International Court of Justice and that concerns were being expressed in many quarters about certain aspects of the campaign.

I have always believed, and have given evidence to this effect to select committees, that the role of the Attorney General is to be candid with his or her employers – the government – and they must be able, if they wish, to rely on this advice. The Attorney General is not there to please but to give sound advice. It must have been very irritating to the Prime Minister. He wanted to get on with the campaign, and his chief lawyer was forever crying wolf, and operating what must have seemed a most conservative interpretation of the law – some might say I was signing my political death warrant but, in view of Blair's comments on my retirement, I have always discounted this. I was again concerned that there was no suggestion of a meeting. I compared what I knew of Elwyn Jones's relationship with Harold Wilson on Rhodesia and Michael Havers and Mrs Thatcher on the Falkland Islands, from what they both told me. She is reputed to have said at the time of the attack on Belgrano: . . . now, Michael, you're a naval man . . . etc'. Michael had served in the navy as a national serviceman.

The following Thursday was my last day before going on what I thought was a well-deserved rest after the sixty-eight day campaign. I was going with my wife to fish in the most extreme part of north-west Scotland. I could not be further away; Iceland or Newfoundland would have been the next stop. However I had foolishly agreed to speak on the Thursday night at the annual dinner of the air force lawyers at their mess in Gloucester, with the intention of returning to London the following morning and catching a plane to Edinburgh.

It was not to be a quiet Thursday afternoon. I hoped to have time to clear my desk of the day to day work of the Attorney. However, there was a further important application, which I shall not expand on now.

The MOD did not get my blessing that day.

The MOD team went away that beautiful afternoon very disappointed and chastened. They should have seen it coming because we had been quite open and transparent in our concerns over the last few weeks. It was the moment to stay stop. I surmised there was a great deal of coming and going between the three sets of lawyers, and the temperature was being taken constantly. After all, all the lawyers came from the same FCO stable. All hell must have been let loose in the MOD. I jumped into the car, a little late, and was rushed to Gloucester. I was now on leave.

As I changed for dinner in the officers' mess, running by this time a little later still, I was telephoned – by my old friend and partner in many defence campaigns within the Labour Party, George Robertson, the Defence Secretary, protesting about my decision.

'You can't do this to us', he said. I replied they had not made out a proper case. He knew what was needed – I had repeated many times my concerns and how close to the line we had gone. He said, 'We will come again tomorrow'. Obviously, following previous applications they had fully expected a decision that day, for action that night. I followed this up by saying, as I recollect, 'I'm sorry, George, but I am now on leave and it will be for others to decide. I am going to Scotland to fish.'

Permission was given the following day on the basis of a further application. I was not a party to it.

In view of the strong pressure from one of my successors I am inhibited for the present from giving further details. I am also anxious to complete my book.

For my purposes, it is sufficient that the statement that 'all that was being done was legal on the advice of the Attorney General', is demonstrably not the whole story as it has transpired.

On the same day, 28 May, the Prime Minister wrote to me regarding my decision the previous Friday:

> As you know, I entirely agree that our policy must be carried out by lawful means. I note what you said about the use of UK bases last Friday. It was obviously a difficult judgment to make. It underlined the need to continue to apply conscientiously the legal criteria to targeting and the use by the US of UK bases.

This comment was reassuring and welcome. It was a pity that it had not been received before the fatal decision that same day. Was it written to ensure the 'slate was clean' so far as Downing Street was concerned?

I went off to fish, and because of the cold weather was not at all successful. Neither Margaret nor I caught anything. The only comfort was that the gillie did not catch anything either.

No one was more relieved than I was to hear on the TV while in Scotland that Milosevic had caved in and that the war was over. On 12 July the Prime

Minister minuted his thanks to ministers, civil servants and members of the armed forces involved in the Kosovo crisis. It was particularly well deserved for my department. Throughout my career, politics had taken precedence over the law. During my period as Attorney General, and particularly during the Kosovo campaign, the roles were reversed. The law dominated that period of my life.

The American refusal to involve ground troops other than in a permissive environment probably encouraged Milosevic to hold out longer against NATO. It was only when the momentum started to build behind other ground operations in early June that Milosevic backed down. Some commentators formed the view that the American performance was generally unimpressive, with long periods of indecision and policy incoherence punctuated by bursts of ill-considered and sometimes counter-productive activism.

NATO decision making involved eighty-two councils in seventy-two days, and it appeared that the NATO machinery was slow and cumbersome. At any rate by the end I wondered a great deal if it was a lack of trust and fear of leaks that resulted in my always being asked rather late in the day and almost each day for my views. The targets, unless they were all mobile, must have been in place some time before.

Nevertheless Milosevic eventually came to heel because he realised that the Russians offered no more than tepid support and that key allies in NATO were seriously planning a ground invasion of Kosovo: the eventual statement from President Clinton that 'no option was ruled out' was not the greatest of clarion calls, but it was enough.

It was noteworthy that of the 440 air attacks carried out, there were apparently only three civilian casualties. By contrast Serb activities in Kosovo had killed and burnt alive many thousands. It was NATO's task to prevent this and restore thousands of refugees to their homes.

Over the previous weeks of the campaign there had been three full-scale debates in the House of Commons and five major statements by ministers. Questions were asked about the rationale for our actions, and Baroness Symons replied on 9 March 1999 in the House of Lords:

> My Lords, all NATO operations must have a basis in international law. Each case needs to be looked at on its own merits. In many cases a United Nations Security Council resolution would be needed to authorise the use of force. But force may be used to defend a non-NATO state . . . or, in exceptional circumstances, to avert an immediate and overwhelming humanitarian catastrophe.

My Lords, cases have arisen, for example, in northern Iraq in 1991, when, in the light of all the circumstances, a limited use of force has been justifiable as the only means to avert an overwhelming humanitarian catastrophe in support of purposes laid down by the Security Council but without the Council's express authorisation. Such cases, by their very nature must be exceptional and would depend on an objective assessment of the factual circumstances at the time and of the relevant decisions of the Security Council bearing on the situation. It is important to stress that all NATO decisions are taken by consensus. Not a single member of the alliance can force the other members to act if the allies are opposed. All our allies would not agree a NATO operation, I believe, unless they considered it was in accordance with international law.

She was asked further on 18 May by Lord Jenkins of Putney:

Whether the NATO bombing of Yugoslavia is in breach of the Geneva Conventions Act 1995.

The minister replied:

My Lords, action by our forces is in strict conformity with international humanitarian law, including the 1949 Geneva Conventions and their additional protocols of 1977. It is therefore also in strict conformity with the Geneva Conventions Act which implements these treaties.

Very soon we faced legal action in the courts. Yugoslavia applied for the equivalent of an injunction to stop the bombing in the International Court of Justice in the Hague. The Bankovic case in 2001 redefined the European Court of Human Rights law on jurisdiction.

I was in Trinidad at an international conference of Attorney Generals. I had hardly taken my place there when there was a call from home for my advice as the case against the UK and eight other NATO countries had been put in the International Court of Justice for urgent decision. It was due to be heard within days, and I was summoned back.

As soon as I got back to London I had urgent consultations in my chambers and work had already been put in hand to prepare our submission. Many of the senior Foreign Office lawyers and MacLeod had worked exceedingly hard.

We had two grounds to submit to the court in our defence. First, we would advocate our belief that an overwhelming humanitarian disaster was taking place in Kosovo and that there was no other way, if the world was at all civilised, except to unleash an attack on Yugoslavia.

The second ground, though technical, proved to be the winning one. Yugoslavia was not a signatory setting up or adhering to the International Court and therefore could not be a party to any proceedings.

I agreed to advance the two defences. We got to the Hague with a day or so to spare so that we could beaver away on the final draft of my speech. I was pleased that despite such a limited knowledge of the advocacy of international law, I was able to grapple quickly with quite complicated issues. The 'jury' points – setting out in fairly dramatic terms the width and breadth of the human disaster were mine. This is what I had been brought up to do. We hoped that whilst the legal issues were cardinal, a little colour would not detract from them.

I opened my case to the International Court on 11 May 1999 opposing the application of Yugoslavia for an 'Indication of Provisional Measures', that is an injunction against the UK and eight other defendants concerning the legality of the use of force against Yugoslavia.

The first pillar of our defence was one of jurisdiction – I suggested that the application by Yugoslavia was an abuse of the process of the court, as the present Federal Republic of Yugoslavia was not a party to the statute of the court, and had not filed to apply for membership of the United Nations when it succeeded the former Yugoslavia. Only a party to the statute could make a valid declaration under the appropriate provisions of the statute: as the FRY had only deposited an acceptance of the court's compulsory jurisdiction only three days before the present application, and so under the rules it could not provide even a prima facie basis for the exercise of the jurisdiction of the court. There were other jurisdictional objections too.

I continued my argument based on the overwhelming humanitarian disaster that had been witnessed in Kosovo. I quoted Mrs Ogata, the United Nations High Commissioner for Refugees, when she briefed in person the members of the Security Council on 5 May, a week after these proceedings were started:

The situation of women, men and children fleeing the Province of Kosovo and Metohija, in the Federal Republic of Yugoslavia, is increasingly desperate. Kosovo is being emptied – brutally and methodically – of its ethnic Albanian population. In the last three days alone about 37,000 new refugees and internally displaced people have arrived in Albania, the former Yugoslav Republic of

Macedonia, and the Republic of Montenegro. More trains with thousands of refugees have arrived last night at the Yugoslav/ Macedonian border. Ethnic cleansing and mass forced expulsions are yielding their tragic results faster than we can respond . . . fragile and unprepared countries are bearing the brunt of one of the largest refugee flows Europe has seen in the twentieth century. Seven hundred thousand people have already been forced to leave their homes.

This refugee crisis is not new. Last year, more than a quarter of all asylum requests in Europe were by people from Kosovo. Up to 23 March, when UNHCR had to reluctantly leave the province following a decision of the United Nations Security Coordinator, it was providing assistance to 400,000 people displaced or otherwise affected by fighting inside the province, and to 90,000 refugees and displaced people outside Kosovo.

I adopted the words of the UK's permanent representative when he addressed the Security Council on 24 March, describing our military action as:

an exceptional measure to prevent an overwhelming humanitarian catastrophe ... under present circumstances in Kosovo there is convincing evidence that such a catastrophe is imminent. Renewed acts of repression by the authorities of the Federal Republic of Yugoslavia would cause further loss of civilian life and would lead to displacement of the civilian population on a large scale and in hostile conditions. Every means short of force has been tried to avert this situation . . . The force now proposed is directed exclusively to averting a humanitarian catastrophe, and is the minimum judged necessary for that purpose.

I ended my speech by formally requesting the court to summarily dismiss the request for the indication of provisional measures submitted by the Federal Republic of Yugoslavia.

The judgment of the court in respect of the case of the applicant and the nine defendant countries was delivered on 2 June 1999 in the following terms:

In an order issued in the case concerning legality in the use of force (Federal Republic of Yugoslavia (FRY) v the United Kingdom) the court rejected by twelve votes to three the request for an indication of provisional measures submitted by the Federal Republic of Yugoslavia.

As we had learned, Yugoslavia had not deposited its declaration of the acceptance of the compulsory jurisdiction of the court within the obligatory twelve months prior to the filing of its application. It had only done so three days before it brought its dispute to the court.

The court concluded that in the circumstances it had no jurisdiction on the case, and that it lacked prima facie jurisdiction to entertain Yugoslavia's application and 'it cannot therefore indicate any provisional measures whatsoever'.

The court could not adjudicate on the main issue – the legality of our actions. Much as I was relieved by our success on the jurisdictional point, I was disappointed that the opportunity could not be taken to judge legality of actions such as ours and other NATO countries.

Before Kosovo and Iraq 1, litigation about the use of force was in practice highly unlikely. I believe my predecessors who were law officers had mentioned the possibility, but more as a remote threat than a realistic prospect.

The Prime Minister had been warned following the TV station incident that legal action could conceivably occur in the European Court of Human Rights, the UK courts and the International Court of Justice, but none of that seemed likely. In fact, within a year, there had been legal action in all these courts.

The warning to the Prime Minister was justified to the hilt. I knew the UK had kept within the law. What the verdict might have been on US activities, I have no idea. I sincerely hope that they were punctilious too.

The whole episode proves the value of the independent judgment of a law officer. What would have been the judgment of the court had the mission to bomb the infrastructure of half of Belgrade gone ahead, I cannot venture to think.

Now following the Human Rights Act, everything has changed, and any use of force in future seems certain to be conducted against the very real prospect of legal action, under the Human Rights Act in domestic courts, and in Strasbourg, and perhaps even before the International Criminal Court. It follows that the role of the Attorney General in all aspects of the use of force by the United Kingdom has therefore become even more central than it was. Any government committed to the rule of law, any minister bound by the ministerial code, any of our servicemen bound by both domestic and international law, can no longer fondly believe that the law officers are the fifth wheel of the coach – they are at the heart of the mechanism to ensure a safe journey for all who are involved in the use of force.

Looking back on events in Kosovo, it is regrettable that there has been no systematic attempt to develop further the theory and practice of humanitarian intervention. The basic criterion for intervention is that the violations of human rights within a particular state have reached a situation where they shock the conscience of humanity. Action was taken in Kosovo by a number of states who justified their use of force where there was no explicit Security Council authority.

Professor Christine Gray, in her book on *International Law and the Use of Force* relates some of the disagreements on the interpretation of Article 2(4) of the UN Charter and whether new circumstances have caused it to be evolved since 1945.

The Secretary-General of the UN in his '1999 Report on the work of the Organisation' states:

> What is clear is that enforcement action without Security Council authorisation threatens the very core of the international security system founded on the charter of the UN. Only the Charter provides a universally accepted legal basis for the use of force.

On another occasion he had said:

> Emerging slowly, but I believe surely, is an international norm against the violent repression of minorities that will and must take precedence over concerns of state sovereignty.

Professor Gray concludes:

> Thus the controversy over the legality of humanitarian intervention continues.

It will continue to be a matter of controversy, whether a new doctrine of intervention without Security Council authority has been established. The validity of the doctrine will be strengthened by similar action and I foresee it becoming established as customary international law. The greater the number of states to validate the doctrine, the greater its claim to be customary international law.

States who acted to intervene did not believe that they did not have legal authority to act. They emphasised in the Security Council debates in March 1999 that they were supported by Security Council Resolutions 1160 (1998), 1199 (1998) and 1203 (1998), adopted under Chapter VII of the Charter. Six non-western states voted with Slovenia in comprehensively defeating criticism of NATO's bombing. The vote in the Security Council was historic in that the Russian draft resolution was defeated by a majority of its non-permanent members.

There will always be critics of NATO tactics. The most powerful military alliance in history could not put together a credible ground option. It might be said that the bombings later accelerated the killing of Serbians by the Kosovars, inflamed by the desire for revenge. Certainly it was only luke-warm Russian support to Serbia and threats of a ground force that brought the conflict to an end.

twenty-four
AFTER 1999

SINCE I DID NOT KNOW when my term of office would come to an end I had made no preparations for life after ministerial office. I assumed I would go back to the Bar. In any event I needed a good rest and I could concentrate on my constituency's problems, which was so necessary after my years in government as Attorney General. One such issue was a desperately needed new hospital in Port Talbot. Previously I had called on three or four Tory secretaries of state and even promised William Hague, who was very cordial and understanding, that he could drive a JCB to cut the first sod if he gave me my hospital. But no hospital was forthcoming. No hospital, no JCB ride.

I fear I was a nuisance to more than one secretary of state and 'promises, promises' meant nothing to me. Poor Alun Michael, the First Minister of the Assembly, would be rung up at home many Sunday mornings and I eventually got my hospital financed via the Public Finance Initiative (PFI) through his good offices. I was invited to mark the commencement of the work by cutting the first sod. I insisted the Assembly's health minister should share the honour. The Assembly deserved it.

What else was I to do? I was in no hurry to return to the Bar. I had noted how many ex-law officers had done so, but not all. Elwyn Jones did so most successfully. It is not easy if you have been away too long. Various other possibilities were dangled before me; one was that of a high court judge. The appointments system was more informal in those days. How serious the suggestion was I did not question but I believed it was put seriously and I took it at face value. My experience of practice, since my devilling days in Swansea, where I worked mainly in personal injury cases, was wholly in crime. I was steeped in criminal practice and nothing else. I had sat as an assistant recorder and recorder on and off since 1972. Occasionally in my younger days I would be sent for a day or so to the county courts in London to sit as a judge if I were not otherwise engaged, but charter parties and similar litigation were way beyond my knowledge and experience.

Realistically it would be a steep climb to take on anything other than crime, and frankly I got bored with sitting. I also had in the forefront of my mind the enormous difficulties I had experienced in returning to the Bar after an absence of more than six years in 1979. I was re-learning each and every day, and I would not recommend it. After some thought, I discouraged the kind suggestion. Governorships of various colonies, not that there are many, were also mentioned. I was a little more interested but I took no steps to further the suggestion. I suppose if they were formalised I might well have been seriously tempted. But nothing came of them and I noticed that one which had been specifically mentioned in the Caribbean was then snapped up by a permanent secretary. I suppose he had had his eyes on it for some time and the Civil Service do not like interlopers taking their prizes. It was rather different in the late 1940s when it was not unusual for ex MPs to be offered governorships, particularly if they had good majorities.

In retrospect, I had no real enthusiasm for any of the suggestions that were canvassed, and similarly no real interest in exploring possibilities in the private sector. I suppose an ex Attorney might have found a suitable non-executive role. However, I did not even engage a headhunter. I had got to where I was through being asked to do a job, and hawking my credentials around had never been my style.

After some months of recovering I decided to restart my career at the Bar. My eyes were obviously on a return there and it would have been difficult to combine any appointment with the uncertain calendar of court appearances.

In the meantime instructions arrived for me to advise Mrs Benazir Bhutto on charges pending against her in Pakistan. The fact that I was instructed was in the public domain and to my surprise my advice was published on her country's TV. She came and saw me in my chambers and was impressive, as always. It was so very depressing and saddening when, years later, I heard the appalling news that she had been assassinated. What a tragedy.

John Grimmer, my clerk, sent me to Lincoln to defend a serious child cruelty case. The trial judge was my former Treasury devil, Stephen Richards, and John, I suspect, believed that I would be in safe hands there, despite my recent absence from the Bar. And so it turned out. There followed about three crowded years when I was able to make up professionally for the years as Attorney. I was particularly lucky in that quite a few cases did not go further than the first day, they either pleaded or were dropped, for one reason or another, the work having been done and the fee earned. One of the earliest was a drug case expected to last some months in Woolwich and, since Margaret was recovering from her first hip operation, I was able to go home to nurse her very much sooner than expected.

They were full and enjoyable years and I endeavoured not to leave the home counties as I was still an MP. Probably one of the most demanding cases I did at this time was defending a railway engine driver at Liverpool Crown Court on a charge of manslaughter. Relying on the signalling, he had reversed his engine in the early hours of the morning, believing it was safe to do so, and so killed a colleague. My client was shattered and I worried myself stiff as to whether I would ever dare to put him in the witness box, given his state of health. The good man was in a pitiful condition. The trouble was that four or five different agencies had a role to play in their use of the track, which was closed to other traffic in the early hours of the morning. It seemed there was no one in sufficient overall charge: hence the tragedy.

I found my experience in chairing a railway inquiry, and learning a lot about railways when I was at transport in 1967, not unhelpful. It had never crossed any of our minds then that you could separate ownership or responsibility of the track from those who actually ran the trains. The architects of the present system of running railways with different ownership and franchises must have been out of their minds. Whether this particular tragedy would have occurred had the split not taken place is questionable. It is my gut feeling it would not have happened with just one owner in control. To the immense relief of my poor client, the defence counsel for the other defendant, and myself, the judge heeded our earnest pleas at the end of the Crown's case that we had no case to answer, and stopped the trial. 'I was very pleased that one poor railwayman and his family had been put out of their misery by our victory.

My pupil master had told me more than once not to go on at the Bar as long as he had. I asked him on one occasion 'how long did you go on for Alun?' He replied that he had retired as Recorder of Cardiff and from the Bar at seventy-two. I was over seventy-one and decided to take my bat away or, as they say in the pits, 'put my lamp on the bar', or more accurately perhaps, 'put my wig back in its box'. I had enjoyed three full years.

When I retired as Attorney I had immediately arranged for a general management committee of my constituency to be called, to begin to choose a suitable successor. My lifelong colleagues in Aberavon were very, very kind. I had served them as best as I could for forty years. I could count the role I had played in ensuring jobs in the area as a positive achievement: the new harbour at Port Talbot; new lines at the steelworks, one of which I was privileged to open; as well as the reconstructed old harbour – the management at British Steel had been very positive in their appreciation. Completing most of the M4, I hoped, would encourage employment. I had chosen the site to build the DVLA headquarters at Morriston, which benefited thousands of families over a wide area, including Aberavon. One failure had been to get more investment up the valley. Occasional successes after the closure of the pits did not last long. The biggest employer at Glyncorrwg was the school.

There was one curious battle when I was Attorney, for the siting of a gas-fired electricity producing plant in Port Talbot. The curtain had come down on any more of these plants as they were thought to be a wasteful way of producing electricity. The American firm GEC wanted to come to the splendid site at Baglan, but ministers could not be shifted. A bizarre idea was seriously canvassed to build a coal-fired plant on the same site, which could use coal from the Neath Valley. I could well imagine ructions on the vast and well-established housing estate at Sandfields. It would be built over my dead body. It would have been sheer madness to site a coal-powered station there and I had to make sure it did not happen.

How to unlock the situation? I approached a good friend – Pat McFaddan, then on the Prime Minister's staff, later a minister. I was able to say that I had heard that Mr Jack Welch, the Chief Executive of GEC was minded to go to Brazil, Berlin – anywhere but Port Talbot – if he were not allowed to build the gas-fired plant. It was cutting-edge technology and could provide cheap electricity for a whole range of industries, and Baglan Industrial Park badly needed the development. Through the good offices of my friends at Number 10, Mr Welch was able to see Tony Blair, who lifted the embargo. Not for the first time industrial South Wales benefitted from being able to access decision makers and my constituency was grateful to Tony Blair, to whom I gave full credit.

Curiously I was nearly shut out of the cutting of the first sod, or equivalent ceremony. I think the date had been moved and having been tipped off by the council leader, Noel Crowley, I managed to get down in time, driving down in the very early hours of the morning.

I did my duty as a loyal back bencher after retiring as Attorney, the first time I had sat on the back benches since I was sacked in 1981–2. I was privileged as a senior back bencher to be asked to move the vote of thanks for the Queen's Speech and, as is the custom, was able to pay tribute to my constituency, which had returned me to Parliament for forty years.

twenty-five
NEW PASTURES

FOLLOWING THE 2001 ELECTION I became a life peer and sat on the Labour bench in the House of Lords graced by privy counsellors. I had a little trouble in agreeing my title. Geoffrey Howe had written to me many years before to say that although he had as a local boy taken the title of Lord Howe of Aberavon, (we were both freemen of Port Talbot) there would be no difficulty in my being Lord Morris of Aberavon, if I so wished. He had kindly checked the position. The story is told of a Swansea jury being brought to Aberavon beach to view the scene of a case, and one of their number asking a bystander if there was a pier at Aberavon, to which the reply is said to have been, 'Yes, there are two peers in Aberavon – one on the left and one on the right.'

I wanted to be known as Lord John Morris, as I was still in practice and the legal profession still knew me as John Morris. But the man in charge – the Garter King of Arms – would not agree to anyone having his Christian name in his title. He had not allowed for it in his time, although there were ample precedents before this. In any event, he volunteered that John was a very common name and it might be thought I was the second son of an earl. I gave up the battle and settled for Lord Morris of Aberavon in the County of West Glamorgan, but wished to have as a second title 'of Ceredigion in the County of Dyfed'. This was agreed to. My very old friends, Lord Merlyn Rees and Lord Prys-Davies were my sponsors. Over the years we had done a great deal together and we could not have been closer friends.

For the first time I could take part in many International Parliamentary Union (IPU) conferences from Mexico to Manila, and I returned to South Africa which I had visited earlier in the 1980s. I became a member of the first Standing Committee on Peace and International Security of the IPU, and from time to time I chaired its drafting committee. I found this both invigorating and demanding, trying over many hours to get some twenty to twenty-five delegates from different countries to agree on around 150 amendments to a draft document. In due course I was appointed one of the joint rapporteurs for a report on 'The Role of Parliament in Striking a Balance between National Security, Human Security and Individual Freedoms and in Averting the Threat to Democracy'. The IPU delegates agreed to our report, emphasising the role of Parliament in being eternally vigilant in monitoring the balance between freedom and security. To my pleasure we affirmed our belief 'that torture has no place in the twenty-first century as it is one of the most abhorrent violations of human rights and individual freedoms'.

I sat on two select committees in the Lords and particularly enjoyed the constitutional committee. We were the only body in the Lords who could handle proposed legislation from the Welsh Assembly. Lord (Ted) Rowlands and I took the firm view that our role was only to consider whether there were any constitutional principles involved, and if the Assembly complied with those we could clear their proposals in minutes. We set a useful precedent and agreed to all proposals immediately, except one which we had to return for poor drafting. There were so many 'exceptions to exceptions' that it was unintelligible. I think the lesson was learnt. I understand now from the First Minister of the Welsh Assembly that it is Whitehall that should be blamed for this.

The constitutional committee delivered extremely valuable reports, the most valuable and far-reaching being on 'The Surveillance Society'. I regret I do not think the government's response was adequate, and this will be an issue which the future will return to time after time. Constant vigilance by Parliament on the balance between the safety of the state and the freedom of the individual is of the utmost importance in our country as well as in all democracies. It was an abuse of terrorist legislation when it was used by local authorities to check dustbins and catchment areas of schools.

A very pleasant duty was 'imposed' on me in 2006–8 to chair the trustees responsible for erecting a statue to David Lloyd George, my hero, in Parliament Square. Cledwyn Hughes and Mr John Grigg, the author of so many authoritative books on Lloyd George had initiated the matter many years before. Some money had been raised for it, but the project had faltered. It was now an almost impossible task to raise a substantial amount of money. We were fifty years too late, and recollections had dimmed.

Gareth Williams, Lord Williams of Mostyn, then Leader of the House of Lords, had chaired the trustees but his untimely death necessitated a new chairman. I believe that Lord Hooson was the senior member of the group and not for the first time, he twisted my arm. He had done so many years earlier when he got me to start a successful campaign to raise money for the Welsh school in London. Emlyn, a most persuasive advocate, was difficult to resist.

I honestly thought the task was impossible. As time wore on I began to lose heart as the money was extremely slow in coming in. I told the chairman and secretary of the Executive Committee I would do the job for one more year. Then suddenly, over lunch in the House of Lords, a most generous benefactor of so many causes in South Wales, Mr Stanley Thomas, my guest, said he would give me £200,000. It was manna from heaven; we were on our way and could contract Professor Glyn Williams who, after a public competition, was to be the sculptor.

It was gratifying to see the remarkable sculpture unveiled in Parliament Square by the HRH Prince of Wales and the HRH Duchess of Cornwall in the presence of the Prime Minister, former prime ministers, the leaders of the political parliamentary parties and many of the donors. I felt I had repaid my debt to a very great Welshman whom I had read such a great deal about in my grandfather's home as a boy, and to whom the country owed such a huge debt as the originator of the welfare state and his role as Prime Minister in the First World War.

Another enjoyable task came my way when I was invited to be Chancellor of Glamorgan University in 2001, when I left the Commons. The post had formerly been carried out by my friend Merlyn Rees and I surmise he had a great deal to do with the invitation. Glamorgan University was originally a polytechnic, based on the old school of Mines in Pontypridd. Merlyn had been an ideal appointment for the chancellorship which he did for a good part of ten years, before ill health caused him to consider retirement.

I was an adopted son of the county of Glamorgan. My maternal grandmother was born in the Rhondda, my grandfather, his brothers and my great grandfather had gone down from Cardiganshire to cut coal there. My mother was born in Aberdare and one of her sisters in Port Talbot. I had served the county for many years as one of its Members of Parliament and now I was to start many happy years as Chancellor of one of Glamorgan's universities, albeit one of the newest.

One of the fascinations to me was that the university sought to widen access to university education and it drew the majority of its students from the county and from Gwent next door. The Chancellorship is only a titular role, but the post holder is there to be consulted. The Chancellor presides over most degree ceremonies, which can be quite demanding as we graduate some thousands each year. The role also includes presiding over important lectures by distinguished visitors, receiving royalty and taking an interest in the standing of the university. I am delighted when it is seen as at the cutting edge of some of its disciplines in newspapers and media commentaries. The Chancellor takes considerable interest in those the university seeks to honour but does not run it. That is for the professionals.

I also served as a member of the Council of the Prince's Trust (Cymru). The work done is outstanding and I would be moved to tears sometimes by the testimony at prize-givings from some of those from extremely under-privileged backgrounds who have benefited from its initiatives. It is an immensely important investment in young people who need help. I wish governments would take on board the Trust's initiatives and apply some of them generally. I fear my contribution was limited. My knowledge of con-temporary courses and the like was on the margin. I could only watch the struggle for money and sponsorship. What I could do, and it was a very small contribution, was to advise on the interface between the Trust and political decision makers. I did what I could, but I felt for some time that others could make better contributions than I.

I was asked by Tony Blair from 2002–9 to serve on the Prime Minister's Business Appointments Committee under the chairmanship of Lord Mayhew, a former Attorney General among other offices. We were an inde-pendent body with a remit to provide advice to the Prime Minister and Foreign Secretary respectively on applying the rules on very senior mem-bers of the Civil and Diplomatic Services accepting outside appointments within two years of leaving Crown service. The ministerial code also obliged ministers to seek the advice of the committee. Hardly a week went by with-out applications from senior civil servants, servicemen and former minis-ters. It was important that as many as possible, where it was appropriate, could be fitted back to serve the country in some other capacity so that their skills and experience could be used, but sometimes conditions and restrictions had to be imposed. I regarded this as of key importance and any criticisms made are against this background.

We all approached our tasks with great diligence and reached our deci-sions judicially. Occasionally a person disappointed by our decision would request an oral hearing and we did our utmost to reach a fair decision. However I was getting quite concerned that persons who had been allowed to take up a post would sometimes claim we had 'approved' it. We had done no such thing. All we could do was to state that according to the rules we could have no objection to their taking up the post and that we saw no rea-son why they could not take up the appointment at the specified time. I was not happy that our decision was being treated as a badge of approval and I persuaded our colleagues to change the wording of the decision to what it exactly was. No more, no less than that we had no objection according to the rules laid down for us.

I was also becoming more and more unhappy with the long list of former ministers going to posts which, to my way of thinking, were a little too close to the work of the ministries in which they had served. We imposed conditions to prohibit lobbying, and according to the rules we could not object to the posts being accepted. We could advise the minister against taking up an appointment for a period and further, whether the post was suitable at that time. Whether the rules were tight enough was another matter and our regular plea to Downing Street to get the rules revised went unheeded. I told the chairman and the committee that there seemed to be a 'revolving door' philosophy developing so far as ministers were concerned – although we were always on our guard as regards the dangers of this – going from one post to another outside government where the connection was uncomfortably close. I was bothered by the current smoothness of the transition. Outside organisations foolishly believed that ex-ministers might have some influence on their former colleagues. Knowing how the contractual systems work, I was extremely doubtful of this. However, the perception was there, particularly where former ministers glided to posts where their real experience and value was questionable. I would ask myself, why did these organisations engage them and sometimes at quite high salaries. To remove any lingering doubt I argued for a *cordon sanitaire* to be erected in the form of a suitable gap of time between office and a job which was too close to a ministerial position. I had in mind at least a year – and in difficult cases up to two years – as a period when the post could not be taken up. We did impose limits forbidding the lobbying of government departments – usually a year and sometimes more.

I fear I was unable to persuade my colleagues at that time. I note with pleasure that the new ministerial code lays down that on leaving office an ex-minister is prohibited from lobbying for two years and must also seek advice from the advisory committee about any job within two years. To move from a voluntary system to a mandatory one is a step forward, but I would have wished for a stronger code for actually taking up a post where there is an issue of perception of possible influence. My seven years' service on the committee was quite demanding and after my time it was appropriately rewarded.

The most interesting appointment I had was to become HM Lord Lieutenant for Dyfed, which included my native county of Cardiganshire, now called Ceredigion. I knew there would be a vacancy as all Lord Lieutenants have to retire by statute at seventy-five. When it was mentioned to me I expressed an interest. I was a native of Dyfed and had as a young man failed in my endeavours to be a political representative for two parts of it. As a young barrister I would go to Lampeter to the Cardiganshire

Quarter Sessions to appear in minor cases and it had crossed my mind then that if I succeeded professionally I would hope in the fullness of time – many, many years later – to become chairman of the Quarter Sessions. By my time, such chairmanships had been abolished and that opportunity would never come to me. Hence I did not hesitate when the Prime Minister's letter came in 2002 offering a nomination to be Lord Lieutenant of Dyfed.

The Lieutenancy in our part of the world is a curious animal. Peter Walker, a Tory secretary of state for Wales, had sought unrealistically to amalgamate the three counties of Cardiganshire, Carmarthenshire and Pembrokeshire. Some councillors had to do a return journey of more than 100 miles for a sub-committee. The make up of the three counties was quite different. Not many years after the marriage a divorce of the counties had to be arranged, and each of the three old counties reverted to being individual all-functions authorities. However, the functions of the Lieutenancy were untouched by the divorce. The Lord Lieutenant was the Lord Lieutenant for all three counties, but each of the three county clerks remained as clerks to the Lieutenancy and a personal appointment of the Lord Lieutenant. For the appointment of magistrates there were three Lord Chancellor's advisory committees, one for each county, which the Lord Lieutenant chaired in turn. It was quite time-consuming but it worked.

I doubt if any of my predecessors in the county as Lord Lieutenant had been fluent Welsh speakers for decades if not centuries. I sought to practise what I preached to ensure the equality of both languages. The proceedings of the Ceredigion Advisory Committee were conducted wholly in Welsh with appropriate translation facilities for the small minority whose knowledge of Welsh was limited. I enjoyed these sessions as I had only once before been able to conduct a meeting in my constituency in Welsh and that was a Pontrhydyfen, Richard Burton's birthplace. The odds were very much on that everybody in this village spoke Welsh, they did one evening and I took advantage of it. It could only have happened there as only about eight per cent of my constituents spoke Welsh fluently at that time.

In Carmarthen I opened all my advisory committees by inviting contributions in either language. On one occasion for the appointing of new members all the sub-committee present spoke Welsh. I took advantage of this too, perhaps to the surprise of some of those being considered, although they were all fluent. These were but small steps in making the use of Welsh in hitherto new fields the norm whenever it was possible, and no one was disadvantaged. My precept of equal validity meant to me equal opportunity if one wished, without disadvantage, to use our language. I always read the lesson in the many church services that I took part in as Lord Lieutenant officially in Welsh – the language of the Bible that I was brought up in.

I encouraged High Sheriffs where they could to swear their rather long oath in Welsh. One perhaps equally significant breaking of new ground was my insistence that the commissions for my Deputy Lieutenants were drafted in both English and Welsh. I was quite pleased with my small contribution for equality in the languages. How far we had moved from the tentative but firm proposals in my report to the Welsh Parliamentary Party of 1962, where I first used the expression 'equal validity'.

At seventy-five, by statute, these duties came to an end.

One particular telephone call, an absolute and utter surprise, was made to me shortly before Easter 2002 from the Queen's Private Secretary. I had gone to a garage a few miles away from Garthwen for some minor repairs and, told about the call when I returned; I wondered what it could be about. What major blunder had I committed in the six months I had been Lord Lieutenant? I rang up Buckingham Palace and to my utter astonishment was told the Queen was minded to offer me the Garter – a Knight Companion of the Order. The press statement made it clear that it was not a political appointment.

I did not have to be knighted again as I had already been dubbed when I received my first knighthood in 1999. I was rather pleased that the collar (or chain) that I wore on ceremonial occasions was formerly worn by Prime Minister Attlee. I made a particular point in ensuring that the brochure for the service at Windsor mentioned my background, including my farming forefathers in Cardiganshire and my maternal grandfather who went down the pit at an early age and was chairman of his miners' lodge.

Jim Callaghan rang me up to congratulate me and said I was entitled to wear so many different outfits that I would not know which to put on in the morning. I told him I would try to wear my white bardic robes! He did not often come to Garter ceremonies in those days, he was around ninety, but he came to my installation in his own words, 'to keep an eye on me'. He was true to his word and gave me invaluable advice that day.

When I got the Garter Knighthood, Garter King of Arms came and told me that I now had to have a coat of arms – I had declined one when I was given my peerage – as it would be necessary to have one so that my banner could be designed to hang high up in St George's Chapel, Windsor. I accepted the inevitable. In honour of my ancestors a Welsh black bull was designed to stand below my banner and a magnificent one it is. He would stand on a small pile of books in honour of my wife's ancestry as daughter and granddaughter of Gomer Press, the Welsh publishers. Below, there are three swords of justice, one as Attorney General, one as Queen's Counsel and one as a Recorder of the Crown Court. As background there is the Portcullis of Parliament, where I have spent more than fifty years. The

Garter motto, *Honi soit qui mal y pense* (roughly translated as 'Evil to him who thinks evil') surrounds the shield. My own motto is, not surprisingly, *Bid ben bid bont* – 'He who seeks to be a leader must be a bridge', from our old Celtic *Mabinogion* tales.

In the Lords I decided it would not quite be appropriate, having been a Lord Lieutenant, if I returned to everyday political battles. I decided I would intervene only occasionally as an ex Attorney on legal matters, such as the preservation of the right to trial by jury and limiting the loss of freedom in terrorist cases to the barest minimum. I would be able to draw on my life-time experience of the criminal law and the criminal courts. In any event, to pour over the minutiae of bills in committee would be doing similar work to that which had taken up so much of my time in the 1950s, 1960s and 1970s in the Commons. I had done my share. I decided that I would be economic in my contributions.

twenty-six
CONCLUSION

L OOKING BACK OVER MORE THAN FIFTY YEARS in Parliament and the law, the inevitable question I ask myself is – 'What have I done to make things better than they were?' and 'Could I have done more?'

My legal career can be disposed of quickly. Every man is as good as his last case and I was fortunate to practise in a branch of the law that gave manifest opportunities – criminal practice: regrettably a growth industry. I would, of course, have wished to have spent more time on my profession and thereby improve my skills. However, since I was riding two horses, politics and the law, at the same time, I comfort myself that I managed to pass the whole of my working life without too many falls. I fear I was one of the last of my generation to attempt to be a serious politician and a practising silk at the same time, which I did up to the moment I became Attorney General, and for three years after I retired from that office. The physical strain of following two professions was heavy, but it had its compensations. When I got tired and temporarily disillusioned with the Parliamentary scene I could always go away for a little while and pick up some professional work. I always returned to Parliament refreshed and reinvigorated and did what Lloyd George, it is said, asked himself each morning: 'What shall I do this day?'

Since I lived professionally in the world of criminals and their professional advisers there were many corners of the darker sides of society with which I was very familiar, which kept me very much in touch. Whether it is right to describe our society as a 'broken one' – far too much of a generalisation – is arguable. There are certainly parts of it that are deeply deprived and at considerable disadvantage and hence a breeding ground for antisocial behaviour. One difficult family on a decent housing estate can make life a real misery for all others, as I heard too often in my constituency surgeries. All I could do was to give every encouragement for councillors and councils to be contacted. It was a real problem.

It is with the young, it is with their ill-equipped mothers and with the early offenders that we need to deploy time and resources better in the interests of society as a whole. 'Prison works,' said one Home Secretary, but only to the extent of isolating wrongdoers temporarily from reoffending. Regrettably, the lack of resources for education and training in prisons reduces the opportunity to provide the basis for a second chance. Much more medical help would be an investment that I have no doubt would reap substantial dividends.

Canvassing in by-elections across the country, which I have done on many occasions over the years, can also be very educational. Councils having to destroy comparatively new council blocks and move the occupants out because they have become part of estates which are uninhabitable is a waste of resources and the sums involved are colossal. I remember Jim Callaghan making a speech, unreported, in Cardiff stating that it was in the interests of the better off to be taxed at a higher rate to create a society that was better educated, in better health, and in which it was safe to move freely in our streets.

I was saddened to read a recent report of the National Inequality Panel commissioned by the Labour government, entitled 'An anatomy of economic inequality in the UK' (January 2010). It said:

> Inequalities in earnings and income are high in Britain, both compared with other industrialised countries and compared with thirty years ago . . . over the most recent decade, according to some measures, earnings inequality has narrowed a little and income inequality has stabilised, but the large inequality growth between the late 1970s and 1990s has not been reversed.

The Labour government commented that 'the report shows clearly how inequality is cumulative over an individual's lifetime and is carried from one generation to the next'. It adds that the Labour government's public policies succeeded in halting the rise in inequality, in narrowing gaps in educational attainment, narrowing the gap between men and women's pay and tackling poverty in retirement.

So much done, but so much still to do.

The target of halving child poverty by 2010 was missed, though there were 600,000 fewer poor children than in 1998. The Annual Report (2010) from the Department of Work & Pensions shows that child poverty fell by 100,000 in 2008–9, and this in the first year of the current recession. As I have said, so much still to do, but I hope I will be able to watch further progress.

During the period when we had National Service, I recollect that there was a far higher rate of rejection for unfitness north of a line drawn from Bristol to the Wash than south of that line. That generation was still paying for the ravages of their industrial past. Recent reports underline that the expectation of longevity is considerably dependent on an individual's material resources.

I recognise progress. Throwing money at the problems is not the only way to tackle deprivation. Teaching communities and individuals how to live better is equally important. But the reminiscences I heard at some of the Prince's Trust awards ceremonies, tear-jerkers as some of them were, showed what can be done, albeit in a small way, to give some of the deprived young a chance. I only wish the template of some of the Trust's work could be adopted by government to include far more young people being given similar practical help.

Things that many take for granted – breakfast before school and a helping hand for homework – can go a long way to remedy deficiencies in families and give hope to free some children from social immobility.

I am proud with what has been achieved by governments that I have been a member of to make some headway in my first aspiration: to 'strive for equality of opportunity for the individual'.

In my second aim of establishing 'a better and more democratic government in Wales', I can claim to be a member of a government that has had a fair measure of success. Sometimes painfully, always slowly, we in the Labour Party developed our ideas, and they are no one else's, which resulted in an elected Assembly in Cardiff. I have played a part over so many years, sometimes against heavy odds, in constructing the architecture for a devolved assembly. No other party would have attempted to legislate at Westminster for either a Scottish Parliament or a Welsh Assembly. It has also been my lifetime's work.

We had a major setback when the Welsh nation rejected our government's proposals in 1979. After a gap of eighteen years others took up the baton and eventually we got national acceptance, just about, for our ideas. On so many occasions the odds were stacked against us in the Cabinet discussions when, under the leadership of Harold Wilson, to whom Scottish and Welsh democracy owes so much, the minority views became the Cabinet's decisions. He wore down the opposition among colleagues. As it transpired the odds were also stacked against us in popular opinion in Wales. We were obviously moving ahead too quickly. Public opinion just would not follow us at that time.

By the time we were returned to power in 1997, to the 'unfinished business', to use the late John Smith's terminology, of the 1974–9 government, there had been a significant turnaround of view, both in the Party and in Wales. A huge movement of view, almost a seismic change, is one of the curiosities of the Labour movement, and not only in this field. The Labour Party has usually one great strength, which unfortunately failed me when I tested it, and that is its desire for unity and for its elected government to carry through its policies.

I do not know of a Labour candidate, particularly in Wales and Scotland who would today actively oppose devolution. The 1997 manifesto bound us all together. Probably most elected politicians in Wales today would not wish to turn the clock back, a massive change from the time when, as a young aspiring politician, I used to stand up in Welsh Labour conferences in the early and mid 1950s, demanding very modest improvements in better and more accessible democratic government in Wales.

There have been similar seismic changes of view within the Labour Party on defence and on Europe. In defence, from the pacifism of George Lansbury or the multilateralism of Ernest Bevin, one of the founders of NATO, or the unilateralism of Michael Foot, to more recent and equally controversial aspirations to be at the United States' side as the world's policemen. Even in my own constituency, I had to contend for a short time with deeply held views on unilateralism which were completely contrary to the longstanding multilateralism of the main stream of the Labour Party, which had been our position historically since the 1930s.

I have seen similar flows of views on Europe, and the majority of Labour's foot soldiers in the parliamentary party have tramped through the lobbies over the years in support of whatever is the perceived political wisdom of its leaders at various times.

We had not completed our task in constructing a fully devolved Assembly for Wales. My successors have had to compromise too. I have been exceedingly doubtful in the past about the prospects of winning a referendum so as to further devolution. Having had my fingers burnt, or more accurately, having seen the elephant on my doorstep and the Labour government only just avoiding defeat the second time around, perhaps I could be forgiven for my caution. As it turned out, the Legislative Powers Referendum was a resounding victory and my caution was unnecessary, an endorsement of the Assembly's success as an institution.

There are other outstanding problems too. I am a late convert to the idea that substantial Home Office powers over the police in Wales should go to the Assembly. I may still be in a minority. The police are so involved with social services, the probation service and with local authorities that it will be odd if government responsibility for it is not coterminous with the other services. This is the same argument that I deployed in setting up the boundaries of the Crown Prosecution Service to be the same as the courts and the police when I was Attorney General.

At the time of writing, the Conservative government has proposed new funding arrangements, quite contrary to the existing statue, for S4C, involving a considerable diminution in finance over the years. I deeply regret that our political leaders in Cardiff have not taken the initiative when economic conditions were so much better to obtain the transfer of responsibility for broadcasting in Welsh, with appropriate compensation, to the Welsh Assembly, as I proposed in 2002 at my initiation as Chancellor of Glamorgan University. In my view the inertia over the years has been the fear by the Assembly to take over financial responsibility. They would, of course, have had to negotiate compensation. Meanwhile S4C preferred to be supervised by remote Whitehall rather than Cardiff. There cannot be anything more Welsh and suitable for devolution than Welsh broadcasting. Would I be unfair in suggesting a failure to understand what we were setting out to do as devolutionists? I hope it is still not too late to move forward.

The main outstanding devolution problem is that of the unanswered West Lothian Question, first formulated by my Cambridge contemporary and sparring partner in the Cambridge Union, Tam Dalyell MP, in his speech during the Second Reading of the Scotland Bill on 14 November 1977:

> For how long will English constituents and English Hon Members tolerate . . . at least 119 Members from Scotland, Wales and Northern Ireland exercising an important, and probably decisive, effect on English politics, while they themselves have no say in the same matters in Scotland, Wales and Northern Ireland. (The English Question)

The answers range from special parliamentary procedure to provide for 'English votes for English laws' to some form of federalism. Sir Malcolm Rifkind MP, the chairman of the Conservative taskforce under Kenneth Clarke MP, various select committees and the Commons Liaison Committee have pondered on it. One of the hurdles to be overcome is the fact that England, as a constituent part of the state, has eighty-four per cent of the population and there appears to be no appetite for devolved assemblies in England.

The Labour government's reply to the commons select committee reporting in May 2009 stated:

> The governance of England is seen by many as the unfinished business of devolution, but the perception is not accompanied by any widespread agreement on what should be done.

Whether we have moved forward in the latest statement from 'the Coalition' on our programme for government (20 May 2010) remains to be seen:

> . . . we will establish a commission to consider the 'West Lothian Question'.

In my time there has been a fundamental change in the structure of our national products. It is the financial services sector, rather than the man-ufacturing industries that are the centrepiece of our economy. Given the size of the financial sector it is a cause of considerable anxiety to me that we have so little control over it. I, of course, fully understand that it is an international industry. The proposals of left-wing politicians in the 1980s to nationalise the banks were treated with scorn. Perhaps we should have listened more so as to devise appropriate machinery to have some control over the 'commanding heights of the economy' which both Aneurin Bevan and Tony Crosland wrote about. The 'light touch' of recent years has been found wanting. I also find depressing the swallowing up of British compa-nies by foreign interests, without any governmental restraint. Some means should be found, if necessary by amending international obligations, to pro-tect vital national interests. I doubt very much if British companies enjoy a level playing field elsewhere. From what I have heard a British credit organi-sation, a subsidiary of a major British company, had enormous difficulties in setting up business in France and eventually withdrew.

From long experience, whenever public money is an issue there is a significant danger of its stewards adopting a cavalier attitude to it. I heard of bonuses for the Civil Service for the first time when I became Attorney General and I was asked to consider one for a senior government lawyer. How could I, with six months' experience as Attorney, reach a fair decision? Undoubtedly there has been, both in Whitehall and Cardiff, both job and grade inflation. The Cabinet Office now has six permanent secretaries, and the distinguished post of the Prime Minister's private secretary under the Labour administration, has been upgraded to permanent secretary. There certainly was a more rigorous approach when, as a Cabinet minister, I had personally to make my case for the salary of the chief executive of the Welsh Development Agency to a Cabinet committee headed by Ted Short as deputy Prime Minister. How times have changed!

In the hope that my grandchildren, when they grow up, will read this book, I trust they will take on board the breadth of my interests, from try-ing to persuade my constituents in Glyncorrwg to re-align their rugby pitch to provide space for an advance factory (which was built and filled, though later became empty) – to persuading more than a hundred countries at the International Parliamentary Union Conference in Cape Town in 2009 to reaffirm the principle of a report, of which I was the joint author, condemning torture.

To conclude, I can say that I have been fortunate to lead a rich and varied life, supported by my family and my constituents. The occasional downsides, sharp and acute, were fortunately relatively brief and my family and I were able to move on.

APPENDIX ONE

*Memorandum sent from John Morris to Harold Wilson
on 19 June 1968*

I have kept in touch with the discussions relating to the work of the Ministerial Committee on Devolution, and I have spoken to the Lord President about some of the issues raised. I am now taking the unusual step of enclosing a memorandum to you, to express my views on a subject which is obviously of first importance to me as a Welsh MP though it has no connection with my work in the Ministry of Defence.

In the absence of any machinery for consultation with Welsh MPs who happen to be ministers, I am writing to express my views on the Draft Conclusions of the Ministerial Committee on Devolution (2nd Revise) which I have studied.

This, to say the least, is a sad document, not only for its conclusions, but worse, for its sheer argument on and lack of philosophy. There appear to be colleagues who do not wish to do anything, and others who, when specific proposals are put, be it on functions or decentralisation of administrative centres, if their own departments are affected seek to reject them. Lastly, like the Secretary of State for Wales, I hold the suggestion that certain proposals 'would give offence to loyal supporters of the UK government' as quite unworthy, and whatever conclusion is come to I would hope that this be not one of the arguments put up for it.

Briefly, I would make the following points:

1. <u>Transfer of Functions</u> Our election pledge in Wales makes it quite clear what we are pledged to do. To resile from this, unless there are unarguable practical difficulties, is just not on. Indeed, as the months go by, we are hard put to put up

a case why we have not yet carried out our promises. While I do not reject the offer of the minister of agriculture for the moment, I find his arguments basically the same arguments that could be put up by any department, and when my former officials in Transport were asked, I believe for the purposes of the Gordon Walker Report, whether there was less or more efficiency following delegation, I believe the answer was neither. It must come down as to what is politically right. Unless functions on the scale which we envisaged are transferred, it calls into question the whole existence of the Welsh Office.

2. <u>The Council for Wales</u> If the argument against this is, quite contrary to the views of the secretary of state, who, after all, is close to the ground in these matters, that it would make a nonsense of local government reform proposals, then it is the local government proposals that need looking at. The Welsh Labour Movement is tired of nominated organisations, and I had thought, as with the PTAs [Passenger Transport Authorities which I had helped to set up in England], we were at last moving away from this. This body would be a useful drawer-together of (sic) many strands in Wales, it could be the forerunner of regional administration in England, and could satisfy some of the aspirations of the Welsh people. I have no doubt likewise that it would be a great help to get over the idea of remoteness and whatever Welsh committees are continued or set up, that they should meet in Cardiff.

3. <u>The Welsh Office</u> Its present difficulty lies, as I see it, in that it has not the functions to justify a sufficiently large staff, and it must experience great difficulty in exercising its supervisory powers. It would be interesting to know the resources available for ministers to be briefed. I do not share the confidence of the minister of agriculture that his proposals will either work over a period of time or satisfy anyone. It does not mean the transfer of one official and the secretary of state is not trusted to appoint on his own even the chairman of a county AEC. I fail to understand, incidentally, why the Welsh Office has no formal supervisory powers over Power, if the position remains the same. (Official Report Vol. 702, Cols 623–4, of 19 November, 1964.)

I would not seek to advance the case for a more realistic Welsh Office by way of examples which could be endless, but in an era where there is discontent with the remoteness of government I would have thought it is politically right for Welsh ministers to be associated with government activity, eg plans for new roads in Wales. I can hardly believe that the wholly misplaced anger with the Rural Development Board in Wales would have arisen to the extent it has if the project had been mothered ministerially in Wales. The failure to sell various hospital decisions, without commenting on their merit, is evidence that all is not right politically. And how education escapes the transfer net in a nation which is so passionately devoted to it, and for which evidentially, if lack of differences is one of the main arguments against transfer, there is persuasive case fortified by even the setting up of a separate Gittins Committee for Primary Education, passes all understanding.

4.   For the future, I am confident that we must look hard at the whole pattern of Regional and Scottish and Welsh Development. Given that we reject economic separation, and given at the same time that ultimately we will become part of a European set-up, radical steps will need to be taken to ensure adequate and effective machinery of government in Wales, Scotland, and the English regions if they wish it. If there is fear that Whitehall does not always know best, how much greater this will be so far as Brussels is concerned, hence the greater our involvement in Europe, the greater the need for people to be closer to and involved with the 'local' Whitehalls. I would also hope that when already old wounds lose some of their remaining scars, Eire should be encouraged to come closer to us. This of course is a long task, but after all, if we cannot effect this, no wonder that historically we have not always been reasonably successful elsewhere.

5.   It would be a grave error to suppose that present problems are transient. Our aspirations certainly manifest themselves with different force at different periods. But they continue to recur after 500 years. For the purposes of this argument, I have deliberately not canvassed some of the underlying problems, and the need to involve people in decision making, but I am saddened at the conservatism of the approach of the present document.

APPENDIX TWO

Letter from George Thomas of 25 August 1969 to the Prime Minister

If we reject parliamentary devolution, it is the more necessary for us to advance in administrative devolution. I am convinced that an elected or partly elected Welsh Council dealing with administrative functions is both practicable and advisable.

Membership of the Welsh Council could be either on the basis of direct election by constituencies, or by indirect election by local authorities, or by a combination of both, with nominees appointed by the secretary of state. We would have to consider the question of payment for Members, since absence from home and work would necessarily be involved if adequate service is to be given.

The functions of the Welsh Council could be partly executive and partly advisory. The following responsibilities are amongst those that could be administered by the council, namely:

(1)   The health services in Wales

(2)   The Welsh Arts Council

(3)   The Welsh Committee of the Forestry Commission

(4)   The Welsh Committee of the Countryside Commission

(5)   The Welsh Joint Education Committee

(6)   The present advisory responsibilities of the current nominated Welsh Council

(7)   The Welsh Committee of the Water Resources Board

(8)   The Central Training Council (Welsh Committee)

(9)   The Youth Employment Council (Welsh Committee)

. . .A Welsh Council such as I have proposed could do what Parliament cannot hope to do, namely to keep a watchful eye on how policy in all these important fields of activity is progressing in relation to Wales. It would do this without encroaching on the responsibilities either of the local authorities or of Parliament.

The suggested council will complete my proposals for local government reform in Wales and will help us to secure for Wales a structure which will improve public participation in government without weakening the United Kingdom ties.

I therefore seek the agreement of my colleagues to the following:

(1) That we concentrate our proposals on administrative devolution, as opposed to parliamentary devolution;

(2) That future Statutory Instruments dealing wholly or overwhelmingly with Wales shall be referred to the Welsh Grand Committee rather than the whole house; and

(3) That we recommend the establishment of a Welsh Council to exercise functions as outlined above.

INDEX

Davies, Alun Talfan 21, 31–2, 55, 102,
    149, 225
Davies, D. H. 29
Davies, D. J. 17, 27
Davies, D. S. 25–6
Davies, Sir Dai 131, 143
Davies, Edmund, Lord Justice, *see*
    Edmund-Davies, Lord
Davies, Elfed 41
Davies, Garfield 149, 150
Davies, Gwyn 29
Davies, Ifor 41, 45, 122
Davies, Ivor 26
Davies, Jennie Eirian 160
Davies, John 149
Davies, Lynn Talfan 31
Davies, Morgan 26
Davies, Ron 126
Davies, Ted 27–8
Davies, W. H. 42
De Peyer, Mr 62
Dear, Sir Geoffrey 185
defence 4, 43, 48, 75, 77–84, 85, 87, 97,
    169–70, 198, 238
Defence and Overseas Policy Committee
    (DOP) 204
Denbigh 146
Department of Work and Pensions
    (DWP) 236
Derelict Land Unit 130
Development Board for Rural Wales
    (DBRW) 132–4, 141, 245
Development Commission 134
Devil's Bridge 159, 162
devolution 11, 13–15, 24, 45, 50–1, 85–95,
    99, 100–1, 102, 103–5, 107, 108, 109–
    11, 113–27, 129, 135, 137, 140, 141,
    149, 151, 152, 154, 155, 165, 166–7,
    168, 173, 185, 237–8, 239, 243–5, 247–8
devolution referendum (1979) 121, 122,
    123–5, 151, 237, 238; (1997) 126, 237,
    238
Devonport 80
Dewar, Ian 103

Dexter, Ted 48
Diana, Princess 190
Dolcniw (Capel Bangor) 1, 3
Dolgellau 18, 20
Donnelly, Desmond 42, 48, 50, 62, 63, 66
Donoughue, Bernard 108, 116, 117, 118
Douglas, Harry 63
Douglas-Home, Sir Alec 95
Drivers' Vehicle Licensing Agency
    (DVLA) 74–5, 226
Dyfed 164, 231–3

Ebbw Vale 49, 143, 146–7, 173
Eden, Sir John 161
Edmund-Davies, Herbert Edmund, Lord
    65, 99
Edmund-Davies, Sarah, Lady 149
education 28, 47, 83, 109, 138–9, 151,
    153–4, 155, 157–8, 163, 164, 245
Edward VIII 184
Edwards, Eliazar (grandfather) 2–3, 4, 5,
    65, 229, 233
Edwards, Huw 174
Edwards, John Ll. J. 195, 196
Edwards, Mary Anne (grandmother)
    3–4, 229
Edwards, Ness 44, 49
Edwards, Nicholas, Lord Crickhowell
    122, 166, 173
Edwards, Owen M. 5
El Adem 82
elections:
    general elections (1945) 48; (1955)
        36; (1959) 36–7, 41; (1964) 13, 44,
        61, 169; (1970) 83, 97, 99, 170;
        (February 1974) 37, 98, 100, 103,
        105, 114, 129; (October 1974) 37,
        105, 108, 114, 129, 130; (1979) 123,
        126; (1983) 36, 173; (1987) 176, 177;
        (1992) 80, 176; (1997) 178–9, 191;
        (2001) 227
    by-elections: Cardiganshire (1921)
        3; University of Wales (1943)
        8; Carmarthen (1957) 23–6,